Participatory Pedagogic Impact Research

Involvement of community partners in the structure and design of services is largely accepted in principle, but its practice is heavily contested. This book argues that the co-production of research is one of the best ways to involve community partners. As well as having intrinsic value in and of itself, research embeds a culture of learning, co-production and of valuing research within organizations. It also creates a mechanism for developing evidence for, monitoring and evaluating subsequent ideas and initiatives that arise from other co-production initiatives.

The book makes a case for research to be a synthesis of participatory research, critical pedagogy, peer research and community organizing. It develops a model called Participatory Pedagogic Impact Research (PPIR). Participatory research is often criticized for not having the impact it promises. PPIR ensures that the issues chosen, and the recommendations developed, serve the mutual self-interest of stakeholders, are realistic and realizable. At the same time this approach pushes the balance of power towards the oppressed using methods of dissemination that hold decision makers to account and create real change. PPIR also develops a robust method for creatively identifying issues, methods and analytic frameworks. Its third section details case studies across Europe and the United States of PPIR in action with professional researchers' and community partners' reflections on these experiences.

This book gives a unique articulation of what makes for genuinely critical reflective spaces, something underdeveloped in the literature. It should be considered essential reading for both participatory research academics and those involved in health and social care services in the planning, commissioning and delivery of services.

Mike Seal is Head of Criminology and Youth and Community Work, and a reader in Critical Pedagogy at Newman University Birmingham. He has worked in the social care field for over 25 years as a worker, manager, trainer and consultant. He has written seven previous books including *Not About Us Without Us: Client Involvement in Supported Housing*, as well as over 30 articles in professional and academic publications. He has conducted 25 major funded pieces of research, all of which were grounded in participatory approaches. He has spoken at more than 80 worldwide academic and professional conferences on co-production and participatory research, and conducted over 25 major pieces of consultancy work in the area.

Routledge Advances in Social Work

www.routledge.com/Routledge-Advances-in-Social-Work/book-series/RASW

Participatory Pedagogic Impact Research

Co-production with Community Partners in Action

Mike Seal

Routledge
Taylor & Francis Group

LONDON AND NEW YORK

First published 2018
by Routledge
2 Park Square, Milton Park, Abingdon, Oxon OX14 4RN

and by Routledge
711 Third Avenue, New York, NY 10017

Routledge is an imprint of the Taylor & Francis Group, an informa business

© 2018 Mike Seal

British Library Cataloguing-in-Publication Data
A catalogue record for this book is available from the British Library

Library of Congress Cataloging-in-Publication Data
A catalog record for this title has been requested

ISBN: 978-1-138-84996-9 (hbk)
ISBN: 978-1-315-72509-3 (ebk)

Typeset in Times New Roman
by Keystroke, Neville Lodge, Tettenhall, Wolverhampton

This book is dedicated to all the peer and participatory researchers we have had the pleasure to work with over the years and especially for Jimmy Carlson (1947–2017), activist, trainer, researcher and friend – 'never give up on anyone'.

Contents

Illustrations

Figures

Tables

Contributors

Nika Balomenou is a senior lecturer in Tourism at the University of Hertfordshire. Her research interests include tourism planning and development, visual methods and the use of participant-generated images in tourism research. She focuses on host community empowerment and experience of tourism, responsible tourism, destinations in crisis, national parks and protected areas. She holds a doctorate in Tourism Planning and Visual Methods (University of Wales, Aberystwyth).

Richard Campbell left school with not much; by his own admission he could just about spell his name. He is now a Master's graduate from Newman University and is a highly motivated creative educational specialist. He is the OCE/Director for BLESS centre. He has worked for 13 years with care leavers, those with mental health issues, young children, those with gang affiliation and those who have been homeless.

Beth Coyne has worked in various sectors with adults with complex needs, including homelessness, drug and alcohol services, and criminal justice. In particular she has worked within service user (client) involvement and employment, and now runs an employment service for a central London local authority.

Brian Garrod is Professor in Marketing at Swansea University. He is the author of eight textbooks and more than 50 research articles, focusing on the marketing and management of tourism destinations. He is co-editor in chief of the *Journal of Destination Marketing & Management* and is on the editorial board of six other academic journals. He has undertaken research for a wide range of organizatons, including the World Tourism Organization (UNWTO) and the Organisation for Economic Co-operaton and Development (OECD).

Simone Helleren is a Doctoral Researcher at the University of Birmingham in the School of Social Policy and Social Work. Her PhD is an exploration of what enables and constrains effective engagement with help, through a longitudinal case study with young people on pathways out of homelessness. Previously, Simone worked with Groundswell UK for over eight years overseeing their peer and participatory research programme. Before Groundswell she worked across the voluntary and statutory sectors with diverse groups focusing on 'involvement and participation' frequently using theatre methods.

Taylor Konkle is an academic staff member for the School of Medicine and Public Health at the University of Wisconsin-Madison supporting healthcare and health systems research. She is a former graduate from the Community and Environmental Sociology major and studied social issues, global health, and environmental studies.

Karen Reece holds a PhD in Physiology granted from the University of Wisconsin School of Medicine and Public Health. She migrated to the world of social science when she saw her analytical skills could complement non-profits struggling to quantify impact. Karen provides programme evaluation, research and strategic support for a social service provider in Madison WI by day. She does programming and organizing in the Hip-Hop community by night. When she's not doing research and/or organizing events, Karen enjoys the local music scene (particularly Hip-Hop), playing the cello and singing, and fighting for social justice.

Randy Stoecker is a Professor of Community and Environmental Sociology at the University of Wisconsin-Madison, with an affiliate appointment at the University of Wisconsin Extension Center for Community and Economic Development. He has a long history of doing, studying, training and writing about various forms of higher education civic and community engagement.

Acknowledgements

Nika and Brian would like to thank all those involved who made their research possible.

Richard feels his achievements would not have been so fruitful without having been mentored by Dr Martin Glynn and Dr Mike Seal with whom he has worked with for many years, helping him to embrace and become fearless in his academic journey.

Beth would thank the participants and staff of the probation trusts and prison whose work is discussed here. In order to protect individuals' anonymity we have chosen not to name them but we are grateful for all your insights and support.

Randy, Karen and Taylor would like to thank the University of Wisconsin-Madison Morgridge Center for Public Service for providing us with a wonderful Service Learning Fellow to support this project, and the University of Wisconsin Extension for providing Randy Stoecker with an academic position supporting community-engaged scholarship.

Simone would like to thank: Mike Seal for giving me the opportunity to make this contribution and teaching me much of what I know about research in particular and working with people in general. Hannah Jones for believing in me and encouraging me to keep writing. Mike (Spike) Hudson and Andrew Campbell for their work on the Escape Plan, and their on-going contribution to Groundswell. All Groundswellians, who allowed me to participate in the brilliant thing that it is, especially Athol Hallé, and Martin Burrows who continues to develop their participatory research. Finally Mark Flynn, who was the most excellent researcher; I wish I had learned more of his secrets and that he was still with us.'

Mike would like to thank all those who created the conditions to make this book and the research contained within it happen.

Introduction

The de-mystification and democratization of research

Client involvement, or co-production, has come to prominence recently in the National Health Service with the statutory requirement for local health authorities to have PPI (Public and Patient Involvement) and the setting up of Healthwatch to monitor health authorities' implementation of this. I have catalogued elsewhere (Seal, 2009, 2016) how parallel duties and expectations have arisen in the housing, social care and youth work fields. At the same time the involvement of those subject to health and social care services, called here 'community partners', in the planning, commission and delivery of those services is something that is rarely contested in principle (Seal, 2009), but its reality is heavily so (Healthwatch, 2013). Similarly, peer research is lauded (Checkoway & Richards-Schuster, 2003), but remains remarkably underdeveloped (Terry & Cardwell, 2016), and is hence often tokenistic (Nestor & Galletly, 2008). At the same time research is expected to demonstrate its impact on the world, and has been criticised for not doing so, the distance between academic research and practice growing ever wider (HEFCE, 2012). The questions therefore arise of how involvement and co-production are best implemented and how research can make a contribution to this.

When done badly, as I explored in 2009 (Seal, 2009), client involvement and co-production fails economically, morally and politically, entrenching existing feelings of them-and-us between communities and the services that are meant to provide for them, making the services less efficient and under-utilised, and social policy distant and ineffective; with the mechanisms developed for involvement and co-production bureaucratic and moribund. However, co-production has the potential to be transformative, for the community partners, the services and policy makers, co-creating more efficient, meaningful and relevant services and policy. It is potentially transformative in that it can cause a paradigm shift in how different stakeholders view themselves, how to create knowledge and keep creating new knowledge, and how they impact on each other and their wider social context.

This book argues that one of the most meaningful and successful ways to involve community partners in health and social care settings is through co-producing meaningful research. It also makes the case that to be meaningful this research needs to be participatory research. The model of participatory research that will be developed in this book places a particular emphasis on research as a pedagogic process, where we all learn from each other and the consequent knowledge we create is richer because of it. The model of pedagogy espoused is critical pedagogy. Finally, this book will also place particular emphasis on research having a meaningful impact, as one of the criticisms of participatory research is that the impact on the wider world, to which it aspires, is often sadly lacking. (Cooke & Kothari, 2001). To these ends this model of participatory research draws on community organizing, as developed by Saul Alinsky (1971), where there is a drive and associated process with an aim to have genuine impact on the lives of community members and in the process become real radicals as opposed to rhetorical ones.

To give an example of how this has worked in practice, in the spring and summer of 2015 I worked with Revolving Doors Agency, in partnership with a team of commissioners from a London borough, to involve individuals with multiple and complex needs, and experience of the criminal justice system, in local commissioning processes. The 'Together We Can' peer research team and commissioners identified research areas, based on their respective priorities and research was conducted at services across the borough. One commissioner went on to say about the project and its impact:

> I would encourage any commissioner to work with this project if they have the opportunity. It was impossible to know how it would all turn out, but my first thoughts were that this idea had great potential. We were used to working very productively with Service Users who have over a number of years been meaningfully involved in procuring services. However, 'Commissioning Together' meant that they would acquire skills and knowledge which would enable them to add greater value to the process and work with confidence in what can be a daunting environment. I was really pleased to see that a good core group stuck with the training and were still there at the end. I have been impressed with the quality of the work, the clarity of their findings and as much as anything else the obvious effect the programme had on their confidence and self-esteem. The group have worked with me to try and improve a specific aspect of our Integrated Offender Management Programme. Whilst the option was there to design and buy in a new support service the recommendations laid out a number of ways which would improve what we already had in order to fulfil the identified need. The recommendations are being implemented in full and have saved a significant amount of money at the same time. My hope and ambition is now that we can continue to work with some more all of the group into the future.
>
> (Commissioner)

The commissioners subsequently set up a permanent community partner group to monitor the implementation of policies and investigate new priorities. One of these involved commissioning some members of the research group to conduct training with staff on the client experience. Other group members went on to become independent researchers through and beyond Revolving Doors Peer Research Network.

The literature

Participatory research is written about quite comprehensively (Brodie et al., 2009; Cooke & Kothari, 2001; Cornwall, 2002; Kesby et al., 2007; White, 1996; Whitehead 1997; Wilcox, 1995). Its theoretical and practical applications are covered particularly in the work of Chambers (2002, 2008, 2010) at the Institute of Development Studies, and in terms of co-enquiry in the work of Heron (1974, 1981, 1988, 1996) and community based research (CBR) (Assaad et al., 1994; Fals-Borda & Rahman, 1991; Hills & Mullett, 2000; Israel et al., 1998; Reardon, 2000; Savan & Sider, 2003). Authors such as Chambers (2010), who advocate for participatory research, claim that traditional processes of research are often rarefied and mystified, and that much research is therefore done 'on' people by 'experts', rather than with, or for them, re-enforcing people's distancing from, and cynicism, towards it. Participatory research seeks to be the opposite of this. Its critics are also prevalent in the literature (Cooke & Kothari, 2001; Cornwall & Brock, 2005; Henkel & Stirrat, 2001; Kapoor, 2002, 2005; Kinpaisby-Hill, 2009; Kothari, 2005; Mohan, 2007; Mosse, 1994; Sanderson & Kindon, 2004).

Similarly community 'involvement', in its myriad forms (co-production, user participation) is quite well documented, both academically and in policy, including within health and social care settings. The work of Beresford (2010, 2016) is respected and comprehensive in this respect. He has also written about the dangers and potential for client involvement within research in his 2002 article *User involvement in research and evaluation: liberation or regulation* and subsequent books with Croft (Beresford & Croft, 2012) and others. His books are very much about the principles involved in survivor research, and the historical account of the development of the survivor movement in mental health.

McLaughlin in 2009 produced a book of user led research in health and social care settings, but its emphasis is more on health, and in terms of research methodology does not come from an overtly participatory perspective. Koch and Kralkin produced another guide in 2009, but this very much focuses on Participatory Action Research in health settings, though it is a good complementary publication to this one, similarly Minkler and Wallerstein, in 2008. What is unique about this publication is its view of participatory research as the most effective means of conducting and embedding community partner involvement, emphasizing its pedagogic potential particularly with the most marginalised groups, and in the process deconstructing our notions of power and peer, and the nature of research itself.

Critical pedagogy was first described by Paulo Freire (1972) and has since been developed, described as either popular education or critical pedagogy, largely in the US, by authors such as Henry Giroux, Ira Shor, Michael Apple, Joe L. Kincheloe, Shirley R. Steinberg and Peter McLaren. It is a broad school of thought, which combines critical theory and educational theory. It grew out of a concern amongst certain educationalists with the way education was being used as a method to re-inscribe power relations in society. The literature on community organizing is relatively rich (Alinsky, 1971; Chambers & Cowan, 2004;

Gecan, 2002; Schutz & Sandy, 2011) although it is mostly from the United States. I will draw upon community organizing as developed in the UK, particularly through the work of Citizens UK, of which I am an active member and leader. As I will later claim, the research element of community organizing, particularly as developed by Chambers and Cowan (2004) is under theorised and underdeveloped. There have been previous attempts to marry community organizing and action research, such as work by the Change Agency in Philadelphia in the mid-2000s, but there has not been a systematic attempt with regards to participatory research in particular.

Intended audience

On one level this book is a monograph based on the research projects detailed in the notes from the third section. As such it has academic concerns and an academic audience, particularly those within the applied social science and health and social care professional fields. However, we wish the readership to reach beyond the academic community, and attract practitioners and managers with responsibility for involvement, and/or research in health and social care settings, and social policy makers throughout Europe, given that some of the research has been done in this context. The statutory requirement for public and patient involvement in health care planning and commissioning will make this an essential book for those involved with Healthwatch, and planners and commissioners within the health and care sectors. We also hope that it will appeal to community members themselves, for if it did not it would fail on its own terms. The book is intended to be for practice usage, not in the sense of a toolkit, but as a point of reflection. Its central idea is that we have to root our research in community members' organic ways of knowing, researching, meaning making and disseminating. That is the nature of something truly co-produced – it has to have resonance with all parties, and particularly those whose ways of being are generally and systematically undermined and marginalised by traditional research approaches.

Aims

The aims of the book aims are as follows.

1)   To argue that one of the most meaningful and successful way to involve community partners in health and social care settings is through co-producing meaningful research.
2)   To argue that the most effective way to conduct research is through a synthesis of participatory research, critical pedagogy, peer research and community organizing, a model I call Participatory Pedagogic Impact Research (PPIR).
3)   To outline how research can be a considered participatory pedagogic process, with all stakeholders being involved in the co-production of knowledge, and that this pedagogic emphasis impacts positively on an organization's culture towards the involvement of community partners.

4) To outline a model for achieving this, giving concrete practice examples.
5) In doing this to explore issues of power, reflection and mindset from a new perspective, including fresh angles such as what we really mean by 'peer' in research, a suggested process for enacting reflexivity, validity and reliability, grounded data and the nature of knowledge.

The book is divided into three parts covering theory, process and practice. Part 1 explores the key debates and dilemmas within the involvement of community partners, peer research in health and social care, participatory research, critical pedagogy and community organizing. It then sets out an agenda for how they could positively inform each other and be combined to resolve their internal tensions. Part 2 examines the PPIR model for undertaking a research project, starting with how to create a common understanding and ownership from all stakeholders in an organization. It then examines all the common processes of research, from ethics to dissemination, but from a pedagogic and participatory angle. The final part (Part 3) examines learning from where PPIR has been put into action in a variety of health and social care setting including homelessness, probation, and those who are multiply excluded. All these case studies will be co-written with practitioners and peer researchers involved in the programme.

Theoretical framework

I am a critical realist. Critical realism has an objectivist ontology and a relativist epistemology (Archer, 2012; Bhaskar, 1993, 2008; Bystag & Munkvold, 2011; Manicas, 2006; Sayer, 2000), whereby a real world exists, but our knowledge of it is contingent, contextual, fallible and socially constructed. In this vein critical realists call for a break between epistemology and ontology. My epistemological stance is that knowledge is something dynamically co-produced by researcher and researched. It is not a fruitless search for some objective truth, nor is it an equally fruitless search for an 'authentic' or 'unheard' voice, somehow untainted by the research process and unique to that context. This book argues that research should be more than the particular, but does not want to stray into making claims about the general. The external world does act upon us, in ways that are hard to articulate but are nevertheless felt. It is from this sense of unease that agency arises, and without agency, there would be little point to participatory research and co-production. It will draw specifically upon the work of Margaret Archer (2010, 2012) and her typology of reflexives and morphogenetic sequences in particular. In terms of a contribution to knowledge, the book develops the concepts of critical reflexive spaces and process, which is underdeveloped in the literature. Theoretically I aim to combine elements of participatory research, co-operative inquiry (including peer research), critical pedagogy and community organizing, as well as drawing on the interrupting techniques of queer pedagogy and Rancière's notion of radical equality (1992, 2004), addressing critiques of participatory methods on, its impact, the tyranny of methods and unaddressed issues of power.

There are many books on research, including participatory research, but what this book does uniquely is:

- set participatory research within the context of the involvement of those subject to services in the planning, commission and delivery of those services
- look at the wider impact of research on the cultural capital of organizations and attitudes towards community partners, emphasizing its pedagogic potential
- look specifically at health and social care settings, detailing real case studies, including working with very marginalised groups; most books on research, particularly on participatory research, look only at wider community and developmental contexts
- seek to mediate some of the tensions within participatory research uniquely incorporating assessing the contribution of authors such as Rancière (1987) and queer pedagogy
- seek to explore issues such as power, reflection, mindset, 'peer' research, notions of validity and reliability and analysis, from a new perspective.

Book structure

Part 1, *The co-production of knowledge with community partners: dilemmas and debates*, examines the key debates and dilemmas within the involvement of community partners (thereafter called co-production), participatory research and critical pedagogy, setting out an agenda for how these could positively inform each other and resolve some of their internal tensions. In doing this it will explore the notion of peer research and review how community partners have traditionally been involved in research to date.

Chapter 1, *Emperor's old clothes: re-contesting the involvement of community partners*, re-examines the debates and dilemmas within involving community partners in health and social care, particularly the dangers of tokenism, the perceived barrier of motivation and ask what constitutes 'meaningful' involvement. It takes a stance that we should see co-production as the culmination of participation and involvement, and that we should settle for nothing less than this. It will examine some of the tenets of critical pedagogy, and the contributions that authors such as Paulo Friere, Giroux and bell hooks can make to co-production. It will also acknowledge that critical pedagogy, particularly in its Freirean formation, is not without critics, particularly that it is not as liberatory as claimed, and retain' patriarchal qualities. It examines the contribution of Rancière, whose notion of radical equality has something to offer in ameliorating issues of power, and Margaret Archer whose typology of different types of reflexives gives us a framework to start to articulate the meta-reflective researcher we want to co-produce.

Chapter 2, The tyranny of transformation: debates and dilemmas within participatory research, examines the debates and dilemmas within participatory research, which again on the face of it, seems hard to argue against in principle. It will re-examine the accusations of tyranny of Cooke and Kothari, and the rebuttals of Hickey and Mohan, three years on, and seek to establish an agenda for participatory research to challenge itself, particularly on issues of power and representation, but also around some of its under theorised elements. These include its pedagogy, particularly the development of mindset and attitude, and the principle of reflection, and its epistemology, with the unfulfilled promise of co-produced transformational knowledge, rather than the seeking out of 'hidden' or 'authentic' voices.

Chapter 3, *Peer research: epistemological symbolism, proxy trust, conscious partiality and the near-peer*, follows on from some of the challenges of the previous chapter and recognises that one of the tenets of PPIR needs to be one of active engagement in issues around power and representation. One of the ways PPIR does this is through the active involvement of peers, in both a symbolic and purposive way. Peer research is another approach that it is hard to disagree with, but is surprisingly under researched and contested. Justifications for using peer research seem to fall into three claims: claims about power and epistemology, claims about the nature of the data that peer researchers can obtain and the emancipatory and empowering impact of using peer researchers for all stake-holders. These claims are explored in this chapter. It will contend that the first of these claims is symbolic, but powerful, that the second is over emphasised, and that the last claim is key, but sets us a challenge for how we make the practice emancipatory, rather than tokenistic, or a tyranny of participatory methods.

The final chapter in Part 1 – Chapter 4, *PPIR's key claim: towards critical peda-gogic reflective spaces* – focuses on the major under theorised and unrealised aspect of participatory research and co-production – the purpose and nature of the critical reflective spaces that is essential for both. It propounds that the purpose of these spaces is to create dedicated meta reflexives with intersubjective con-sciousness. On a more practical level it outlines a number of characteristics of these spaces: that they are liminal rather than safe spaces that are co-contained by all stakeholders; that they are characterised by intersubjectivity, encounter and recognition; that they place an emphasis on and commitment to de-construction of power and the concept of knowledge and democratic decision-making, they privilege spontaneity and working in the moment; and they cultivate hope and a future orientation.

Part 2, *Participatory Pedagogic Impact Research: towards a process*, examines how to undertake a PPIR project, including all the common processes of research including ethics, issue identification, methodology and methods, participations in analysis and dissemination, but from a pedagogic and participatory angle, assessing PPIR's differences from and similarities to other forms of research. It will also examine how to create a common understanding in organizations about research, and how to win stakeholders over to the process.

Chapter 5, *Meaningful organizational impact: winning stakeholders over to the process*, drawing on practical experience, looks at how to sell the concept of research to all stakeholders, as well as how to mediate existing attitudes towards research. It examines what needs to be in place for a research project to have a chance of making an impact on the overall organizational culture, particularly its mindset towards research and community partner involvement. It creates a set of criteria by which to judge if an organizations is truly ready to take on board co-production and participatory research and works through examples of where this has and has not worked in practice.

Chapter 6, *Ethical considerations in PPIR: negotiating power and position*, examines both the ethics of pedagogic participatory research in general and how to approach ethics for a specific project in a pedagogic and participatory way. To these ends it sees ethics, and its amelioration, as a dynamic between researchers and researched, rather than something that we do beforehand. Research should unsettle and occasionally disturb, and in doing so take risks, but it should not humiliate and undermine. It also questions where we should put the emphasis of ethics, and whether this should be equal, taking the stance that ethical considerations should favour those with the least power.

Chapter 7, *Defining your terrain: community member and issue identification*, examines firstly how to identify community member participants, distinguishing between primary secondary and participatory research gatherers. It gives practical ideas for how to make the group meaningfully representative. Secondly it explores how the subject under investigation is initially identified and explored. An emphasis is put on exploring the paradigm PPIR operates within, as many community partners, and commissioners of research, come with a very positivistic view of research that needs to be worked with. Indeed PPIR has post positivistic concerns to influence beyond the subjects in the investigation, but also has critical concerns and an emphasis on allowing unheard voices to emerge. And that these voices are contextualized, and are worked with. PPIR also draws on community organizing principles to discern what are the most potentially meaningful

Chapter 8, *Methodology in action: transforming participant knowledge*, challenges how all too often the methodology and resultant methods are chosen because a researcher has a particular interest or expertise in that approach. Alternatively, often in health and social care research, over familiar tools such as interviews and focus groups are used, forgetting that community partners may have particular associations with such approaches, through key working and group work. It outlines how in PPIR we ground the approach in the medium(s) that are familiar to those being researched, organically building on indigenous ways of knowing. PPIR methods are often creative, but are deliberately not exotic – they are grounded in means by which the researched express themselves.

Chapter 9, *Analysis and making recommendations: grounding your data in community ways of knowing*, critiques how all too often analysis is the point where research stops being participative, and certainly pedagogic. Here we explore this dilemma and seek ways to keep the participation meaningful. The method of analysing PPIR also seeks to find a way between a pre-imposed thematic approach and a purely grounded approach that is in danger of orientalizing and de-contextualizing the researched. Methods of triangulation and grounding the data in the wider community are sought. The chapter again explores how, as well as having local ways of knowing, communities will also have local ways of understanding – i.e. analysing information.

Chapter 10, *Dissemination and impact: accounting for and privileging process*, begins with a deconstruction of the existing Research Excellence Framework's view of impact, and seeks to outline ways that Impact could be more meaningfully reflected for participatory research. Then as well as exploring traditional means of dissemination and trying to assess impact, it looks at how PPIR emphasizes the localized impact on the organization, the researchers and the researched, with the importance emphasis of relationship and capacity building within the organization. It is often the process of doing the research that has greatest pedagogic impact on how workers, community partners and the organization now see each other, and themselves. Implementing the recommendations of the research is important, particularly in embedding this learning, but is not the only criteria of success. It will make a distinction between dissemination products, processes and events. As an example it calls for making the launch event far more than the staid thing it often is, and instead, building go on community organizing approaches, calls for it to be dramatic, a power play between researched, researchers and policy makers.

Part 3, *Notes from the field: research in action*, is a series of case studies, detailing learning from PPIR in action. It covers a variety of health and social care settings including homelessness, probation, working with violent young people and those who are multiply excluded. All these case studies are written by practitioners and peer researchers involved in the programme.

In Chapter 11, *Reflections on peer and participatory research: Groundswell UK and The Escape Plan*, Simone Helleren reflects on her experience in Groundswell, a homeless self-help group that has always involved peer researchers in its research. In particular it explores learning from a study identifying critical success factors that have enabled entrenched rough sleepers to move on from homelessness. It explores three key issues commonly met when approaching peer and participatory research. The first of these is 'Peerness: the "who" of participation', unpicking the role of peer researcher and recognizing the complexity of peer research for the people involved. The second is 'Involvement in decision-making: how and how much?' highlighting some techniques and strategies for opening the space and getting out of the way to enable participation. The third is, 'Working with commissioners: how it helps and gets in the way', considering working within limitations and the benefits of partnering with experts.

In Chapter 12, *Courage of our convictions: participatory research in the criminal justice system*, Beth Coyne presents a brief précis of the methodology and findings of two service user involvement projects in probation settings, and one in a prison. The chapter also sets out a number of key findings that are of interest to the discussion here about participatory pedagogy, its use, its value and its limitations. It begins with some context of the time and the transforming agenda and how the authors undertook the projects before going on to examine the impact of involvement Rehabilitation on service users themselves including the effect of pro-social modelling between peers, the identity theory of desistance and use of language.

In Chapter 13, *The absent lens of the peer researcher: reflections on and beyond a research project into youth violence*, Richard Campbell, one of the peer researchers from the project, expands upon the learning from a two-year participatory action research project (from March 2011 to March 2013) funded by the EU and conducted in Bradford, London, Cologne and Graz. It used peer researchers to examine how street-based youth work can respond meaningfully to street violence, and will specifically look at some of the issues about using peer researchers in such a context. It issues some challenges to those who wish to utilize peers in research including what makes for a successful peer–participant relationship and its limitations, what it takes to break into the circle of trust of participants, the importance of creativity, and the development and contesting of academic language.

In Chapter 14, *From relationships to impact in community–university partnerships*, Randy Stoecker, Karen Reece and Taylor Konkle critically examine what we mean by the university having a relationship with the community, asking whether these relationship have true impact and create social change or advance social justice? The authors undertook a partnership piece of research that sought to investigate and confront the fears of music venue owners about Hip-Hop, with an aim to potentially open up those venues to more Hip-Hop shows. In doing so they ask fundamental questions about how universities and community view each other, and themselves, and show how this can transformed. What emerges is the centricity of trust and respect, and that this needs to be both earned and lived from both sides.

In Chapter 15, *Using Volunteer-Employed Photography: seeing St David's Peninsula through the eyes of locals and tourists*, Nika Balomenou and Brian Garrod explore how Volunteer-Employed Photography (VEP) has been described as a powerful but underused and undervalued research tool. Indeed, there is a growing body of scientific evidence to suggest that participatory photographic techniques such as VEP allow complex meanings to be conveyed and permit study subjects to express their views more efficiently and effectively. It is argued that this is because the medium of photography is more sensitive to the multidimensional nature of experiences than is written text or the spoken word. On this basis, it is argued that VEP proves itself useful in investigating tensions between locals and tourists in tourism destinations. This chapter focuses mainly on the methodological issues that arise from the use of VEP. A critique of the methodology with the view of it being used in different contexts is presented in this chapter.

The concluding chapter brings together the themes of PPIR, looking at its potential and some of the challenges it faces. This will be done within the context of the real life issues and dilemmas thrown up by the case studies, particularly issues of power, the reality and limitations of becoming a researcher, and the impact researching self has on individuals. PPIR sees itself as the most effective means of conducting and embedding 'involvement' in an organizational culture, with an emphasis on pedagogy. In doing this it argues that we must set its standard as reaching the most marginalized groups, not just those that are the most articulate. It must also in the process deconstruct notions of power and peer, and, on an operational level, the nature of research itself, in terms of how it views validity and reliability and what is meant by 'grounded' data and reflexivity. It argues that PPIR's epistemological stance is part of the participatory paradigm shift.

References

Alinsky, S. (1971) *Rules for Radicals: A Pragmatic Primer for Realistic Radicals*. New York: Vintage Books.

Archer, M. S. (2012) *The Reflexive Imperative in Late Modernity*. Cambridge: Cambridge University Press.

Archer, M. S. (2010) *Conversations About Reflexivity*. London and New York: Routledge.

Assaad, M., el Katsha, S. & Watts, S. (1994) 'Involving women in water and sanitation initiatives: an action/research project in an Egyptian village.' *Water International*, 19: 113–120.

Beresford, P. (2016) *All Our Welfare: Towards Participatory Social Policy*. Bristol: Policy Press.

Beresford, P. (2010) *A Straight Talking Guide To Being A Mental Health Service User*. Ross-on-Wye: PCCS Books.

Beresford, P. & Croft, S. (2012) NIHR School for Social Care Research Scoping Review – User Controlled Research, London, UK: NIHR School for Social Care Research.

Bhaskar, R. (2008) *A Realist Theory of Science*. 2nd edition. London: Verso.

Bhaskar, R. (1993) *Dialectic: The Pulse of Freedom*. 2nd edition. London: Routledge.

Brodie, E., Cowling, E., Nissen, N., Paine, A., Jochum, V. & Warburton, D. (2009) *Understanding Participation: A Literature Review*. NCVO, IVR, Involve (www.involve. org.uk).

Bygstad, B. & Munkvold, B. (2011) 'In search of mechanisms, conducting a critical realist data analysis.' Conference proceedings, Thirty Second International Conference on Information Systems, Shanghai.

Chambers, E. with Cowan, M. (2004) *Roots for Radicals: Organizing for Power, Action and Justice*. New York: Continuum.

Chambers, R. (2010) *Provocations for Development*. Rugby: Practical Action Publishing.

Chambers, R. (2008) *Revolutions in Development Inquiry*. London: Earthscan.

Chambers, R. (2005) *Ideas for Development*. London: Earthscan.

Chambers, R. (2002) *Participatory Workshops: A Sourcebook of 21 Sets of Ideas and Activities*. London: Earthscan.

Checkoway, B. & Richards-Schuster, K. (2003) 'Youth participation in community evaluation research.' *American Journal of Evaluation*, 24(1): 21–33.

Cooke, B. & Kothari, U. (2001) (eds) *Participation: The New Tyranny?* Zed: London.

Cornwall, A. (2002) *Making Spaces, Changing Places: Stimulating Participation in Development*. IDS Working Paper 170, Brighton Institute of Development Studies.

Cornwall, A. & Brock, K. (2005) 'What do buzzwords do for development policy? A critical look at "participation", "empowerment", and "poverty reduction."' *Third World Quarterly* 26(7): 1043–1060.

Fals-Borda, O. & Rahman, M. A. (1991) *Action and Knowledge: Breaking the Monopoly With Participatory Action Research*. London: ITDG Publications.

Freire, P. (1972) *Pedagogy of the Oppressed*. London: Penguin.

Gecan, M. (2002) *Going Public*. Boston, MA: Beacon Press.

Healthwatch (2013) *Annual Report 2012/13*. HMRC: London.

HEFCE, SFC, HEFCW, DELNI (2012a) Assessment framework and guidance on submissions (02.2011 updated version) www.ref.ac.uk/media/ref/content/pub/assessment frameworkandguidanceonsubmissions/GOS%20including%20addendum.pdf.

HEFCE, SFC, HEFCW, DELNI (2012b) Main Panel A Criteria (01.2012) www.ref.ac.uk/ media/ref/content/pub/panelcriteriaandworkingmethods/01_12_2A.pdf.

Henkel, H. & Stirrat, R. (2001) 'Participation as spiritual duty: empowerment as secular subjection.' In B. Cooke & U. Kothari (eds) *Participation: The New Tyranny?* London: Zed, pp. 168–184.

Heron, J. (1996) *Co-operative Inquiry: Research Into the Human Condition*. London: Sage.

Henkel, H. & Stirrat, R. (1988) 'Impressions of the other reality: a co-operative inquiry into altered states of consciousness.' In P. Reason (ed.) *Human Inquiry in Action*. London: Sage, pp. 182–198.

Henkel, H. & Stirrat, R. (1981) 'Philosophical basis for a new paradigm.' In P. Reason & H. Bradbury (eds) *Human Inquiry: A Sourcebook of New Paradigm Research*. Chichester: Wiley.

Henkel, H. & Stirrat, R. (1974) *The Concept of a Peer Learning Community*. London: University of London Press.

Hickey, S. & Mohan, G. (2004) *Participation: From Tyranny to Transformation*. London and New York: Zed Books.

Hills, M. & Mullett, J., (2000) *Community-based Research: Creating Evidence Based Practice for Health and Social Change*. Paper presented to the Qualitative Evidence Based Practice Conference, Coventry University, 15–17 May.

Israel, B. A., Schultz, A. J., Parker, E. A. & Becker, A. B. (1998) 'Review of community-based research: assessing partnership approaches to improve health.' *Annual Review of Public Health*, 19: 173–202.

Kapoor, I. (2005) 'Participatory development, complicity and desire.' *Third World Quarterly*, 26(8): 1203–1220.

Kapoor, I. (2002) 'The devil's in the theory: a critical assessment of Robert Chambers' work on participatory development.' *Third World Quarterly*, 23(1): 101–117.

Kesby, M., Kindon, S. & Pain, R. (2007) 'Participation as a form of power: retheorising empowerment and spatialising Participatory Action Research.' In S. Kindon, R. Pain & M. Kesby (eds) *Participatory Action Research Approaches and Methods: Connecting People, Participation and Place*. Abingdon, Oxon: Routledge, pp. 19–25.

Kinpaisby-Hill, C. (2009) 'Participatory praxis and social justice: towards more fully social geographies.' Paper presented to Mestizo Arts and Activism Collective, Salt Lake City, Utah, 21 January.

Kincheloe, J. L. (2008). *Critical Pedagogy Primer*. 2nd edition. New York: Peter Lang.

Koch, T. & Kralkin, B. (2009) *Participatory Action Research in Health Care*. London: Wiley.

Kothari, U. (2005) 'Authority and expertise: the professionalization of international development and the ordering of dissent.' *Antipode*, 37(3): 402–424.

Manicas, P. (2006) *A Realist Philosophy of Social Science*. Cambridge: Cambridge University Press.

McLaren, P. (2016) 'Critical pedagogy and class struggle in the age of neoliberal terror.' In R. Kumar (ed.) *Neoliberalism, Critical Pedagogy and Education*. London: Routledge, pp. 19–67.

McLaughlin, H. (2009) *Service User Research in Health and Social Care*. London: Sage.

Minkler, M. & Wallerstein, N. (2008) *Community-Based Participatory Research for Health: From Process to Outcomes*. 2nd edition. San Francisco, CA: Jossey-Bass.

Mohan, G. (2007) 'Participatory development: from epistemological reversals to active citizenship.' *Geography Compass*, 1(4): 779–796.

Mosse, D. (1994) 'Authority, gender and knowledge: theoretical reflections on the practice of participatory rural appraisal.' *Development and Change*, 25(3): 497–526.

Nestor, P. & Galletly, C. (2008) 'The employment of consumers in mental health services: politically correct tokenism or genuinely useful?' *Australasian Psychiatry*, 16(5): 344–347.

Rancière, J. (2004) 'Introducing disagreement.' *Angelaki: Journal of the Theoretical Humanities*, 9(3): 3–9.

Rancière, J. (1992) *The Ignorant Schoolmaster: Five Lessons in Intellectual Emancipation.* Stanford, CA: Stanford University Press.

Reardon, K. M. (2000) 'An experiential approach to creating effective community-university partnership: the East St Louis action research project.' *Cityscape: A Journal of Policy Development and Research*, 5(1): 59–74.

Sanderson, E. & Kindon, S. (2004) 'Progress in participatory development: opening up the possibilities of knowledge through progressive participation.' *Progress in Development Studies*, 4(2): 114–126.

Savan, B. & Sider, D. (2003) 'Contrasting approaches to community-based research and a case study of sustainability in Toronto.' *Canada, Local Environment*, 8(3): 303–316.

Sayer, A. (2000) *Realism and Social Science.* New York: Sage.

Schutz, A. & Sandy, M. G. (2011) *Collective Action for Social Change: An Introduction to Community Organising.* New York: Palgrave Press.

Seal, M. (2016) 'Critical realism's potential contribution to critical pedagogy and youth and community work: human nature, agency and praxis revisited.' *Journal of Critical Realism*, 15(3): 263–276.

Seal, M. (2009) *Not About Us Without Us: Client Involvement in Social Housing.* Lyme Regis: Russell House Publishing.

Shor, I. (1980) *Critical Teaching and Everyday Life.* Chicago, IL: University of Chicago Press.

Steinburg, S. (2000) *Contextualizing Teaching: Introduction to Education and Educational Foundations.* New York: Longman Publishing.

Taylor, P. (1993) *The Texts of Paulo Freire.* Buckingham: Open University Press.

Terry, L. & Cardwell, V. (2016) *Refreshing Perspectives: Exploring the Application of Peer Research with Populations Facing Severe and Multiple Disadvantage.* London: Revolving Doors Agency.

White, S. C. (1996) 'Depoliticising development: the uses and abuses of participation.' *Development in Practice*, 6(1): 6–15.

Wilcox, D. (1995) *Community Participation and Empowerment: Putting Theory into Practice.* London: Partnership Press.

Part 1

The co-production of knowledge with community partners

Dilemmas and debates

1 Emperor's old clothes

Re-contesting the involvement of community partners

As I have previously noted (Seal, 2009) the involvement of community partners, whether called client involvement, service user participation or co-production, is something that is very difficult to argue against in principle of, but it is even harder to agree on what it should look like in practice. Since my last book on the subject, community involvement in services planning and delivery has come to prominence in the Health Service with the statutory requirement for PPI (Public and Patient Involvement) and the setting up of Healthwatch to monitor its implementation. Since that publication, statutory and voluntary organizations from the Scottish Executive, to Shelter to the National Offender Management Service (who in 2009, had not embraced such ideas to any great extent), have all produced guides and policy extoling the idea, some of which this author has been involved in).

There has also been a linguistic and philosophical shift with the notion of co-production coming to the fore. As we shall explore this signifies a shift from seeing clients as service users, as a group to 'consult', or 'involve' to seeing them as active partners in co-producing services (New Economics Foundation, 2008). However, contradictions and tensions remain. Successive governments have couched client participation in social care in terms of the 'personalization' of services (DOH, 2008.) While this sounds empowering in their rhetoric 'every person who receives support, whether provided by statutory services or funded by themselves, will have choice and control over the shape of that support in all care settings' (DoH, 2008, p. 2) the approach is underpinned by a neo liberal agenda of individualization and consumerism (Beresford, 2016) rather than the implied collectivism of co-production, and symptomatic of the increasing commodification of care services. Also, as Beresford notes, in reality choice is limited, and controlled, and this commodification has actually resulted in 'vast profits made by a small number of providers at the expense of good quality services for those who use them' (Beresford, 2016, p. 89).

At the same time, we have experienced the largest cut in public and social care services in a generation. Taking my own field, homelessness, we had great successes between the mid-nineties and the mid-2000s in embedding the idea of client involvement into the sector. We trained hundreds of agencies, designed numerous client involvement strategies and embedded service user involvement into the quality assessment framework for Supporting People, the main funder of services (albeit as a supplementary standard, meaning in reality it was one of the first to go to the wall). Yet when the cuts came, the Supporting People budget was 'devolved' to local authorities, i.e. pushed down onto a sector with an already stretched budget. After a brief period of ring-fencing services were cut by up to 85% (Homeless Link, 2013), the monitoring of services became minimal and commissioning based on a crude calculation of 'unit' (i.e. people) cost.

Client involvement, while acknowledged as important, was not embedded and lost prominence. This prompted a colleague to reflect recently at a celebration of 20 years of campaigning for client involvement that in many ways we are back to where we were 20 years ago. In hindsight this is partly an inevitable retreat and retrenchment that any social movement experiences in its journey. However, we have to accept that the homeless sector in general only ever saw to client involvement as a worthy add on, rather than an essential key to success and efficiency.

This chapter will re-examine the debates and dilemmas in involving community partners in health and social care as partners in the delivery of services. It will particularly explore the principles and barriers to effective involvement, the dangers of tokenism, and ask what constitutes 'meaningful' involvement, under the principle that true involvement should be transformative for all. It will also seek to foreground and enrich some of the arguments for co-production and client involvement with a more robust theoretical, empirical, ontological, pedagogical and epistemological examination of the process of knowledge creation and the impact that co-production, in particular, seeks to make.

In doing so I am setting out an agenda that the rest of the book will follow, namely that PPIR is the most effective way of involving community members. There are several layers to this argument: our model of involvement should be that of co-production; we should see co-production as a knowledge producing process that is underpinned by critical pedagogy; that the most effective and robust way to produce this knowledge is through joint research; and that this needs, almost by definition, to be participatory research, albeit one that sees itself as a transformative pedagogic process. Lastly that in these times of austerity, where we have to think faster, quicker and across multiple audiences, we also have to have a discernible and meaningful impact. In order to do this I draw on some of the approaches of community organizing, which has a significant history of making real change. It's approach to campaigning led to a governmental policy, ending child refugee detention.

The rationale for involvement and co-production

I have previously emphasized the importance of understanding and developing a clear rationale for client involvement (Seal, 2009). This is for several reasons. It is partly for our own clarity, particularly where there are different agendas for involvement. However, it is mainly for end service users, lest they get pulled around because of said mixed agendas. One of the central themes in that book concerned the ways in which services construct clients, and how they are allowed to participate only in certain ways, are underpinned by certain ideologies that we rarely acknowledge. Having perhaps had negative experiences of client involvement they might have a natural suspicion of an agency's or individual's motivations for inviting them to 'get involved' (Cameron et al., 2005; Seal, 2009; Wilcox, 1995).

In a previous book on client involvement I outlined four primary rationales for community and service user involvement, which are worth summarizing. Consumerist rationales say that as consumers of our services we ought to consult community members, and service users as to what they want so we can better 'serve' them. The professionalization agenda certainly seem to fit into this perspective. Democratic rationales view that the community and service users have a 'right' to be involved, particularly when we are talking about 'public' services. The PPI initiatives in the health services seems to be broadly predicated on this way of thinking. Personal development rationales building on the work of Putnam and others (Putnam, 2000; Groundswell, 2014) tend to say that involvement is good for people per se, it develops agency, self-esteem and self-efficacy. Many recent care initiatives, from developing psychologically informed environments (Breedvelt, 2016), to recovery models (Jacob, 2015), tend to see client involvement using this rationale as a lens.

Before I mention the final, critical, model, it is worth rehearsing the critiques I made of the other models. Consumerist models underestimate the power dynamics in the community/service provider relationship and are limited in scope, with the limits of change being tinkering with the 'product', and there are often rigid assumptions about who is the producer and who is the consumer, which co-production challenges at a fundamental level. Democratic models beg the question of what it means to be democratic and who controls the point at which people have their say. It also raises questions about the tyranny of the majority, and which community we privilege at what point. The personal development model can be dangerous in isolation, and risks becoming over therapeutic and re-inscribing the professional/community power divide 'emphasising the dignity and respect to be sought between user and provider, without any attempt to change the balance of power within it' (Braye, 2000, p. 12). It is not surprising that it is often the most palatable for workers and it can also be the least challenging to their practices and structures (Seal, 2009). In critiquing these models, I am not saying that these perspectives goals are illegitimate. However, I would challenge their driving forces and underpinning rationales. I would say that co-production, done well, will organically address the concerns of these perspectives. Services for clients will becomes better, and more efficient, co-production is democratic, and makes for a more democratic culture in the organization, and co-production will certain develop individuals personally, including workers and managers.

My final rationale was a critical perspective, defining it as a perspective that challenges the very rationale for services and the fundamentals of their structures. In hindsight I under-theorized this perspective, naming some of the model's characteristics rather than its premise. Critical perspectives differ on both an epistemological and an ontological level. They are perhaps best exemplified in the idea of co-production. Professor Edgar Cahn (2004) has developed the idea of co-production since the 1970s, rejecting both a market view of the relations between consumer and producer and a centralized bureaucratized view of production. For him the community, and service users, should not be seen as a drain or passive consumers of products, but as having an essential vitalizing contribution to make. Similarly, producers, particularly front line workers, should not be viewed as faceless bureaucrats, but humanized and encouraged to be innovative (New Economics Foundation, 2008).

Co-production is a capacity based – as opposed to a deficit based – approach to involvement. The community moves from being seen as passive recipients of services and burdens on the system into being equal partners in designing and delivering services (Cahn, 2004). There is an emphasis on reciprocity and mutuality where the community, service users, professionals and managers develop reciprocal relationships with mutual responsibilities and expectations (Nestor & Gallely, 2008). This involves a blurring of professional distinctions between professionals and community, and between producers and consumers of services, through a reconfiguring of the way services are developed and delivered (Cahn, 2004).

Again on an ontological level, public services move from being seen as central providers and deliverers to being catalysts and facilitators (Nestor & Gallely, 2008). Developing peer and personal support networks to work alongside professionals is emphasized as the best way of transferring knowledge. Tellingly, Cahn (2004) draws on the work of Putnam (2000) around social capital, but from an interesting stance, as we shall explore presently. Co-production is good for the health and well-being of all, and this includes the organizations and ultimately the whole economy, for without it they will stagnate, losing the creative core that stimulates growth.

At an epistemological and pedagogical level co-production, and critical stances on community involvement in general, seem to have resonance with the ideas behind critical pedagogy. Within critical pedagogy knowledge and knowledge creation is an evolving process and inherently contextual. It is 'democratic, context-dependent, and appreciative of the value of learners' cultural heritage' (Cho, 2010, p. 315). In this sense we need to be actively democratic, involving the community at all levels and breaking down barriers between the learners and the educators, the community and the professional, not just on principle but because it makes for better knowledge. Similarly, community member's perspectives and expertise on their own experience is needed if we are to understand any particular context (Freire, 1972). Also central to critical pedagogy is the need to actively blur boundaries. This is not necessarily professional boundaries, although many of them are based on re-enforcing unhelpful power dynamics (Seal, 2005). It is challenging the perception about who knows best in a particular situation. Even where the professional is humble about their knowledge, the service user or community member may be intimidated simply by the worker's professional status and may privilege the worker's knowledge over their own. We will also see this dynamic emerging in Chapter 10 when we explore client representation on academic research panels – this is why the barrier of potential perception must be actively undone, to undo years of operant hegemonic forces.

Critical pedagogy also gives other pointers towards how to build effective knowledge, and this includes challenging community perspectives as well as professional knowledge. New synthesized knowledge needs to be co-produced between all, and this will be an at times difficult process. There is another important implication of an allegiance to co-production and critical pedagogy, and it represents a departure from the conclusion of my previous book. There I argued that all of the stances have legitimacy, the important thing being that the agency was clear about which one it has adopted. However, only a critical stance potentially leads to the necessary change in fundamental perception about what makes for better services and between knowledge. On a practical level stances other than a critical one can lead to a surface buy in from agencies, professionals and even community partners that, when times of austerity come along and budgets are cut, co-production is one of the first thing to go, in the erroneous belief that the most important thing is that the client still gets a service. It is not: it is that that service is fit for purpose, and that can only be achieved through the embracing of the core philosophy of having critical stance, focused on co-production – all else is tokenism, and is in the long term inefficient and counter-productive.

Barriers

I broke down my previous chapter on the barriers to community partnership (Seal, 2009) into barriers for the clients, for the workers, for managers and for the organization. While resources were identified as an obstacle, it was attitudinal barriers and perceptual barriers that dominated. Barriers for clients included ingrained cultures of fear and mistrust of systems with a them-and-us mentality towards professionals and ingrained lack of self-belief and self-efficacy. Barriers for workers seemed to be a practical focus and wish to get on with the job rather than 'have all this talking', seeing securing accommodation as their primary function. This was often a projection of their own sense of disempowerment, and lack of motivation, onto the communities and service users they worked with, and a denial of the power they have in the user/worker relationship. Managerial barriers focused on their unrealistic, and unethical, expectation that it is clients who need to change to fit in with existing planning structures. The starting point for many managers is how to enable service users and community partners to engage in their structures, rather than asking themselves how they will need to change their structures and methods of planning to incorporate service users' and communities' culture and languages. As we will see through section three, all three of these levels of barriers are still present and operative.

The underpinning themes of these barriers seems to be the fundamental views taken towards engagement, and to develop a culture of co-production is the key towards addressing them. Active breaking down of them-and-us cultures is fundamental to co-production, as is building up trust, respect and a willingness to think differently. Motivation would seem to flow from this and this all stems from a management recognition that all need to change, and not just clients and workers. Nestor and Galletly (2008) identify the central barriers to co-production thus:

> Overall, the challenge seems to amount to one clear problem. Co-production, even in the most successful and dramatic examples, barely fits the standard shape of public services or charities or the systems we have developed to 'deliver' support, even though [in the UK] policy documents express ambitions to empower and engage local communities, to devolve power and increase individuals' choice and control.

Bovaird & Loeffler (2012) expand on this, identifying three main barriers.

- *Funding and commissioning barriers*, including short termism, a reliance on quantitative measurement and the deception of the reliability of outputs over outcomes. Most funders measure only some of the outcomes achieved from their funding.
- *Issues of scale and replicability* most successful examples of co-production are organic and localized. If we see co-production as allied to critical pedagogy, then this is of necessity the case. However, many understandings of research and commissioning are underpinned by positivist constructions. Even the wishes to replicate 'best practice' are constrasted with the nuances rooting research in local conditions.
- *A lack of systematic evidence and research* of the added value created by co-production for people, professionals, funders, and auditors. Part of this is the need to articulate the kind of research that is needed, and this links to the aims of this book and chapter.

These are not easy barriers to overcome, as Beresford (2016) recognized in his latest book. It will entail a paradigm shift from seeing community members as either consumers, or issues to be dealt with, to seeing them as producers and an essential part of both enterprise and welfare. The aims of this book are more modest in this regard, and largely relate to the third barrier. It puts forward the idea that involving service users and community members in co-producing research into their own experience and services is both one of the most effective ways of undertaking co-production and increases the evidence base. As we shall see from the examples we will developed, it is a way of achieving a paradigm shift, even at the local level, that may in turn build a groundswell for a more general shift in the way service users and community members are viewed.

Principles

Looking back at the 12 values and principles I drew together for *Not About Us Without Us* (Seal, 2009), many of them stand up and dovetail with a co-productive approach. In re-examining them, there seems to be four fundamental principles.

Believing in the importance of user knowledge – let people develop their own ideas and speak for themselves

This seems to speak directly to the fundamentals of co-production. At the time I said that this principle was an article of faith that went across the rationales for involvement. Co-production, and he work of authors such as Cahn (2004) and Beresford (2016), offer a firmer empirical basis for this. Putnam (2000) recognized the impact of social capital, famously citing that engaging in social events that are reciprocal is as powerful, in health terms, as giving up cigarettes. Cahn (2004) makes the link between social capital and co-production thus:

> If social capital is critical to the well-being of society, then we must ask what its home base and source is. Social Capital is rooted in a social economy – and surely, the home base of that economy is the household, the neighbourhood, the community and civil society. That is the economy that co-production seems to rebuild and to reconstruct.
>
> (Cahn, 2004, p. 54)

Incorporating the views of all stakeholders makes for efficiency and innovation at the heart of an enterprise. Aligning ourselves to critical pedagogy also means we have philosophical, epistemological and pedagogical underpinnings, as it has a dynamic, dialectical view of the process of knowledge creation (Aristotle, 1976). Cho (2010) describes knowledge as 'democratic, context-dependent, and appreciative of the value of learners' cultural heritage' (Cho, 2010, p. 315). Knowledge comes about as a result of dialogue between those subject to the experience the potential knowledge relates to. As I have noted before (Seal, 2017) community members have their own theories and ideas about the world, and this needs to be our starting place. As Bolton describes, 'paying critical attention to the practical values and theories which inform everyday actions, by examining practice reflectively and reflexively' (2010, p. 56). I will come back to this notion of reflection later, as it is crucial. Critical educationalists view knowledge, as well as being able to be created by all, as social. We create knowledge through dialogue with each other.

Co-production is a pedagogic transformative process

In my previous work (Seal, 2009) I stated that people need to be educated for participation, to develop understanding of their situation, to see what happened and why. There is limited value in just asking people what they want, people often have to learn how to ask, analyse and question. This is not because community members do not have the potential to analyse and articulate, it is because they have been actively educated not to and told that their ways of knowing and knowledge are not valid until this is internalized. That there is this active dynamic in society that undermines the oppressed in this way is the fundamental premise of critical pedagogy (Freire, 1972; Giroux, 2012; Seal & Harris, 2016; Seal, 2017).

Critical pedagogy propounds that our current education system re-inscribes and continually re-enforces to certain excluded groups, such as most community members, a particular 'common sense'. It creates a narrative along the lines that dominant elites' social positions are 'natural and inevitable', without them life and existence would be 'Nasty, Brutish and Short', that elites' knowledge is superior and that conversely, excluded groups are not intelligent, do not have a contribution to make, and should accept their fates. Critical pedagogy seeks to interrogate received wisdoms and 'go beneath surface meaning, first impressions, dominant myths, official pronouncements, traditional clichés, received wisdom, and mere opinions' (Shor, 1992, p. 125). It grew out a concern about education was being used as a method to re-inscribe power relations in society. Theoretically critical pedagogy draws on Marxism, humanism, existentialism and post-colonialism (Seal, 2014). Giroux (2012) describes it as an 'educational movement, guided by passion and principle, to help students develop *consciousness* of freedom, recognize authoritarian tendencies, and connect knowledge to power and the ability to take constructive action' (Giroux, 2012, p. 1). This is a process that critical pedagogy calls 'concientization'.

As Aliakbari and Faraji (2011) state, critical pedagogy aims to 'transform oppressed people and to save them from being objects of education to subjects of their own autonomy and emancipation'. It aims to get people to 'think critically and develop a critical consciousness which help them to improve their life conditions and to take necessary actions to build a more just and equitable society'. Drawing on Gramsci, 'conscientization' is the aforementioned idea that people need to unlearn received wisdoms particularly about the naturalness and inevitability of their oppressed situations. Critical educationalists work to encourage students to 'develop a critical consciousness of who they are and what their language represents by examining questions of language, culture, and history through the lens of power' (Brito et al., 2004, p. 23).

Freire (1972) names three levels of consciousness: intransitive, semi transitive, and critical consciousness. Those with an intransitive consciousness accept their lives as they are and see changes beyond their control and their life situations as a result of fate, and inevitable. I have previously described how this rings true of client involvement (Seal, 2005, 2006, 2009). It can manifest as a deep cynicism about whether co-production will make a difference. There are also doubts about whether the instigators of co-production are sincere, and whether they will follow through. This is often accompanied with a self-belief amongst client and communities that they are not worth it, that their situations are inevitable or even self-inflicted and even when they rail against the unfairness of fate, this still manifests as a feeling of powerlessness. Often community members will hold contradictory views at the same time, oscillating between them.

Those with a semi transitive consciousness are aware of their problems but think they can change things only at a local level. This is where a community might involve themselves in local actions, speaking up in consultations *provided* for them, or be content to sit on a committee, even where they do not really understand what it going on. They will not make the connection between these actions and wider actions – that aspects of the system, and its methods of involvement, need to be challenged, as should the underlying assumptions and constructions behind services and initiatives. They may also be politically cynical and not see that the struggle at the local levels is paralleled in wider social struggles. Their concern often remains localized and de-politicized.

It is when people meet other community groups with similar ideas that they start opening up and making connections. This is even more marked where there are differences in focus and approach, but the dynamics, particularly of oppression, are similar. They start seeing that the oppressive forces they face are expressions of wider social forces. As an example I worked with a group of homeless people who were being evicted from their substandard B&Bs because social services and local construction companies were using them instead for asylum seekers and building workers. At first there was animosity between the groups. However, when we got them to share their lives they saw parallel, in their experiences. This was particularly so where they saw the unity of the underlying economic exploitation they were all subject to, albeit manifesting differently, and this enabled them to unite in challenging their common fate of being made to live in sub-standard conditions. This is an example of a community starting to develop a critical consciousness, beginning to see the structural dimensions of their problems, and making connections between their problems and the social context in which these problems are embedded. Hopefully they will go on, both in terms of analysis and actions, to challenge their structural oppressions as well as addressing some of their immediate concerns.

However, there are dangers with the idea of conscientization, particularly the idea of false consciousness, and I qualify a critical pedagogic approach with the work of Rancière (1992). He critiques the role is of the teacher, or worker, in critical pedagogy. For him critical pedagogy is in danger of presenting those who are oppressed as not having agency and needing an outsider, or worker, to enlighten them. Jacques Rancière was a disciple of Althusser, the Marxist theoretician, but famously broke with him in 1974 accusing him of having authoritarian tendencies, and preserving of the teacher/student power relationship. Rancière similarly critiqued Bourdieu's notion of reproduction, and Friere's notion of critical pedagogy, for condemning the masses as being unknowing and in need of liberation. Instead of the oppressed having a 'false veil' of the nature of their oppression drawn over them, they may have simply lost the will to act, often in the face of seemingly monolithic social forces where they have been forced to prioritize short term material survival that grinding poverty necessitates (Seal, 2017).

For him the educator should act under the assumption that we are all intelligent enough to understand the world, and that, given access to resources, we can discern the knowledge that will enable this understanding. He invites the educator to become 'ignorant' (his 1992 book is called *The Ignorant Schoolmaster*). He does not intend that the educator denies their knowledge, or hides it, revealing it when the time is right for others to understand their insights. Instead the educator should not privilege their knowledge – we should become ignorant, not by pretending to know nothing, but rather we should 'uncouple our mastery from our knowledge.' A true educator 'orders them (the student) to venture into the forest of things and signs, to say what they have seen and that they think of what they have seen, to verify it and have it verified' (Rancière, 1992, p. 96).

The role of the educator is two-fold – first, to act on the students' will to engage and challenge themselves and others and learn, concurrently with building up their self-belief and efficacy, two of the main components of the will; secondly, to attend to the argument people are creating, not in its content, but to their logic and internal consistency, clarifying and deconstructing the language behind those arguments and the concepts behind the language, to ensure they understand them.

Support those who get involved, preferably mutual support, being humble about the impact of the worker
Support is strange word as it has overtones of dependency (Illich, 1974): I support you because you cannot do it without me, and by implication, never will. Some may counter this by saying that we empower people until we are no longer needed. However, as several authors note (Illich, 1974; Galloway, 2012) the process by which our unequal relationship changes is ill defined, determined by the educator, and consequently often does not happen. This is not necessarily by intent, but if the power differential is not addressed from the outset it is inherent in the relationship. Originally I said that the most important aspect of making co-production accessible is not practical support, and I think this still holds, though practical support is necessary, as without it involvement does not happen anyway.

I said at the time that people need to be helped to believe in themselves, to see that the skills they have are transferable and valuable. The question is whether others are needed to help them realize this. I think there were possible community members need to be self-defining and self-determining, and even if we may help in the short term, what are the long terms consequences of this. I have discussed previously (Seal, 2014) how marginalized groups may need to have a period of self-help and autonomy, even isolation, where they develop a sense of themselves and their identities before they can emerge and engage with others. There is a legitimacy, at least for a time, in women only, LGBT, and black minority ethnic (BME) spaces, and by extension community members and service users. The early work of Groundswell, a client led organization for homeless people, started out with this emphasis, as Simone discusses in Chapter 11. In practice I have found that clients often need less help than we think they do, and what may seem chaos to a professional worker is often a community's organic way of working things through.

This doesn't not necessarily mean leaving the community to work it out for themselves. We have named the role of the educator/facilitator earlier to work on will and self-esteem/belief and to ensure that people are rigorous and logical in their approach, and that people hold each other, and the educator, to account. This means that a worker will need to challenge the structure they operate within including 'rejecting long standing cultural expectations' of the organization and themselves, including the superiority of their own knowledge over the communities. It also means losing the 'power which is given to them through their titles' (Foley, 2007 p. 98). We need to be explicitly humble and challenging of our own privilege. To be a critical pedagogue means challenging the worker's illusion of power.

Many communities have years of experience of using services, such that the worker gets a certain level of authority derived from this common cultural experience, (though not necessarily respect) and this needs to be named, brought into the discussions and challenged.

As Joldersma (1999) notes, there is a certain familiar complacency in dependant relationships for some community members. They do not have to make much effort, or take responsibility, and can apportion blame entirely outside of themselves. Community members and services users can also see themselves as consumers, taking what they want and ignoring what does not immediately resonate. They can also passively resist, taking small chances to undermine the authority of the worker, but often in a non-constructive way, or a way that can in turn be infantilized by the worker. For the learning to be real this 'play' of accepted roles again needs to be named and challenged.

This is an organic contextual process: no one model will work for all

In my previous work (Seal, 2009) I noted that there is no single model for effective user involvement because users are not homogenous and there needs to be a multiplicity of methods. I linked this to the concept of diversity, saying that all co-production approaches will allow certain groups to dominate, that this must be acknowledged and the key is having a diversity of approaches. However, commissioners and planners like models that can be replicated and scaled up, both through positivist assumptions and also simply for convenience. This is why our arguments need to be more robust. The need for localism is on an ontological and epistemological level.

Philosophically and epistemologically this means we are wedded to the idea of Phronesis. Aristotle (1976) talks about three types of knowledge, scientific knowledge that largely does not change ('Episteme'), although this idea is itself heavily contested, the technical knowledge a person needs to put this science to use ('Techne') and 'Phronesis'. This is very different in character, and is often simply called practical knowledge or wisdom. It is where we are applying knowledge to the world, hence the practical, but it is where human beings are involved, and so involves an application of values and ethics. Fundamental to this is that it is relative knowledge. A person is making a judgement about what is *right* to *do* in *particular* situations. Aristotle was clear that we should not try and find universal truths in this as people are infinitely complex, and the variables are great and in flux. I talk elsewhere about the horror expressed by a representative from the business world expressed at a conference I attended where a homeless service was proudly explaining its adoption of models from industry into its evaluation processes – 'but they were designed for machine parts, not people,' the representative exclaimed.

Furthermore, most situations are multi factorial and happen in particular contexts and time. Consequently, knowledge about people is similarly particular and contextual. While we may draw on wider universals, we are seeking to determine what is the appropriate action this particular context and in this moment of time. As Mao says 'the development of each particular process is relative, and that hence, in the endless flow of absolute truth, man's knowledge of a particular process at any given stage of development is only relative truth' (Zae Tung, 1937). There is a political dimension to this for critical pedagogues. Much of what is presented by agencies and services as Episteme – i.e. as facts that are objective, neutral and natural, such as the structures, committees and ways of planning and delivering services – are in actuality 'Phronesis', knowledge that is a result of, and underpinned by, a particular moral view, a choice, and as such, could be different. They stem from a particular ideology.

Many of the other principles from *Not About Us Without Us* stem from an orientation towards co-production the principles of *being holistic: seek to involve people in all aspects of the work,* is a restatement of co-production. Similarly the idea of starting *at the point of interest for the users* is about the remembering to not impose our agendas onto community members. Perhaps in time mutual agendas can be developed but at the start, often where community members and service users are giving up their own time, it must engage them. As I also noted in that book (Seal, 2009) clients have often in the past been asked to respond to the agenda of the agency – why would anyone, unless paid to, want to discuss the infinite detail of a strategic plan, or even the strategic planning process?

The principles of *Cultivating, permission and protection* and *Demonstrating potency and commitment* are again about addressing, continually, issues of power and perceived power. Permission to participate cannot simply be given; it must be accepted and trusted by the user. It is a developmental process. People must also *feel* safe, not only physically but psychologically. They need to feel and *see* that there will not be repercussions from their involvement. Service users and community members must be able to see that they can make a difference (although not necessarily that everything will change) through a clear, accountable system.

I still think the idea of *Recognizing the importance of setting, abandon the idea of 'neutral space'* has resonance. The concept of a 'neutral space' should be abandoned. Instead, take the process to the communities' own space; this acknowledges the power differential between the community and the services meant to enable them. *Reciprocity: being clear how being involved has value for all parties* is, again, fundamental to co-production. It should be clear what users and 'involvers' get out of the process. People are suspicious and feel undervalued if the 'involver's' reason seems too philanthropic. The message that clients' views are fundamentally needed to make a service work is a far better message than we embrace co-production because we are 'nice' people.

Finally, to *recognize that involvement is an ongoing, ever-evolving process* stems from our epistemological stance. As well as being contextual and specific, knowledge evolves. One word for this is praxis and critical pedagogy has consistently described itself as a praxis (Batsleer, 2012; Ord, 2000). Praxis is often interpreted as the synthesis of theory and action. It sees knowledge as an evolving thing. Important here, as we may encounter cynics from both the community and the services, is a recognition that things we have tried, but failed, in the past may work now because the context and circumstances are different, even though they may look the same. This is not to say that we do not subject ideas to critique and reflection, but that this should be a reflexive process.

Developing critical reflection in co-production

We noted earlier in this chapter the importance of reflection. As Freire (1974) says, the creation of evolving knowledge entails 'reflection and action upon the world in order to transform it' (Freire, 1973, p 12). Reflection is a means of mediating and developing praxis. It was present in the work of John Dewey (1933) and was coined as a method by Schön (1983). Schön describes reflective practice as 'the capacity to reflect on action so as to engage in a process of continuous learning' (1983, p. 34). Many others have developed these early formulations (Brookfield, 1998; Gänshirt, 2007; Gibbs, 1988; Johns, 1995; Rolfe et al., 2001). However, in keeping with a Rancierian approach, it is not that the community, or indeed services and workers, do not reflect – we should not rarefy it as a process. However, the way they reflect may not be helpful in creating new knowledge. Archer's work on reflection (most comprehensively expressed in *The Reflexive Imperative in Late Modernity'* in 2012) is of use here. Reflection for Archer is not the reflection of a practitioner emphasized in the helping professions' literature, but the everyday reflections of people and communities – our 'internal conversation' (Archer, 2012). She has developed a typology of reflexive actors, and while this has the limitations of any such schema, it is a useful heuristic device for examining how people do, and do not, create new knowledge.

Only *fractured reflexives* fit into the structuralist view of individuals without agency. Alienated and reified, they are the people to whom things simply happen. Their backgrounds are too fractured and painful for them to truly reflect and develop. Reflection and internal conversations (Archer, 2010, 2012) make them emotionally distressed and cognitively disorientated. As a consequence, their identities are equally fractured and they are often at the mercy of their social environment. When working in homelessness I encountered many who fitted into this category. This was often as a result of the severely disabling experiences leading to their homelessness, but also their experiences going through the system. However, while they have temporarily forfeited control over their own life, and can only passively register what happens to them, this is not a static state: for reflective abilities can be developed.

Communicative reflexives think and talk. Their internal conversations, and personal and social identities need to be affirmed and discussed with others in their immediate circle. They reduce their aspirations according to their context and constraints, and do not engage in projects that exceed their contextual confines. They reproduce their familial backgrounds and show contentment with their lot. From a more theoretical point of view, they can be considered as 'socially conservative Habermasians and contented Bourdieusians' (Atkinson, 2014, p. 125). Workers, community members and agencies who like to avoid conflict, and keep involvement 'cosy' seem to fit into this category. I will come back to this, as one of the underpinning approaches in critical pedagogy is to work with the contradictions of a service or phenomenon. It is working the seam between the liberal desire to focus on the positive and the temptation to wallow in the negative. I have met many workers and community members who pride themselves on being 'good communicators', but the concern is when this means they are also a communicative reflector.

Autonomous reflexives think and act, and are generally more internal in their conversations. They are goal orientated and will challenge and change their context if it is not compatible with their stated goals, rejecting constraints but very accepting of any enablements. They often have projects from an early stage that challenge their received contexts, but not the structures that allow those contexts to arise. Archer also notes that they often have a Rawlsian sense of fairness and justice but have a structural conservatism and engage in actions that re-enforce and re-inscribe the system and strengthen its integration. This reminds me of the services user, community member, or worker who is on a mission, will work the system until they reach their goal, but will often stop at this point.

For Archer, only *Meta-flexives* exercise critical reflexivity. Often idealists, they critically reflect on themselves and their situations, and then reflect on their reflections. Their internal conversation is self-directed. They seek self-knowledge and practice self-critique for the sake of self-improvement and self-realization. They are critical of their context, environment and received social constructions. However, as a consequence they are contextually unsettled, continuously on the move searching for a new job, a new career, a new life, a new self, so they are not as loyal as communicative reflectors: if their family and friends do not share their goals, they move on from them. They are immune to constraints and enablements as they cannot be bought off by inducements and will be downwardly mobile if it realizes their ideals.

While such reflectors have certainly developed consciousness, they also seem somewhat fickle, self-centered and decentered, and ultimately, not very content. It is also a very individually focused view, which somewhat jars with the collective nature of co-creation and critical pedagogy's emphasis on mutuality and the inter-subjective development of knowledge. Perhaps more useful is Scrambler's (2013) vision of a dedicated meta-reflexive 'whose value-driven commitments become central to identity for self and others and transmute into life-long advocacy on behalf of the 'community as a whole' (Scrambler, 2013, p. 146).

Conclusion

I hope I have created an argument in this chapter for community partner and service involvement being best exemplified by a synthesis of co-production and critical pedagogy. I hope I have enriched our empirical and philosophical groundings and paved the way for my subsequent argument about the ways that this synthesis can most effectively be enacted. If the co-production of knowledge is an ongoing, ever evolving process then we need to have a mechanism for doing this on a permanent basis, otherwise we could fall back into co-production's reduction to delivery once the service has been planned. Every co-produced initiative will, in time, need to refresh and even replace itself and we need to have mechanisms, such as research, that can evaluate, hold to account and shape the new services to come. I believe this is best achieved through a concurrent synthesis of participatory research with elements of community organizing, as practiced by Saul Alinsky (1971). The emphasis of the synthesis is to develop a culture of valuing continual co-produced research that has a discernable impact on the object of its concern, which, as we shall see, is one of the traditional criticism of participatory research.

References

Aliakbari, M. & Faraji, E. (2011) *Basic Principles of Critical Pedagogy.* Paper presented at 2nd International Conference on Humanities, Historical and Social Sciences IPEDR vol. 17.

Alinsky, S. (1971) *Rules for Radicals: A Pragmatic Primer for Realistic Radicals.* New York: Vintage Books.

Archer, M. S. (2012) *The Reflexive Imperative in Late Modernity.* Cambridge: Cambridge University Press.

Archer, M. S. (2010) *Conversations About Reflexivity.* London and New York: Routledge.

Aristotle (1976) *The Nicomachean Ethics.* London: Penguin.

Atkinson, W. (2014) 'Review of the reflexive imperative in late modernity.' *European Journal of Social Theory,* 17(1): 122–126.

Batsleer, J. (2012) *What is Youth Work.* London: Learning Matters.

Beresford, P. (2016) *All Our Welfare: Towards Participatory Social Policy.* Bristol: Policy Press.

Bolton, G. (2010) *Reflective Practice, Writing and Professional Development.* 3rd edition. Thousand Oaks, CA: Sage Publications.

Bovaird, T. & Loeffler, E. (2012) 'From engagement to co-production: how users and communities contribute to public services.' In T. Brandsen & V. Pestoff (eds) *New Public Governance, the Third Sector and Co-Production.* London: Routledge, pp. 35–60.

Braye, S. (2000) 'Participation and involvement in social care.' In H. Kemshall & R. Littlechild (eds) *User Involvement and Participation in Social Care: Research Informing Practice.* London: Jessica Kingsley Publishers, pp. 9–28.

Breedvelt, J. F. (2016) *Psychologically Informed Environments: A Literature Review.* London: Mental Health Foundation.

Brito, I., Lima, A. & Auerbach, E. (2004) 'The logic of nonstandard teaching: A course in cape verdean language, culture, and history.' In B. Norton & K. Toohey (eds) *Critical Pedagogies and Language Learning.* Cambridge: Cambridge University Press, pp. 181–200.

Brookfield, S. (1998) *Becoming a Critically Reflective Teacher.* San Francisco, CA: Jossey-Bass.

Cahn, E. (2004) *No More Throwaway People: The Co-production Imperative.* New York: Essential Books.

Cameron, A., Harrison, L., Burton, P. & Marsh, A. (2005) *Crossing the Housing and Care Divide.* Bristol: Policy Press.

Cho, S. (2010) 'Politics of critical pedagogy and new social movements.' *Educational Philosophy and Theory,* 42(3): 310–325.

Department of Health (2008) *Putting People First: Personalisation Toolkit.* London: HMSO.

Foley, P. (2007) *A Case For and Of Critical Pedagogy: Meeting the Challenge of Libratory Education at Gallaudet University*. Paper presented at the American Communication Association's annual conference. Taos: New Mexico, 2007.

Freire, P. (1972) *Pedagogy of the Oppressed*. London: Penguin.

Galloway, S. (2012) 'Reconsidering emancipatory education: staging a conversation between Paulo Freire and Jacques Rancière.' *Educational Theory*, 62: 163–184.

Gänshirt, C. (2007) *Tools for Ideas: An Introduction to Architectural Design*. Boston, MA: Basel.

Gibbs, G. (1988) *Learning by Doing: A Guide to Teaching and Learning Methods*. London: Further Education Unit.

Giroux, H. (2012) *On Critical Pedagogy*. New York: Continuum Press.

Groundswell (2014) *The Escape Plan: Creating an Evidence Base of the critical Success Factors That Have Enabled People to Successfully Move on From Homelessness*. London: Groundswell.

Homeless Link (2013) *Survey of Needs and Provision 2013*. London: Homeless Link.

Illich, I. (1974) *Disabling Professions*. London: Penguin.

Jacob, K. S. (2015) 'Recovery model of mental illness: a complementary approach to psychiatric care.' *Indian Journal of Psychological Medicine*, 37: 117–119.

Joldersma, C. (1999) 'The tension between justice and freedom in Paulo Freire's epistemology.' *Journal of Educational Thought*, 35(2): 129–148.

Nestor, P. & Galletly, C. (2008) 'The employment of consumers in mental health services: politically correct tokenism or genuinely useful?' *Australasian Psychiatry*, 16(5): 344–347.

New Economics Foundation (2008) *Co-production: A Manifesto For Growing the New Economy*. London: New Economic Foundation.

Ord, J. (2000) *Youth Work Curriculum*. Lyme Regis: Russell House Publishing.

Putnam, R. D. (2000) *Bowling Alone. The Collapse and Revival of American Community*. New York: Simon and Schuster.

Rancière, J. (2004) 'Introducing disagreement.' *Angelaki: Journal of the Theoretical Humanities*, 9(3): 3–9.

Rancière, J. (1992) *The Ignorant Schoolmaster: Five Lessons in Intellectual Emancipation*. Stanford, CA: Stanford University Press.

Schon, D. A. (1983) *The Reflective Practitioner: How Professionals Think in Action*. New York: Basic Books.

Scrambler, G. (2013) 'Resistance in unjust times: Archer, structured agency and the sociology of health inequalities.' *Sociology*, 47(1): 142–156.

Seal, M. (2017) *Trade Union Education: Transforming the World*. Oxford: Workable Books, New Internationalist.

Seal, M. (2016) 'Critical realism's potential contribution to critical pedagogy and youth and community work: human nature, agency and praxis revisited.' *Journal of Critical Realism*, 15(3): 263–276.

Seal, M. (2009) *Not About Us Without Us: Client Involvement in Social Housing*. Lyme Regis: Russell House Publishing.

Seal, M. (2006) *Working with Homeless People: A Training Manual*. Lyme Regis: Russell House Publishing.

Seal, M. (2005) *Resettling Homeless People: Theory and Practice*. Lyme Regis: Russell House Publishing.

Seal, M. & Harris, P. (2016) *Responding to Youth Violence Through Youth Work*. Bristol: Policy Press.

Shor, I. (1980) *Critical Teaching and Everyday Life*. Chicago, IL: University of Chicago Press.

Wilcox, D. (1995) *Community Participation and Empowerment: Putting Theory into Practice*. London: Partnership Press.

World Health Organization (2002) *Community Participation in Local Heath and Development: Approaches and Techniques*. Geneva: World Health Organization.

Zae Tung, M. (1937) *On Practice: On the Relation Between Knowledge and Practice, Between Knowing and Doing*. Bejing: Communist Party of China, Philosophical Papers.

2   The tyranny of tyrannical discourses

Debates and dilemmas within participatory research

Introduction

This chapter will outline the development of participatory research, and then examine the debates and dilemmas within it. It will pay particular attention to accusations of 'tyranny' made by Cooke and Kothari in 2001 and the rebuttals of Hickey and Mohan some years on. In doing so it will seek to establish an agenda for participatory research in the belief that participatory research can exemplify best practice for co-production. Pertinent issues of power and representation arise from the tyranny debates, and I claim that incorporating critical pedagogy goes some way to ameliorating these concerns. Similarly, critical pedagogy may address other pedagogical issues, particularly how we develop a mindset and attitudes needed for engagement in participatory research. It may also help to enrich and elaborate on the principles and practices of reflection, which are under-theorized, including establishing participatory research's epistemology. I claim that participatory research may create a pathway to the unfulfilled promise of co-produced transformational knowledge, and goes far beyond the limiting aim of trying to seek out 'hidden' or 'authentic' voices, characteristic of phenomenological approaches.

Participatory research – an overview

As with the concept of community involvement, the idea of involving people subject to research in doing that research is a hard principle to argue against in principle, yet its reality is continually contested and colonized. In the last 30 years, a variety of forms of participatory research (e.g. Participatory Action Research, Participatory Rapid Appraisal, Rural Rapid Assessment and Participatory Learning in Action) have grown in prominence across the world and are mainstream in international development agencies such as the World Bank – although for some, including those from the critical pedagogy field, this is not to be celebrated, and is where the critique begins (Cooke & Kothari, 2001).

Participatory research as a body of knowledge and practices arose in the 1970s as a critique of large-scale survey studies that were perceived to give insufficient attention to people's local knowledge (Cooke & Kothari, 2001; Kumar, 2002;

Petty et al., 1995) and led to inappropriate development initiatives. The methods are therefore intended not just to enable the voice of local people to be heard, especially those who are marginalized, but also for them to develop an analysis of their own conditions. As Petty et al. (1995) note:

> The method encouraged the active involvement of local people with perspective and knowledge of the area's conditions, traditions and social structure in data gathering activities, using a variety of informal techniques that could be employed within a short timescale.
>
> (Petty et al., 1995, p. 5)

As such participatory research has an intention to accurately represent the perspectives of the researched and to uncover and to ameliorate possible power relations between the parties to the research. Its links to the agenda of co-production are manifest. Participatory research similarly believes that the end user of services, who stands to be affected most by the outcomes of research and tends to be the 'subject' of the research as well as the 'reason' for commissioning the research, continues to be marginalized in the research process. To give a further flavour of participatory research it seems worth looking at some of its criticisms, which participatory research would see as its strengths. Rath (2012) notes traditional research's criticisms as the following:

- *Participatory researchers do not formulate hypotheses that can subsequently be tested, and even the research questions emerge only gradually during the process of engagement with the research partners* – indeed participatory research rejects positivist models of testing hypotheses conceived a priori, priorities and methodologies should emerge from research participants.
- *The closeness between the research partners prevents scientific distance on the part of the academic researchers, who are so entangled with the researched persons that it is not possible to separate the researchers' contribution to the collected data from that of the researched; hence the quality criterion of objectivity cannot be fulfilled.* Participatory research rejects notions of objectivity and therefore the need to create professional distance, indeed doing so makes one's results less resonant and authentic.
- *Exact planning is not possible because the negotiation of the various decisions during the research process prevents the estimation of the duration of the project and the expected findings.* Planning is indeed a challenge to planning participatory research, but only if we say that pre-planning is preferable. If we take a stance the evolving knowledge is more valid, then privileging preplanning is a negative position. To stay within budget and a timeframe can be just as effectively managed in process as prior to it, it set ones parameters to be continually negotiated.
- *When 'classical' quality criteria are applied, the research is not acceptable because it is neither objective, nor reliable, nor is it valid* (Rath, 2012, p. 78).

Similarly to objectivity being rejected, participatory research has different measures to validity and reliability which are positivism centric – it is, however, no less rigorous.

The rest of this chapter will expand upon these ideas, set out some challenges and seek some solutions.

Paradigms and epistemological positions

Participatory research does not sit easily within the traditional research paradigms (Chambers, 2008, 2010). It shares with the interpretive paradigm a desire to break with the positivistic scientific approach, and shares phenomenologists belief that many phenomena are socially constructed (Cohen et al., 2000). However, participatory research differs significantly in its epistemology from interpretative approaches (Lather, 1985, 1986) and in its aims (Morley, 1991). Participatory research is grounded in post-structuralism, believing that self cannot be separated from research or practice (Cochran-Smith & Lytle, 2004; Cole & Knowles, 2000; Cuenca: 2010). Some authors place participatory research within a third, critical, research paradigm (Cohen et al., 2000). Indeed, as part of interrogating our practice we seek to reveal contradictions and disguised power structures, which the actors, and we will need to reflect on in the process of the research. However participatory research's aims and epistemology often go beyond a wish to illuminates the hidden power within research processes, and seek to impact on these process, although, as we shall see, this is also one of the major sources of critiques of participatory research.

The knowledge it wishes to explore and create is not objective or neutral, as positivism make a claim to, nor does it privilege marginalized voices and life-worlds, as one operating within an interpretive paradigm may wish to do. It will uncover unheard voices, and as a political project it will undoubtedly wish to do this, and within the research that these voices that are normally foregrounded. However, it will also act upon these voices, interact with them and even seek to change them. It takes the stance that marginalized voices are no less subject to prevailing hegemonic discourses, and the difference between privileging and orientalizing (Said, 1978) such voices is a thin line. This throws up huge ethical debates about how the challenging of marginalized voices is done ethically. Power in participatory research is a permanent tension, but one to be worked through and ameliorated, rather than avoided. There is potential power dynamics in challenging community views, but also in not doing so. Within participatory research if one does not challenge some community perception there is real potential to re-inscribe micro level power relations present within the community, and between the community and peer researchers. If one does challenge, then one is in danger of re-inscribing power relationships between professional researcher and peer researchers. On a meso level we have to challenge some of the hegemonies within the academy, and on macro scale the hegemonic tyranny of western research paradigms. Many of the criticisms of participatory research focus on such issues of power (Cooke & Kothari, 2001). Chapter 4 will explore the nature of meaningful critical reflective spaces and how they emerge, where such power can be ameliorated.

However, participatory research challenges some phenomenological approaches for being content to simply allow voices to be heard, and views this itself as avoidance. Not analysing these voices for fear of tainting them, or not outlining policy implications for fear of misinterpreting them, is an understandable concern, but ultimately to not do so is an evasion of responsibility. A participatory researcher would say that this is passing the epistemological buck onto either the researched or the reader. In doing so interpretivism is itself in danger of re-inscribing existing power relations in that the researcher is not taking responsibility for the consequences of the actions of undertaking research. This is particularly so when, as is often the case, the researcher has more power than the researched to enable the research to have impact and better the lives of the researched, even if in doing so it will inevitably become interpreted, misconstrued and compromised. As Alinsky (1971) says on the dangers of being over principled, 'He who sacrifices the mass good for his personal conscience has a peculiar conception of 'personal salvation'; he doesn't care enough for people to 'be corrupted' for them' (Alinsky, 1971, p. 25). As a colleague of mine of mine bluntly put it 'phenomenology is voyeurism at best and pornography at worst'. It is pornography in the sense that it will reveal lives and voices, but not take responsibility for changing them, and in purely presenting them allow others to be voyeuristic, to sensationalize and to orientalize. Conversely participatory research is about actively challenging and creating knowledge, and not in a neutral sense, but with a particular moral stance and set of beliefs. I will come back to the nature of these beliefs later.

Participatory research invokes the notion of praxis in relation to knowledge. Participatory research is said by some to be situated within a paradigm of praxis (Ahmed, 2006; . In a Freirian (1972) sense praxis is the interplay between theory and practice – they are not opposites, but two facets of knowledge creation that interact. Moreover, this interplay needs to be active and therefore needs action. Aristotle makes the distinction between 'Theoria' and 'Praxis'. Theoria is knowledge for its own sake, and is neutral and passive. Praxis has political and moral dimensions and need to be acted upon; it is 'the art of acting upon the conditions one faces in order to change them' (Friere, 1972, p. 12). As such it does not share with positivism or interpretivism the desire for the researcher to be objective, bracketing off their views, or for the researcher to be a passive collector and interpreter of data, rather it is to be an active creator of it (Ahmed, 2006).

Participatory research also differs in its aims from interpretative perspectives. The goals of the research go beyond theorizing the specific and relative constructions of meaning of the players in the research. As such it echoes post positivist concerns. (Gelphart, 1997). To take an example from the Touch project that Campbell describes in Chapter 13, and which the author was involved in, we wished to inform others' practice, to see what detached street based practitioners, and the policy makers that frame these interventions, could learn from our project. However, we did not intend to discover any objective truths, or develop positivist theories, but hoped that the research could serve as a point of reflection for others on their own work and illuminate their practice (Higgs & Cherry, 2009).

Challenge 1: the tyranny of action and transformative claims

Action and change are both central to, and hotly contested, within participatory research. Cooke and Kothari (2001), in their seminal book *Participation: The New Tyranny?*, had three criticisms of participatory research, which I have re-framed as challenges. First, they refute whether many participatory research projects have enacted real change. In actuality they either leave structural inequalities unchallenged, or over-privilege local impacts, denying that they themselves are constrained by prevailing hegemonies. They accuse participatory research of simplifying the dynamics of structure and agency in social change, questioning the transformative claims of much participatory research.

Hickey and Mohan (2004), in *Participation: From Tyranny to Transformation*, attempt to rescue the participatory research project and re-conceptualize participation, empowerment and development. Adopting a Foucauldian approach, they say we need to see power as stratified and differentiated. To judge participatory research as being a failure, or manipulative, unless it affects structural change, re-inscribes a binary view of power. For them we need to recognize that marginalized people have limited control, influences and access, but they still have agency. There is power and significance in local action, push-back and resistance. Feminist action researchers such as Brydon-Miller et al. (2003) and Reid et al. (2006) concur and have interrogated the idea of 'action' in PAR, saying it is often used interchangeably with the notion of 'social change' (Reid et al., 2006, p. 325), and that this is not helpful.

PPIR builds on Hickey and Mohan's ideas, and propounds that we need to find a way between an overemphasis on the individual that ignores the structural, and an over emphasis on the structural that denies any individual agency, and can leave people with a 'knowing hopelessness' and structural pessimism – something we will explore more in Chapter 4. PPIR incorporates Margaret Archer's (2010, 2012) notion of the morphogenetic sequence, whereby there is a time delay between our agential actions now, and social and structural change. Current social and cultural structures are a result of past social interaction between agents, which condition the current context within which social agents operate. We will return to this idea in Chapter 4's section on cultivating hope and a future orientation.

The emphasis on the morphogenetic sequence and the power of symbolic change means we need to interrogate what we are trying to achieve within a research project in a nuanced way. We need to explore and integrate Alinskian (1971) approaches which say we should make our goals achievable, but meaningful, such that they always push the boundaries and leave the powerless more powerful and the powerful slightly less so. Also, borrowing from critical pedagogy, the themes to be explored need to be generative. Generative themes have certain characteristics. First, they should be a galvanizing force for the community, something about which there is passion and feeling. Secondly, generative themes must have tensions and contradictions within them: things that do not add up, that need to be worked through and have a potential to create new ideas to resolve them. These tensions should not be seen as negative, although there will be a tendency for them to become so. Instead their negative energy should be turned into a positive incentive to change. Generative themes should open up discussion about, and relate to, wider social issues, and this is where their more political and critical edge come in. In this way one generative theme has the seed of other generative themes within it. Finally, generative themes must have the potential for action, meaning that something concrete can be done about them. As generative themes develop, and more actions are taken, the morphogenetic sequence is revealed – i.e. present agent's actions leading to future social and structural change.

To be meaningful, these actions and themes require strategy, compromise and a long-term view – we cannot jump the morphogenetic sequence. This concern to take appropriate time echoes Cooke and Kothari's concerns (2001). They echo the dangerous phenomena of 'rhetorical radials' who want to make this jump, and when they cannot, almost glorify their failures to change the 'real' structural issues. Their self-justification is one of remaining ideologically pure in not compromising their principles. Alternatively, such radicals have a disquieting sense of failure and leave their communities with a re-enforced sense of hopelessness. I would agree with Cooke and Kathari (2001) that participatory research has a lot to learn about effective community action, and will explore further how participatory research can learn from community organizing.

Levels and dimensions of participation

The degrees to which community partners participate in research is crucial. Perhaps unsurprisingly, analysis of levels of participation mirror the literature on client involvement and co-production. Also, as with co-production and client involvement, the literature is similarly multitudinous and conceptually confusing. Examples of schemas and typologies include Biggs (1989), writing in the field of agriculture, who distinguishes four modes of participation – contractual, consultative, collaborative and collegiate. White (1996) identifies Nominal, Instrumental, Representative and Transformative, and would reject all but Transformative, and the collegiate approach of Biggs (1989,) as tokenistic. There are many more such schemas. Both Unger (2012) and Cook (2012) offer an overview of different conceptual frameworks. Goeke and Kubanski (2012), Caspari (2006) and Berghold and Thomas (2012) all identify pseudo-participation as a phenomenon, focusing on the degree to which participants are involved in decision-making within the research as the distinguishing factor between pseudo and true participatory research.

I think the degree to which community members are involved in decision-making is a useful and a helpful distinction between participatory research and non-participatory research. An alternative criteria to decision-making could be that the research is mindful of issue of power and representation. However, while highlighting and ameliorating issues of power is integral to participatory research, it is possible to have research that attends to these issues that is not participatory

(Cohen et al., 2000). Indeed the whole critical theory paradigm in research was long examining such issues long before the emergence of participatory research (Cohen et al., 2000).

However, what is meant by decision-making in research is itself nuanced. Should community partners be all involved, and to the same degree, in every decision from the topic, to the methods, to project structure, analysis and dissemination. Crucially if any of this is not so, is the project not participatory? Given how contested participatory research is, it would be difficult to start making definitive statements about what is and is not participatory research. This book takes a different angle, and a makes a difference claim. It says that certain principles need to be present in the research to be able to make a claim that it is a positive example of co-production.

The issue of peers is an interesting example we will discuss more in the next chapter. It is quite possible to have a peer led project that is not participatory. Groundswell, which Simone Helleren will discuss in greater length in Chapter 11, has had many peer led, but none participatory, research projects. The distinction for me is that in participatory research projects community members that are being researched are active researchers in the process, not just research participants, and not represented by peers. In a moment I will make a distinction between primary, secondary and active research participants, but suffice to say that to make a claim as a participatory research project, community members being research need to be at least secondary researchers.

In a similar way participatory research does not have to involve peers, although we would suggest it does. It is also quite possible to have a piece of research that involves participatory practices, such as having focus groups when formatting questions, and having verifications focus groups at the end for the recommendations, without them being participatory research. Good practice in conducting narrative interviews (Given, 2008) can mean checking out if the themes the interviewer has identified are resonant, or even that the questions being asked and style of interview are conducive. However, those being researched do not undertake a pedagogic process, or are involved in decision-making in a systematic and meaningful way. To be meaningful this book will claim that community member have to be engaged in critical reflection and become meta-reflectors with intersubjective consciences, something that Chapter 4 explore in great detail.

One of the criticisms commonly aimed at participatory research is that the issue or push for the research did not came from the community itself. A dilemma is that many marginalized communities, or sections of those communities, who we may want to 'reach' are not in a material or psychological position to participate in research, and certainly not to instigate it (Berghold & Thomas, 2012), such is the power of oppression and hegemony. Ironically a community, or section of a community, who are in a position to lobby for a particular issue to be researched, and demand to be in a participant in it, are often those who already dominate. For this reason, I am sometimes suspicious about claims that the community instigated the demand for research, and would counter those who condemn projects where the idea did not 'emerge' from the community. I would argue that ideally preceding any research should be some community development, such as a period of community organizing to build a community to this point. However this is not always possible, and for this reason PPIR tries to incorporate elements of community organizing.

In a few of the projects described in Part 3 the research was pushed for by the community, but we deliberately partnered with community-based organizations who had already been developing capacity within communities. Indeed capacity building is needed with community organizations to see the benefits of, particularly research and the skills they have organically in this area. In most of these cases, the idea for a participatory project was suggested, sometimes through discussions with some sections of the community, and participants were then recruited. This has implications because community members did not have a say in the overall subject, if there was one, and often the broad scope of the project is predetermined. I think this can be worked through as long as the professional researchers are honest about it. In the case of the Touch project (Chapter 13) and the Escape Plan project (Chapter 11). Participants were told that this first part had not been participatory, and we discussed why this was, what the implications were and whether the project was still legitimate. The key is to make sure that other participatory principles remained, and the community was involved in research decision, such as the detail of the themes to be explored, methods and methodology. Even when there was no predetermined subject, as in the Commissioning Together project (Chapter 12) and the Probation projects (Chapter 12), there were implications because the timescales and overall structures had not been negotiated with clients, something we will return to in the ethics chapter (Chapter 6).

Kothari (2005) also problematizes who gets to make decisions within communities, accusing many participatory approaches as having simplistic and homogenized notions of community that re-enforce local hierarchies, often with gender and cultural dimensions – they only talk to the usual *male* suspects. Conversely we do not want to end up in a position whereby unless we have the perfect sample, that is wholly demographically representative, and represents the 'genuine' community, we cannot proceed – because we probably never will achieve such perfection. As I have said elsewhere (Seal, 2009) we have to start with what and who we have and build from there, using our community and clients who are involved to build the links to others who are not (Unger, 2012; Caspari, 2006, p. 375). While there is a danger if we 'rely on the utterances of the local participants or the client' entirely and if 'the sample is inadequate or faulty as a result' (Berghold & Thomas, 2012, p. 3) there are dangers of becoming unrepresentative. A key seems to be in building the right mindset with participants, with an attitude that embraces the inclusion of others, and that after we have recruited, community members are genuinely involved in research decisions.

Primary and secondary researchers and those involved in participatory data gathering

There is also a danger of assuming that everyone is involved to the same level in every decision. Again the literature is vague on this, implying that this is possible, and thus opening itself to criticism. I think the idea of everyone who has any involvement with the project is fully, meaningfully, involved in all decisions is unrealistic. Aside from making decisions it would entail everyone being fully conversant in participatory research techniques, having developed critical consciences and become meta reflectors. In the Touch project, the Escape Plan, and to a degree, the Commissioning Together project, a distinction was made between primary participatory researchers, secondary researchers and participants who engaged in participatory research gathering.

Primary researchers were involved in all significant decisions, received comprehensive training in all research techniques, and were involved in all major research decisions and data analysis. There was also a conscious effort to ensure that they developed a critical consciousness and became meta reflectors, a process explored in much greater detail in Chapter 4. Secondary researchers were not involved in all decisions, such as the research questions and themes, but were involved in specific areas of investigation, sometimes the choice of method to investigate their themes and analysis of data in broad thematic terms – i.e. they were presented and asked to comment on, or verify, themes that the primary researcher had gathered from the data. They also received research training, but mainly in the specific method that they had chosen, or had been chosen, for the specific theme they were researching. Again, critical consciousness and being meta reflectors would be desirable, but the focus was on ameliorating power relationships between them and professional researchers and primary researchers, so that their data was genuine and had integrity. For all participants involved in data gathering the principles behind participatory research are explained, and the emphasis is on ameliorating power relations, unearthing and valuing local ways of knowing, and deconstructing and reconstructing any existing conceptions of research. Of course critical engagement is encouraged, but it is not always the case that all those in data gathering develop critical consciousness, although the hope is that through their engagement in the research they may go on to do so. Participation, in the sense envisaged in the principals in this chapter, is therefore stratified to a degree and mediated through primary and secondary researchers. It is for this reason that the role of the peer is emphasized and explored in greater detail in the next chapter, and the orientation towards ethnopraxis, to keep the research as grounded as possible in the community's ways of knowing.

General processes of participatory research: developing an ethnopraxis

Many traditional research projects, after having established themselves in relation to the research paradigms, and having outlined their overall research approach and methodology, will move quickly onto discussions of method. Participatory research criticizes this 'privileging of methods' (Chambers, 2010; Kumar, 2002) as being anti-participatory and colonial. To decide the methodological approach for a piece of research, its methods and what the ethical issues are, a priori, is to impose one's research framework upon those you are researching. It does not allow for local knowledge to come to the fore, or more importantly, local ways of knowing to influence the process of the research. Chambers (2010) calls for equal consideration to be given to the cultivation of the attitudes, mindset and behaviour of those involved in the research and the principles of sharing, dialogue and critical reflection. Hence, as well as its distinctive epistemology and orientation towards action, participatory research also differs in its processes. Participatory research is an evolutionary approach. At the beginning you only really have a broad topic, and sometimes less than that, and have maybe identified key players who are to be involved (although this may change). How you conduct the research will need to be negotiated with the organizations and participants, at all times, as we will describe.

Many authors outline the general processes of participatory research (Chambers, 2010; Fals-Borda & Rahman, 1991, Petty et al., 1995). This is typically portrayed as an iterative cycle of research, action and reflection (Kindon et al., 2007). I find Krishnaswamy's (2004) work useful. He outlines a five stage process that precedes this cycle, although elements of this prior cycle will continue to have relevance once one is in the research cycle proper. He identifies the preparatory stages of clarifying the purpose of the research, identifying and involving diverse stake-holders, building trust, building common understanding and identifying the research questions. I would say that these are rarely experienced as linear or dis-crete processes, and certainly not stages. Identifying stakeholders mutually builds trust, and developing a common understanding involves clarifying the purposes of research. What is also not emphasized enough in the literature, is the degree to which these processes are educative ones.

Community members often have a perception of research that needs to be worked with, particularly if working in urban western settings, and this it is often a positivist perception. Integral to all of the participatory research projects I have been involved in has been education on the nature and practice of research, often with an emphasis on challenging and changing perceived wisdoms about research, including on the part of the professional researchers – this process is exemplified in Chapter 12. Participatory research's stance towards the nature of knowledge needs to be articulated to participants, and constantly affirmed. Participatory research must be a process of creating knowledge, rather than merely of discovering or uncovering it, and participants have a right and the ability to be active partners in its creation. As our process evaluation in the Touch project (see Chapter 13) noted, 'the dominant and guiding metaphor that represented the Touch project and which was offered throughout the conversations and interviews with partners was that of the "journey", emphasizing process, connection, transi-tion and change' (Bradford, 2013, p. 6). This process of affirming and articulating participatory research's epistemological stance was, and needs to be, built into the design of the research.

Discussion about the process of building trust is also under largely absent in the literature, beyond stressing its importance. It seems particularly important when working with marginalized communities who either have research and consultation fatigue, often from having had little follow up or evidence of change, or where there are natural suspicions of any perceived authority (Christopher et al., 2008).

Many participatory guides (Petty et al., 1995; World Bank, 2005) have sections and associated exercises on trust building. While a good start, I am not convinced that they will fathom the depth of the issues around trust. In the violence research detailed in Chapter 13, we frequently encountered fractured reflexives (Archer, 2010, 2012), and one of their characteristics was shattered trust (Seal & Frost, 2014; Seal & Harris, 2016) – it was not simply that they did not trust people, they did not have a grasp of the concept, never having experienced it.

Christopher et al. (2008) suggest that trust building has five elements: (1) acknowledge personal and institutional histories, (2) understand the historical context of the research, (3) be present in the community and listen to community members, (4) acknowledge the expertise of all partners, and (5) be upfront about expectations and intentions. These seem a good start, and we will see elements of these present in the latter case studies. However, as a precursor to this, we need to understand participants perspective on trust. Building trust entails understanding participants own cultural constructions of trust, and working with them. In the case of fractured reflexives, we will need to enable them to build a concept of it from often contradictory and conflicting elements.

In the Touch project we talked about *ethnoconflictology* (Seal & Harris, 2016). We built on the work on ethno-conflictologists such as Lederach (1996) and Avruch and Black (1991, 1993) who stressed the importance of developing a historical and cultural understanding of a community's construction of violence as a first step to involving them in tackling it. Avruch and Black (1991, 1993) advocate a preliminary cultural analysis that makes explicit the underlying assumptions and understandings of violence held by all parties. *Ethnopraxis* goes beyond an ethnographic approach, saying we should apply the method to all aspects of research, with the communities cultural constructions of issues like ethics, dissemination analysis, being our starting point for research development. Ethnopraxis also represents a different orientation from traditional ethnography in that it may seek to act upon the communities cultural constructions that are unearthed. Once we have unearthed participant's views on a topic we sometimes extend them, such as where research is viewed by community members in only positivist terms, or where there is incoherence or danger in people's conceptualizations (which we often found with violence) – we seek to act on them –but together. In cases where conceptualizations are non-existent, such as with shattered trust, we co-create them.

General principles of participatory research

While they could be considered to be part of the developing of a mindset, principles that emerge from a participatory ethnopraxical approach to research include:

- *Participation and Democracy* opening up the design of the process to include those most directly affected and giving the intended beneficiaries the chance to speak out about local impacts.
- *Negotiation* between the different stakeholders to reach agreement about what will be monitored and evaluated, how and when data will be collected and

analysed, what the data actually means, and how findings will be shared, and action taken.

- *Learning* focusing on cumulative learning by all the participants as the basis for subsequent improvement and sustained action. This action includes local institution building or strengthening, thus increasing the capacity of people to initiate action on their own.
- *Flexibility* in adapting the evaluation to the wider external environment and to the set of local conditions and actors, as these factors change over time (Petty et al., 1995).

However, the important thing is an exploration of what these principles mean to participants and they may well need to be reframed within the cultural understandings of participants, and we may find that they foreground certain issues. For instance, in the Probation research, ethics was very much in people's foreground, as were power relations within the research.

Returning to Krishnaswamy's typology (2004), other elements need expansion and critical pedagogy again has potential illuminate these processes. The idea of generative themes (Aliakbari & Faraji, 2011; Freire, 1972) discussed in this chapter is useful for exploring the purpose of the research and identifying research questions and themes. To remind ourselves, generative themes should galvanize the community, contain tensions and contradictions that need working through, have a potential for actions that will resolve these tensions and in doing this, open up discussion about, and relate to, wider social issues and lead to other generative themes. In one piece of research, described in more detail in Chapter 12, the research group initially wanted to explore their experiences of reception at a probation service. This was because they had found reception to be rude and unpleasant, and they united in their objection to their treatment. Initially they thought it was because the receptionists were 'bad people', but on reflection they realized that it was more complex. They saw people who had entered jobs with good intentions, but suffered from a lack of training and supervision, bad pay and an office wide culture of them and us, at all levels of hierarchy and not just client worker. This exemplified that reception was the interface where these dynamics were played out, often in messages passed from client to workers and vice versa of which the receptionists bore the brunt. This opened up a very different discussion about pay, office cultures, how workers and clients constructed each other, and power dynamics. Positive measures were put in in the form of training about how people viewed each other, an honest appraisal of office culture and policy changes that made reception less of a political interface.

Beyond the privileging of methods

Having built trust, established stakeholders and identified some tentative themes, Chambers (2010) then places emphasis on attending to the behaviour, attitudes and mind-sets of the stakeholders needed to conduct participatory research, including the adoption of the principles of sharing and reflection, and only then

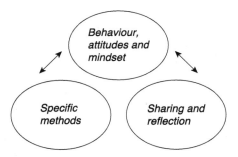

Figure 2.1 Behaviours, attitudes and mindset; specific methods; and sharing and reflection

do we get to an examination of specific methods. Chambers (2010) sees these components as having a symbiotic relationship and while initial work is needed on behaviour attitudes and mindset, these processes are ongoing and continue to inform each other.

Chambers says we must attend to behaviours, attitudes and mindsets needed to make a research project possible. Kumar lists these attitudes as:

> self-critical awareness of one's behaviour, bias and shortcomings; respecting others; not interrupting, not lecturing, but being a good, active listener; not hiding but embracing error; passing initiative and responsibility to others; having confidence in the ability of others and open-ended flexibility.
>
> (Kumar: 2002, p. 45)

These are attitudes not only for the research team to have, but also for the participants. In previous research I have developed and adapted these principles into a set of groundrules for conducting research, to be negotiated and stated early on in the process. One version of them reads as shown on Table 2.1.

However, as I have noted previously, setting groundrules does not necessarily change people's attitudes and behaviours (Seal, 2006). As I have also noted previously (Seal, 2005) setting groundrules is something many practitioners have done before and it may have therefore lost meaning as an exercise, particularly in a UK context (people just putting up 'confidentiality', 'respecting each other', etc.). Kothari (Cooke & Kothari, 2001) criticizes the sometimes 'ritualistic' ways of conducting participatory research, particularly with those who have some familiarity with it, and advocates 'breaking' some of it's conventions. With this in mind, and to set the tone for the workshop, we challenged the convention of groundrules and made it a detailed point of discussion.

In the aforementioned session, before setting groundrules we discussed participants' experiences of such exercises and whether this is a familiar exercise for them. It was indeed a familiar exercise and there was then a follow-on discussion about the nature of groundrules and participatory research. To help facilitate the

Table 2.1 Kumar's principles of participatory research

Kumar's principles of participatory research	Groundrules set in the workshops
Self-critical awareness of one's behaviour, bias and shortcomings	*People will be critical, but open and respectful towards others about their own, and others opinions*
Respecting others; not interrupting, not lecturing, but being a good, active listener	*People will not talk over each other, give each other space but also take responsibility to not hogging the space (and above)*
Not hiding but embracing error; passing initiative and responsibility to others	*People are allowed to make mistakes, but have to accept challenge, including the lecturers!*
Having confidence in the ability of others	*We all have a contribution to make and should support each other in bringing these ideas out*
Open –ended flexibility.	*People will take responsibility for their own learning and behaviour in the workshops and lecturers will allow the group input into the direction and content of the sessions*

groundrules the workshops, conferences and the final event had built in sessions to reflect on the processes of the group and the intended content of the sessions, again a mechanism recommended by Kumar (2002, 002).

Chambers (2008) stresses the importance in developing a learning environment of overcoming what Freire calls the 'habit of submission' – 'the frame of mind that curtails people from fully and critically engaging with their world and participating in civic life' (Freire, 1972). Within critical pedagogy (Freire, 1972; Giroux, 2012) we need to deal with submissive habits, created by prevailing hegemonies by creating such environments, and to do so is a precursor to developing a context in which, open, critical and democratic dialogue can be fostered. Participatory research challenges the separation of the researcher from the researched. Both researcher and participant are actors in the investigative process, influencing the flow, interpreting the content, and sharing options for action (Chambers, 2010). However, how this is to be achieved in not as simple as wishing it to be so. It involves both parties being able to have a power free, or at least power acknowledged, conversation, where both parties have de-colonized their minds (Smith, 1999).

Challenge 2: tyranny of the group and ignoring issues of power

Cooke and Kothari's (2001) second group of challenges is a critique of the reality of these principles in action. They found that many participatory practices obscures local issues of power and sometimes contribute to the maintenance and exacerbation of local power differentials. They found that on a micro and meso level there is often a group level tyranny, and there is therefore a need to address the well-known social psychological dynamics of group functioning 'which are largely ignored in the participation literature' (Christens & Speer, 2006, p. Authors within that volume detail further nuances, exploring how participatory practices have manipulated findings (Mosse, 2001) underestimating the power dynamics within relationships (Hildyard, Hedge, Wolvekamp & Reddy, 2001) ignored cultural difference (Hailey, 2001) and treated communities as homogenous entities.

More attention is obviously needed on ameliorating power dynamics between the researcher and researched, and between different groups of the researched. Some of this was debated within the previous chapter's discussion when we examined the importance of education for participation and conscientization (Freire, 1972). However, Friere himself has encountered criticism for ignoring power, (Elias & Merriam, 1980; Illich, 1972; Zachariah, 1986), and for absence of analysis of colour (Ellsworth, 1993; Ewert, 1977; Oliveria et al., 1974) and gender (Brady, 1994; hooks, 1994;) in his work. We will return to these issues on numerous occasions. The last chapter in this section tries to build conditions for reflection and sharing to ameliorate some of these concerns. The next part of the book will then explore how to continue to do this at each stage of the research.

Sharing and reflection, and its relation to validity and reliability

The notion of sharing and reflection has two dimensions to it, and both are directly related to ideas about validity and reliability. For Chambers (2008), the organic nature of participatory approaches can liberate the researcher from an external authority that imposes a pre-determined process, with its orientation towards experiential learning. However, in doing this the responsibility for research integrity does not disappear. Responsibility for the reliability, validity and ethics falls back on the reflective judgement of researchers and participants. In common with several authors (Key & Kerr, 2011; Lincoln & Guba, 1985), 'trustworthy', 'authentic' and 'resonance' are more relevant concepts in participatory research than 'reliability' and 'validity' (Lincoln & Guba, 1985). However, such terms are again contextual and subjective, and need to be unearthed, articulated and ameliorated. Consequently 'questions of context, process, and relationship' are again at the centre of inquiry' (Lincoln & Guba, 1985, p. 34). They go on onto say, 'This lies in the humanistic commitment of the qualitative researcher to study the world always from the perspective of the interacting individual' (Lincoln & Guba, 1985, p. 575). Researcher, researched and subject/object relationships are, to a degree, merged (Chambers, 2008) in that they are not binary, but we should be a pains to ensure that power dynamics are again not ignored. Part of the adoption of the idea of a morphogenetic sequence (Archer, 2010, 2012) is the belief that these processes can also be separated, examined and critiqued.

As a process reflection is seen as both the central mechanism for mediating different understandings (Chambers, 2008) and the engine of participation, and we will presently explore it in more detail. Specifically, some authors talk about 'reflective' validity (Waterman, 1998), which has a number of dimensions. First, authors such as Clarke (2010) and Waterman (1998) say that participatory research

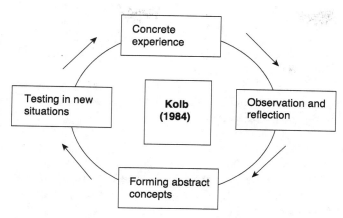

Figure 2.2 Learning as a cycle, Kolb (1984)

needs to present an analysis of decisions made during the conduct of the study to facilitate judgement of validity. We will show examples of this in the third section of this book. Second, there are ongoing reflective processes done by the research team, partners and other colleagues involved (Chambers, 2008; Kumar, 1996, 2002; Petty et al., 1995). A process of managing the reflective, sharing process needs to be constantly attended to and articulated. Part of this articulation is an explicit theoretical model of reflection, for there are many. This will include an articulation of its formal and informal processes, and what the reflective process should have as a focus. Theoretically, models of reflective learning are numerous in learning theory; the most commonly used being those of Kolb (1984) or Lewin (1948, 1951) where learning is seen as a circle, and it is a useful starting point.

Kolb (1975) thought we could enter this cycle at any point, the point being to abstract from our experiences and then keep testing and refining them. Later authors such as Jarvis (1995) develop Kolb's model identifying different routes such as non-learning and non-reflective learning, as well as reflective learning, illuminating the knee jerk reactions we want to avoid.

However, Kolb is criticized for his lack of development of the process (Boud & Walker, 1998, 2013) developed his ideas, and identify three aspects to reflection:

- *Returning to experience* – that is to say recalling or detailing significant events.
- *Attending to (or connecting with) feelings* – this has two aspects: using helpful feelings; and removing or containing obstructive ones.
- *Evaluating experience* – this involves re-examining experience in the light of one's conceptual framework, integrating this new knowledge into it.

What seems important here is the attending to feelings and their impact on our rationalizations. Schon (1983) is famous for creating the idea of reflective practice, now one of the mainstays of professional development from nursing to law, makes a distinction between reflection on-action, and in-action. He aimed to make the link between reflecting on previous actions, in the hope that subsequent decisions made the next moment would be informed ones. In terms of focus, Berghold and Thomas (2012) suggest four domains of reflection: 'reflection upon personal and biographical attributes and dispositions', 'reflection upon social relationships among research partners', 'structural reflection upon the social field of the research project' and 'reflection on the research process itself'.

Chambers (2008, 2010) also recognized the need for critical reflection *within* sessions. 'Sharing without boundaries' was a principle that emerged from a workshop of PRA practitioners in 1994 (Absalom et al., 1995) and is an extension of the idea of the mindset one needs to bring to the research. The researchers need to be responsive to the changing needs, and ways of thinking, of participants beyond using a diversity of methodologies. This goes beyond reflecting in formal times for reflection and sharing, and sometimes means responding in the moment. Chambers epistemologically sees parallels between the need for such responses and theories of chaos (Gleick, 1988), complexity (Waldrop, 1994) and emergence (Johnson, 2002), In particular he draws on self-organizing systems on the edge of chaos (SOSOTEC). Within SOSOTEC the edge of chaos is the zone of diverse, self-organizing and emergent complexity that lies 'between top-down rigidity and random chaos' (Chambers, 2008, p. 174). Chambers (2008) describes how ideas of deep simplicity (Ibid., p. 3), as in the few shared principles stated, with the minimal role given to the facilitator, underlie the 'complexity, diversity, dynamism and unpredictability' (Ibid, p. 3), of the progress of the research and the methodologies employed. However, beyond this reflection in session is underdeveloped both theoretically and practically. As we can see models of reflection are myriad, and need to be brought together move comprehensively within any piece of research.

Challenge 3: creating reflective pedagogical spaces and reflection in action

While all participatory research notes the importance of reflection and reflective spaces, beyond the work mentioned earlier there is little discussion of the process in the literature. Work is needed on how researchers can cultivate their reflection in action, and Chapter 11 will start to do this. More widely the model of reflective practice has sustained heavy criticism on numerous grounds: for lack of precision (Eraut, 2004) that it is unachievable (Moon, 1999), particularly reflection in action (Ekebergh, 2007); that it is individually focused (Solomon, 1987); ignores context (Boud & Walker, 1998); and is atheoretical and apolitical (Smyth, 1989). It has also come under criticism for becoming technocratic and something people know they have to do, or say they do (Trelfa & Trelfa, 2014), rather than something they embody. It has become, or is in danger of becoming, a defensive practice, and 'remain at the level of relatively undisruptive changes in techniques or superficial thinking' (Fook, 2006, p. 9). The concept of critical reflective practice (Brookfield,

1998; Finlay, 2002, 2008; Fook, 2006) goes someway to addressing the above criticisms, particularly the contextual and political ones, though ultimately, as I will argue, not far enough.

Finlay proposes five overlapping variants of reflexivity with critical self-reflection at the core: introspection; intersubjective reflection; mutual collaboration; social critique; and ironic deconstruction (Finlay, 2002, 2008). Finlay rightly points out that most reflection covers the first level, the probing of personal emotions and meaning. There is a need for 'Intersubjective reflection' which focuses on the 'relational context, on the emergent, negotiated nature of practice encounters' (Finlay, 2008, p. 7) and also for 'mutual collaboration', engaging participants, in a 'reflective conversation' (Ghaye, 2000) that takes account of wider political and social contexts, including institutional, student/tutor and student/student power relations. Of particular appeal is 'ironic deconstruction' that 'cue(s) into postmodern and poststructural imperatives to deconstruct discursive practices and represent something of the ambiguity and multiplicity of meanings in particular organisational and social contexts' (Finlay, 2008, p. 7).

However, we need to go beyond the five dimensions of critical reflective practice as established by Finlay (2002, 2008). We need to work at a sixth level, beyond social critique and ironic deconstruction and make a commitment to developing an active dialectical epistemology and pedagogy, with reflection at a philosophical level that contests, seeks out, and is an active contributor to paradigm shifts, being mindful or how this effects our praxis and pedagogic practice. We need to move from being a critical reflective practitioner to a pedagogical one.

We also need to examine how we create such critical reflective pedagogical spaces within research contexts. Finlay (2008) raises two main pedagogic concerns in developing them: developmental readiness and the extent to which the process becomes formularized, forced and a hurdle. She says guiding principles are that we should (1) present reflective practice(s) with care, (2) provide adequate support, time, resources, opportunities and methods for reflection, (3) develop skills of critical analysis and (4) take proper account of the context of reflection. These will serve as points of refection in our findings.

However, as with other authors on critical reflection (Brookfield, 1998; Pollard et al., 2005) this is a typology of the principles to employ rather than an account of the actual pedagogical practice of creating research spaces. Such accounts are remarkably absent in the literature, as Luhmann says 'teachers dedicated to critical pedagogy when speaking about their pedagogy might refer to little else than their teaching style, their classroom conduct, or their preferred teaching methods' (Luhmann, 1998, p. 120). Other authors make vague calls for pedagogical practice to be student centered (Finlay, 2008), to focus on building autonomy (Morley, 2007 or give list of tools, such as analysing critical incidents, case studies, peer assessment, small group work and reflective diaries (Brookfield, 1998; Finlay, 2008; Pollard et al., 2005). There is therefore a need for more accurate modelling on how to develop critical pedagogic research spaces and this is the subject of Chapter 4.

Methods of participatory research

Most descriptions of participatory research are understandably reluctant to define particular methods, saying they should be negotiated with participants and that participatory research is an approach to research, rather than a set of methods. However, Cooke and Kothari (2001) challenge this, saying there is a hidden orthodoxy of what constitutes participatory methods, and that this needs to be made explicit and challenged. Many methods used within participatory research have an emphasis on visual and kinaesthetic methods of learning, but they will also often use more traditional approaches like interviewing, focus groups and even more quantitative approaches including surveys and questionnaires. Petty et al. (1995) divide these into *semi structured interviewing* (including focus groups), *diagramming and visualization* and *ranking and scoring*. Many of these methods, and their relative merit, are explored in the case studies section of the book (Part 3).

While many of the issues in interviewing and focus groups are common to all qualitative approaches, the nature of the interaction is in keeping with a participatory approach in that 'the outcome of an interview must be perceived as a situation-dependent co-construction on the part of the interview partners' (see McCartan et al., 2012, p. 45). Taking this further, and because of the imagined audience of the other research participants and the communities within the research, Berghold & Thomas (2012) view that the interview is part of a wider system of communication. Rath (2012) contends that an interview is not purely a private conversation between the interview partners, but that it is, in a sense, public.

Berghold & Thomas (2012) further note that many methods in participatory research are multi-functional beyond just data gathering. This can be in other aspects of research, including validation (Russo, 2012). But in the process of this we can have other effects, Russo goes on to note that, 'Focus groups in survivor-controlled research set off a collective process whereby participants start to take ownership of the research' (Russo, 2012, p. 72). McCartan et al. (2012) similarly notes that they are an essential part of trust building. Russo (2012) also notes focus groups use in participants getting to know each other (Russo, 2012). Other researchers have found that focus groups can open up a taboo theme in the community (Cook, 2012; Dentith et al., 2012; Unger, 2012). This similarly applies to professional researchers (Borg et al., 2012).

There is often an emphasis within participatory research on diagramming and visualization, with a further emphasis on things like transect walks, where community members explore a community and its geographical relationship to the issue at hand (Petty et al., 1995). Other methods include art, photo voice, drama, theatre and music. This emphasis is often put down to issues of language and culture, to get past language barriers and find other ways of exploring meaning, or where a culture determines a different way of expressing oneself, or of creating and embodying knowledge (Berghold & Thomas, 2012).

These methods can also be used in analysis. In one piece of research I used Diagnostic Role Play (DRP). DRP was designed to 'examine behaviors, spoken words and interactions and understand why people behave as they do' (Change

Project, 2002, p. 2). It holds that with certain sensitive issues, such as interpersonal conflict, people may be more willing to act them out and discuss them when they are not portraying themselves. Similarly, Augusto Boal (2000), building on Freire's work, developed Forum theatre, or theatre of the oppressed, which encourages audience participation to change the direction of a play and explore oppression and how to counter it. It has been adopted and adapted by many participatory research project as a forum of analysis (Wrentschur, 2008).

Ranking and scoring exercises are rarely intended as a quantitative representation, but as a method of exploring participant's perceptions, and as a democratic exercise, asking them to score and rank their priorities for issues within the research. They can be used a test of resonance with issues. In the Touch research we asked people to go to the workshop they wanted to, identified from issues they had previously prioritized. If no one went to a workshop it was deemed not to be of sufficient priority for participants. While there is a danger here of a popularity contest, there are ways of checking out people's priorities within them, and reincorporating ideas where appropriate. In Chapter 11 we will explore some examples of this being in used in practice.

Conclusion

> Insofar as one of the primary purposes of inquiry is to heal the alienations that characterize modern consciousness, participation provides a throughway to relationality and healing that objectivist and Cartesian methods necessarily reinscribe via the distance and fragmentation that they evoke.
>
> (Dentith et al., 2012, p. 110)

This quote also illustrates the power of participatory research as an example of co-production. If two of the principal aims are to be transformative of both how agencies and community partners view each other on a fundamental human level and how the knowledge produced by co-production is viewed, then participatory research has the potential to do this. The examples we explore later show how this happens in practice, how paradigm shifts are possible on a local level, with the potential to go wider. Nevertheless, for now, and in practice, it seems useful to keep certain ethical question in mind. Wadsworth (1998, p. 5) notes that participatory research has action effects, and the group needs to be mindful of these. These action effects include the effects of, 'raising some questions and not others; involving some people in the process . . . and not others; observing some phenomena and not others; making this sense of it and not alternative senses and of deciding to take this action . . . rather than any other action' (Wadsworth, 1998, p. 107). As we shall illustrate, conflict management and an ability to work with group processes are essential aspects of a participatory worker's skill set. We have dedicated Chapter 6 to further explore issues around ethics in participatory research.

Hopefully this chapter has given the reader an understanding of the nature of, and challenges within, participatory research. I also hope the reader can see the potential links and dovetailing of co-production, community organizing and critical pedagogy with participatory research. I am making a grand transformative claim here and in subsequent chapters in Part 1, and in Part 2 I will foreground the theory behind this claim. In Part 3 we will explore how we can be transformative in practice. In the meantime, participatory research, and in turn co-production, have some challenges to meet.

First, we need to establish what participatory research means by action, whether it can truly fulfil its social justice claims, and what can it realistically claim to impact upon. Second, we need to articulate how participatory research can address issues of power, groupthink and the 'tyranny of the articulate'. We may need to think beyond critical pedagogy; it has its own critics in these regards. In the process concern around issue identification, stakeholder identification and trust building will be to be foregrounded. Third, we need to theoretically develop a framework for reflective practice that can accommodate the necessary paradigm shifts, but at the same time can create new knowledge. An important aspect here seems to be the space in which these critical reflections are operationalized and sustained. We need to articulate their characteristics, nature and dynamics for they are also the spaces within which power and domination operate. Finally, we need to find a way to continually re-invigorate our methodologies and methods lest they solidify into a new orthodoxy, dogma and, ultimately, tyrannical discourses.

References

Absalom, E. et al. (1995) 'Sharing our concerns and looking to the future.' In PLA Notes 22, February 1995. London: IIED.

Aliakbari, M. & Faraji, E. (2011) *Basic Principles of Critical Pedagogy*. Paper presented at 2nd International Conference on Humanities, Historical and Social Sciences IPEDR vol. 17.

Alinsky, S. (1971) *Rules for Radicals: A Pragmatic Primer for Realistic Radicals*. New York: Vintage Books.

Ahmed, S. (2006) *Queer Phenomenology: Orientations, Objects, Others*. Durham, NC: Duke University Press.

Archer, M. S. (2012) *The Reflexive Imperative in Late Modernity*. Cambridge: Cambridge University Press.

Archer, M. S. (2010) *Conversations About Reflexivity*. London and New York: Routledge.

Avruch, K. & Black, A. (1993) 'Conflict resolution in intercultural settings.' In H. der Merwe & D. J. D. Sandole (eds) *Conflict Resolution: Theory and Practice*. Manchester: Manchester University.

Avruch, K. & Black, A. (1991) 'The culture question and conflict resolution.' *Peace & Change*, 16(1): 22–45.

Berghold, J. & Thomas, S. (2012) 'Participatory research methods: a methodological approach in motion.' *Forum Qualitative Sozialforschung/Forum: Qualitative Social Research*, [S.l.], 13(1): January.

Biggs, S. D. (1989) *Resource-poor Farmer Participation in Research: A Synthesis of Experiences from National Agricultural Research Systems*. OFCOR, Comparative Study No. 3. International Service for National Agricultural Research, The Hague, The Netherlands.

Boal, A. (2000) *Theatre of the Oppressed*. London: Pluto Press.

Borg, M., Karlsson, B. K., Hesook, S. & McCormack, B. (2012) 'Opening up for many voices in knowledge construction.' *Forum Qualitative Sozialforschung/Forum: Qualitative Social Research*, 13(1): Art. 1.

Boud, D. & Walker, D. (1998) 'Promoting Reflection in Professionals Courses: The Challenge of Context.' *Studies in Higher Education*, 23(2), 191–206.

Boud, D., Keogh, R. & Walker, D. (2013) *Reflection: Turning Experience into Learning*. London: Routledge.

Brady, J. (1994) 'Critical literacy, feminism, and a politics of representation.' In P. L. McLaren & C. Lankshear (eds) *Politics of Liberation*. London: Routledge, pp. 154–173.

Brookfield, S. (1998) *Becoming a Critically Reflective Teacher*. San Francisco, CA: Jossey-Bass.

Brydon-Miller, M., Greenwood, D. & Maguire, P. (2003) 'Why action research?' *Action Research*, 1(1): 9–28.

Caspari, A. (2006) 'Partizipative Evaluationsmethoden – zur Entmystifizierung eines Begriffs in der Entwicklungszusammenarbeit.' In Uwe Flick (ed.) *Qualitative Evaluationsforschung. Konzepte, Methoden, Umsetzungen*. Reinbek: Rowohlt, pp. 365–384.

Chambers, R. (2010) *Provocations for Development*. Rugby: Practical Action Publishing.

Chambers, R. (2008) *Revolutions in Development Inquiry*. London: Earthscan.

Chambers, R. (2005) *Ideas for Development*. London: Earthscan.

Chambers, R. (2002) *Participatory Workshops: A Sourcebook of 21 Sets of Ideas and Activities*. London: Earthscan.

Chambers, R. (1997) *Whose Reality Counts, Putting the First Last*. London: Intermediate Technology Publications.

Change Project (2002) *Guide to Diagnostic Role Play*, London: Save the Children.

Christens, B. & Speer, P. W. (2006) 'Tyranny/Transformation: power and paradox in participatory development.' *Forum Qualitative Sozialforschung/Forum: Qualitative Social Research*, 7(2): 438–452.

Christopher, S., Watts, V., McCormick, A. K. H. G. & Young, S. (2008) 'Building and maintaining trust in a community-based participatory research partnership.' *American Journal of Public Health*, 98(8), 1398–1406.

Clarke, T. (2010) 'On "being researched": why do people engage with qualitative research?' *Qualitative Research*, 10(4): 399–419.

Cochran-Smith, M. & Lytle, S. L. (2004) 'Practitioner inquiry, knowledge, and university culture.' In V. K. LaBoske & T. Russell (eds) *International Handbook of Self-study of Teaching and Teacher Education Practices*. Dodrecht: Kluwer Academic Publishers, pp. 817–869.

Cohen, L., Manion, L. & Morrison, K. (2000) *Research Methods in Education*. London: Falmer-Routledge.

Cole, A. & Knowles, G. (2000) *Researching Teaching: Exploring Teacher Development through Reflexive Inquiry*. Boston, MA: Allyn Bacon.

Cook, T. (2012) 'Where participatory approaches meet pragmatism in funded (health) research: the challenge of finding meaningful spaces.' *Forum Qualitative Sozialforschung/ Forum: Qualitative Social Research*, 13(1): Art. 18.

Cooke, B. & Kothari, U. (2001) (eds) *Participation: The New Tyranny?* London: Zed.

Cuenca, A. (2010) 'In loco paedagogus: the pedagogy of a novice university supervisor.' *Studying Teacher Education*, 6(1): 29–64.

Dentith, A. M., Measor, L. & O'Malley, M. P. (2012) 'The research imagination amid dilemmas of engaging young people in critical participatory work.' *Forum Qualitative Sozialforschung/Forum: Qualitative Social Research*, 13(1): Art. 17.

Ekebergh, M. (2007) 'Lifeworld-based reflection and learning: a contribution to the reflective practice in nursing and nursing education.' *Reflective Practice*, 8(3): 331–343.

Elias, J. L. & Merriam, S. (1980) *Philosophical Foundations of Adult Education.* Malabar, FL: Krieger.

Ellsworth, E. (1993) 'Why doesn't this feel empowering?' In K. Geismar & G. Nicoleau (eds) *Teaching for Change.* Cambridge, MA: Harvard Education Press, pp. 43–70.

Eraut, M. (2004) 'Editorial: the practice of reflection.' *Learning in Health and Social Care*, 3(2), 47–52.

Ewert, D. (1977) *Freire's Concept of Critical Consciousness and Social Structure in Rural Zaire.* Madison, WI: University of Wisconsin Press.

Fals-Borda, O. & Rahman, M. A. (1991) *Action and Knowledge: Breaking the Monopoly With Participatory Action Research.* London: ITDG Publications.

Finlay, L. (2008) *Reflecting on Reflective Practice.* Milton Keynes: Open University Practice Base Learning Centre.

Finlay, L. (2002) 'Negotiating the swamp: the opportunity and challenge of reflexivity in research practice.' *Qualitative Research*, 2(2): 209–230.

Fook, J. (2006) 'Beyond reflective practice: reworking the "critical" in critical reflection.' Keynote speech for conference 'Professional lifelong learning: beyond reflective practice', 3 July.

Fook, J., White, S. & Gardner, F. (2003) 'Critical reflection: a review of contemporary literature and understandings.' In S. White, J. Fook & F. Gardner (eds) *Critical Reflection in Health and Social* Care. Maidenhead, Berks: Open University Press.

Freire, P. (1972) *Pedagogy of the Oppressed,* Harmondsworth, London: Penguin.

Gelphart, R. P. (1997) 'Hazardous measures: an interpretive textual analysis of quantitative sensemaking during crises.' *Journal of Organizational Behavior*, 18: 583–622.

Ghaye, T. (2000) 'Into the reflective mode: bridging the stagnant moat.' *Reflective Practice*, 1(1): 5–9.

Giroux, H. (2012) *On Critical Pedagogy.* New York: Continuum Press.

Given, L. M. (2008) *The SAGE Encyclopedia of Qualitative Research Methods.* Thousand Oaks, CA: Sage 10.4135/9781412963909.

Gleick, J. (1988) *Chaos: Making a New Science.* London: Cardinal.

Goeke, S. & Kubanski, D. (2012) Menschen mit Behinderungen als GrenzgängerInnen im akademischen Raum—Chancen partizipatorischer Forschung. *Forum Qualitative Sozialforschung/Forum: Qualitative Social Research,* 13(1): Art. 6.

Hickey, S. & Mohan, G. (2004) *Participation: From Tyranny to Transformation.* London and New York: Zed Books.

Higgs, J. & Cherry, N. (2009) 'Doing qualitative research on practice.' In J. Higgs, D. Horsfall & S. Grace (eds), *Writing Qualitative Research On Practice.* Rotterdam, the Netherlands: Sense, pp. 3–12.

Hildyard, N., Hedge, P., Wolvekamp, P. & Reddy, S. (2001) 'Pluralism, participation and power: joint forest management in India.' In B. Cooke & U. Kothari (eds.) *Participation: The New Tyranny?* London: Zed, pp. 56–71.

hooks, b. (1994) *Teaching to Transgress. Education as the Practice of Freedom.* London: Routledge.

Illich, I. (1972) *Disabling Professions.* London: Penguin.

Jarvis, P. (1995) *Adult and Continuing Education. Theory and practice* 2e. London: Routledge.

Jarvis, P. (1994) 'Learning.' *ICE301 Lifelong Learning*, Unit 1(1). London: YMCA George Williams College.

Johnson, S. (2002) *Emergence: The Connected Lives of Ants, Brains, Cities and Software.* London: Penguin Books.

Key, D. & Kerr, M. (2011) 'Towards an intersubjective-heuristic method for ecopsychology research.' *European Journal of Ecopsychology*, 2: 61–75.

Kindon, S., Pain, R. & Kesby, M. (eds) (2007) *Participatory Action Research Approaches and Methods: Connecting People, Participation and Place*, Abingdon, Oxon: Routledge, pp. 19–25.

Kolb, D. A. (1984) *Experiential Learning. Experience as the Source of Learning and Development*. Englewood Cliffs, NJ: Prentice-Hall.

Kothari, U. (2005) 'Authority and expertise: the professionalization of international development and the ordering of dissent.' *Antipode*, 37(3): 402–424.

Krishnaswamy, A. (2004) 'Participatory research: strategies and tools.' *Practitioner: Newsletter of the National Network of Forest Practitioners*, 22: 17–22.

Kumar, S. (2002) *Methods for Community Participation: A Complete Guide for Practitioners*. New Delhi: Vistaar Publications.

Lather, P. (1986) 'Research as praxis.' *Harvard Educational Review*, 56(3): 257–277.

Lather, P. (1985) 'Empowering research methodologies.' Paper presented at *Annual Meeting of the American Educational Research Association*, Chicago, IL, 31 March – 4 April.

Lederach, J. P. (1996) *Preparing for Peace: Conflict Transformation across Cultures*. Syracuse, NY: Syracuse University Press.

Lewin, K. (1951) *Field Theory in Social Science; Selected Theoretical Papers*. D. Cartwright (ed.). New York: Harper & Row.

Lewin, K. (1948) *Resolving Social Conflicts; Selected Papers on Group Dynamics*. Gertrude W. Lewin (ed.). New York: Harper & Row.

Lincoln, Y. S. & Guba, E. G. (1985) *Naturalistic Inquiry*. Newbury Park, CA: Sage Publications.

Luhmann, S. (1998) 'Queering/querying pedagogy? Or, pedagogy is a pretty queer thing.' In W. F. Pinar (ed.) *Queer Theory in Education*. Mahwah, NJ: Lawrence Erlbaum Associates, pp. 141–155.

McCartan, C., Schubotz, D. & Murphy, J. (2012) 'The self-conscious researcher – postmodern perspectives of participatory research with young people.' *Forum Qualitative Sozialforschung/Forum: Qualitative Social Research, 13*(1): Art. 9.

Moon, J. (1999) *Reflection in Learning and Professional Development: Theory and Practice*. London: Kogan Page.

Morley, C. (2007) 'Engaging practitioners with critical reflection: issues and dilemmas.' *Reflective Practice*, 8(1): 61–74.

Morley, D. (1991) 'Resource analysis as action research.' In P. F. Wilkinson & W. Found (eds) *Resource Analysis Research in Developing Countries*. Toronto: York University, pp. 1–16.

Mosse, D. (2001) '"People's knowledge", participation and patronage: operations and representations in rural development.' In B. Cooke & U. Kothari (eds) *Participation: The New Tyranny?* London: Zed Books, pp. 16–35.

Mosse, D. (1994) 'Authority, gender and knowledge: theoretical reflections on the practice of participatory rural appraisal.' *Development and Change*, 25(3): 497–526.

O'Brien, R. (2001) 'An overview of the methodological approach of action research.' In Richardson, R. (ed.), *Teoria e Prática da Pesquisa Ação [Theory and Practice of Action Research]*. João Pessoa, Brazil: Universidade Federal da Paraíba (English version).

Oliveira, R., Dominice, D. & Dominice, P. (1974) *The Pedagogy of the Oppressed: The Oppression of Pedagogy*. Geneva: Institute of Cultural Action.

Petty, J., Guijt, I., Scoones, I. & Whompson, J. (1995) *Participatory Learning and Action: A Trainer's Guide*. London: International Institute for Economic Development.

Pollard, A., with Collins, J., Simco, N., Swaffield, S., Warin, J. & Warwick, P. (2005) *Reflective Teaching: 2nd edition*. London: Continuum.

Rath, J. (2012) 'Poetry and participation: scripting a meaningful research text with rape crisis workers.' *Forum Qualitative Sozialforschung/Forum: Qualitative Social Research*, 13(1): Art. 22.

Reid, C., Tom, A. & Frisby, W. (2006) 'Finding the "action" in feminist participatory action research.' *Action Research*, 4(3): 315–332.

Russo, J. (2012) 'Survivor-controlled research: A new foundation for thinking about psychiatry and mental health.' *Forum Qualitative Sozialforschung/Forum: Qualitative Social Research*, 13(1): Art. 8.

Said, E. (1978) *Orientalism*. New York: Panthanon Books.

Schon, D. A. (1983) *The Reflective Practitioner: How Professionals Think in Action*. New York: Basic Books.

Seal, M. (2017) *Trade Union Education: Transforming the World*. Oxford: Workable Books, New Internationalist.

Seal, M. (2016) 'Critical realism's potential contribution to critical pedagogy and youth and community work: human nature, agency and praxis revisited.' *Journal of Critical Realism*, 15(3): 263–276.

Seal, M. (2009) *Not About Us Without Us: Client Involvement In Social Housing*. Lyme Regis: Russell House Publishing.

Seal, M. (2007) *Working in the Homeless Sector: Worker Perspectives*. London: YMCA George Williams College Occasional Paper.

Seal, M. (2006) *Working with Homeless People: A Training Manual*. Lyme Regis: Russell House Publishing.

Seal, M. (2005) *Resettling Homeless People: Theory and Practice*. Lyme Regis: Russell House Publishing.

Seal, M. & Frost. S. (2014) *Philosophy in Youth and Community Work*. Lyme Regis: Russell House Publishing.

Seal, M. & Harris, P. (2016) *Responding to Youth Violence Through Youth Work*. Bristol: Policy Press.

Smith, L. (1999) *Decolonising Methodologies: Research and Indigenous Peoples*. London: Zed Books.

Smyth, J. (1989) 'A critical pedagogy of classroom practice.' *Journal of Curriculum Studies*, 21(6): 483–502.

Solomon, J. (1987) 'New thoughts on teacher education.' *Oxford Review of Education*, 13(3): 267–274.

Trelfa, J. & Telfer, H. (2014) 'Keeping the cat alive: "getting" reflection as part of professional practice.' In Z. Knowles, Dr D. Gilbourne, Prof. B. Cropley, & Dr L. Dugdill (eds) *Reflective Practice in the Sport and Exercise Sciences: Contemporary Issues*. Abingdon (Oxon) and New York: Routledge, pp. 47–56.

Unger, H. (2012) 'Participatory health research: who participates in what?' *Forum Qualitative Sozialforschung/Forum: Qualitative Social Research* [S.l.], 13(1).

Wadsworth, Y. (1998) *What is Participatory Action Research?* Action Research International, Paper 2.

Waldrop, M. (1994) *Complexity: The Emerging Science at the Edge of Order and Chaos.* London: Penguin Books.

Waterman, H. (1998) 'Embracing ambiguities and valuing ourselves: issues of validity in action research.' *Journal of Advanced Nursing*, 28(1): 101–105.

White, S. C. (1996) 'Depoliticising development: the uses and abuses of participation.' *Development in Practice*, 6(1): 6–15.

World Bank (2005) *World Bank Participatory Research Sources Book.* Geneva: World Bank.

Wrentschur, M. (2008) 'Forum theatre as a participatory tool for social research and development: a reflection on "Nobody is perfect" – a project with homeless people.' In P. Cox, T. Geisen & R. Green (eds) *Qualitative Research and Social Change*. London: Palgrave Macmillan, 94–111.

Zachariah, M. (1986) *Revolution Through Reform.* New York: Praeger.

3 Peer research

Epistemological symbolism, proxy trust, conscious partiality and the near-peer

Introduction

One of the tenets of both participatory research and co-production is that they engage actively in issues of power and representation between researcher, researched and wider social forces (Cahn, 2004; Chambers, 2008). One of the ways they do this is through the active involvement of peers within research in both a symbolic and purposive way. Peer involvement, particularly in research, is another approach that it is hard to disagree with but is surprisingly under researched and contested. Justifications for using peer research seem to fall into three camps: claims about power and epistemology (Wahab, 2003; Beresford, 2016; Fine & Torre, 2004, 2006); claims about the richer nature of the data that peer researchers can obtain (Fine & Torre, 2004, 2006; Harding et al., 2010); and the emancipatory and empowering impact of using peer researchers for all stakeholders (Beresford, 2016; Wahab, 2003). Wahab (2003) identifies a tension between goals of empowerment and academic rigor of which we need to be mindful and to ameliorate, although I think this is a false distinction, as we explored in chapter one. It is these claims that I wish to explore in this chapter. It will contend that the first of these claims is largely symbolic, albeit powerful, and that the second is over emphasized, but pertinent at particular points and for nuanced reasons. For me the last claim is key, but sets us a challenge for how we make the practice emancipatory, rather than a tokenistic re-inscribing of a tyranny of participatory methods (Mosse, 1994).

Background

The idea of peer research, particularly with young people, has gain credence in the last few decades, both within the academic community (Burns & Schubotz, 2009; France, 2000; Kaseniemi, 2001; Griesel et al., 2002; Winton, 2007) and amongst practitioners (NYA, 2010; Tyler et al. (Banardos), 2006; Kirby (Involve), 2004). Other drivers have been a commitment to Articles 12 and 13 of the United Nations Convention on the Rights of the Child (1989), whereby children have the right to express their views and to seek and receive information of all kinds through any media of their choice. Some practices, such as youth and community work and informal education, explicitly draw on educational traditions which try and develop the voice of marginalized communities, which traditional educative and research practice can try and silence (Friere, 1972).

Peer research, epistemology and power

As we have seen, there are issues of power between the researchers and the researched, and by extension, epistemological concerns with who creates the knowledge stemming from the research. This concern is one of the central tenets of participatory research involving peers (Cooke & Kothari, 2001; Kumar, 2002; Petty et al., 1995), originally arising from insights of feminist research into the construction of knowledge (Bowles & Duell, 1983; Coppock, 2011). Broadly the claim, as Kilpatrick outlines, is that peer research reduces the inherent power imbalances within research by involving peers in the process and research participants as they therefore have a stake in knowledge creation (Kilpatrick et al., 2007).

In the Touch project (see Chapter 13) our process evaluator, Dr Simon Bradford (2013), cast a critical eye over our use of peer researchers, and helped us to focus on the power and dangers of their use. Ultimately using peer researchers seemed most powerful symbolically. They were signifiers in terms of the perception of research participants of our seriousness about their right to be involved in knowledge creation, which in turn impacted on their own view of their legitimacy. As Bradford says:

> The Touch Project's deployment of peer researchers seems to be a serious attempt to mediate the social distance created by established professional/ client relations, establishing respect between young people and providers and in so doing legitimating the work of the Touch Project.
>
> (Bradford, 2013, p. 2)

Bradford found that because we were using peers, had trained them as researchers and valued their local knowledge, it meant that the young people at least entertained the idea that we might also value the young people's and local practitioners' knowledge. The symbolism of the peer researcher involvement also had practical impact as it meant that the non-peer researchers gained 'proxy trust'. Having a peer whom the research participants trusted meant they extended trust to the professional research team. Involving peers also had cultural and racial impacts on gaining access. One Asian young man explained that he had only engaged with one of the white researchers because the peer researcher trusted him, so he trusted him in turn, although contingently. Lucero (2013) says this type of trust 'occurs when members of the partnership are trusted because someone who is trusted invited them. In this type, a third party, which may be a person or a group, influences trust' (p. 46).

Deutsch (1958) defined it thus: 'If two people are both in the same relationship to a third party, a bond may be established between them which might not otherwise exist' (p. 277). Lucero (2013) goes onto explore how early knowledge about partners or knowledge about a partner's reputation is thought to effect trust in small group teams (McKnight, Cummings & Chervany, 1998) and that there is also 'proxy mistrust' based on participants' previous experience of that research team, and perceptions of research in general and of the academy. Certainly in the Touch project we experienced generalized proxy mistrust in that young people and those involved in violence had mistrustful conceptions of perceived authority figures, including educational establishments (Decker & Van Winkle: 1996) and university researchers. Proxy trust is only a starting point; Webber (2008) found familiarity from prior experiences to be positively associated with early development of trust in a team environment, but it did not predict trust at later stages of a team's functioning. The Asian man mentioned above said that quite quickly he trusted the white researcher on his own merits, but the 'in' was through the peer researcher.

Peer researchers and the genuineness of data

A second claim by advocates of peer research (Alderson, 2001; Kirby, 1999) is that that the quality of data collected is enhanced as peer researchers share commonalities with research participants enabling the participants to feel safe enough to open up. This implies that some form of mutual understanding and shared language enables peers to communicate with research participants, and in turn allows both parties to bring their own understanding to the data and co-create richer, more representative knowledge. As Alderson says, 'Peer research is justified in terms of efficiency in that it encourages closer intimacy and fuller discussion between researchers and researched, and fuller understanding of the data' (Alderson, 2001, p. 140).

Clarke (2005), specifically researching young people's experiences, worked from the assumption that the young people would be 'experts on their own lives', able to relate to other young people better than adults, less intimidating than other adults, able to talk the same language, more able to know when the respondent was 'pissing about' or not, and able to make the interview situation 'informal'. Kirby (2004) similarly says that peers, as opposed to non-peer researchers, have the ability of talking the same 'language', are able to talk about 'taboo' subjects with peers, are able to share common experiences, be on the same side and may give access to other potential research participants. The concepts of having a common language, informality and being less intimidating are generally borne out by the literature (Terry & Cardwell, 2016). Terry and Cardwell go on to sum up the process well.

> Initially, the presence of a peer should relax the participant, knowing that the interviewer understands what they are going through. This should improve the reliability and honesty of the data. As the interview process continues, peer researchers have the 'insider knowledge' to ask the right follow up questions, understand slang and particular terminology, and to judge the interviewee's honesty and truthfulness, perhaps probing where necessary.
>
> (Terry and Cardwell, 2016, p. 20)

The claim about research participants being experts on their own lives has resonance with much of the research I have been involved in. As we note, in the Touch Project 'Partners argued strongly that young people are experts in their own circumstances and lives and that their knowledge should be regarded, therefore, as 'expert knowledge' (Seal & Harris, 2016, p. 63). For example, their understanding of the processes and dynamics of street violence was felt to be something to which young people have privileged and unique access in a way not possible for professional workers (Bradford, 2013, p. 8). However, Bradford (2013) points out that there are also potential dangers in the assumption of expertise. There is a danger or orientalizing (Said, 1978) community partners' perspectives. In privileging such perspectives one can set up tensions between professional, or universal, knowledge and locally situated knowledge and also that privileging local knowledge can lead to the result being inward focusing. As we noted in the last chapter, one of the criticisms of participatory research is that it is subject to the tyranny of the group (Cooke & Kothari, 2001) and Groupthink (Janis, 1982).

At one point in the Touch research the steering group thought we were in danger of simply reproducing tales that youth workers, and young people, tell about youth work. Bearing this in mind, when interrogating the data we used a number of strategies. We tried to keep the initial data analysis grounded (Glasser & Strauss, 1967), especially in relation to young people, and to a large extent, workers, in keeping with action research approaches (McTaggart, 1996). However, we also employed Critical Discourse Analysis and focused on the ways social and political domination were reproduced in text and talk (Caldas-Coulthard et al., 1996; Fairclough & Wodak, 1997). We found particular empty categories, concepts which rather than being grounded in the data arose at points where people, particularly workers, were being challenged, or feeling tensions and were struggling to back up their perspectives. An example was the concept of relationship. Workers emphasized its importance, particularly in developing relationships before engaging in interventions with young people, but struggled to define their positive characteristics, or give accounts of how relationships were built; they just knew they were important. Similar empty categories were respect, trust and building hope. The difference between more traditional usages of critical discourse as our practice was to feedback these empty categories to participants, and work together to define them and consider the reasons why they caused tension (Caldas-Coulthard et al., 1996).

Community members are undoubtedly experts in living their lives, but whether they can articulate the nature of that lived life is a different consideration. As Terry and Cardwell (2016) note, there is a danger in assuming that having lived an experience, means you are going to be good at researching it. As explored before, critical thinkers such as Gramsci (1971) and Freire (1972) would argue that structural forces have an investment in ensuring that those who are oppressed are actively denied the tools to understand their oppression, else they might want to do something about it. If many of our research participants are not meta-reflectors (Archer, 2012), and some are fractured reflexives, it will take some support and development for them to be able to reflect on their experiences effectively, a process we will return to several times in this book.

In contrast, more traditional approaches would want to maintain a separation between researcher and researched so that the researcher should not 'contaminate' the other (Seal & Harris, 2016). This contamination can either be from the researchers sharing of their experience in order to establish themselves as peer, or even simply from their own introduction as a peer – the researched may react to what they imagine that means. In contrast, Mies (1983, p. 122) argues that we need to take our own experiences, and the community's, as a place to start and use these experiences to guide us. While objectivist researchers would say that this is precisely what we should avoid, participatory researcher would argue that we do this in any case, and that trying to escape it, to be neutral, or to 'bracket' our own experiences, are neither possible or desirable. Beresford (2016) also challenges the attention given to peer researchers and their possible bias. He and other authors note that while a peer researcher may have bias because of the closeness of their lived experience to the subject of the research, the professional will have 'blind spots due to their lack of experience and investment in the subject' (Devotta et al., 2016, p. 3).

In order to co-create mutual understanding, participatory research advocates the sharing of these mutual experiences between researcher and researched. While contested (Behar, 1996), the legitimacy of self-revelation on behalf of researchers has a long tradition in feminist research (Oakley, 1981). Du Blois argues that 'The knower and the known are of the same universe, they are not separable' (1906, p. 111). For him, to set objectivity and subjectivity as polar opposites is a false dichotomy. Oakley (1981) argues that principles of commitment and egalitarianism should guide interviews, and that intimacy and self-disclosure are key features of establishing both principles. Similarly, Lather (1985, pp. 23–24) suggests that the most emancipatory approaches to research include interactive interviews with self-disclosure.

In the research described in this book we found that those being researched are a part of, and will react to, any relationship dynamic that professional researchers set up. What is important is that we can foreground these dynamics and subject them to examination. In the Touch project (Seal & Harris, 2016), we found that those researched reacted to the 'peers', and projected onto them, creating an imaginary of their experiences. However, we also found that they did this to all those who researched them. They often had particular perceptions of the academy and professional researchers, this projected onto the dynamic of the 'interview'. This is supported extensively in the literature (Cunningham & Diversi, 2012; Kilpatrick et al., 2007; Shier, 2001; Ward et al., 2005). Interviews can be seen as symbolic interactions (Cohen et al., 2000), and not just between participants, but implicating the communities and society that sit outside the 'interview' process, but are reflected within it. Benjamin says we need to be attentive to these processes, and speaks of taking account of 'intersubjectivity' (1998, p. 94) in the interview process. We will come back to intersubjectivity in several chapters, as it is an essential part of ethnopraxis. For now it suffices to say that there is a dialectical relationship between subjects that necessitates the researcher to constantly compare their data with their own experiences and to share this with the researched. Mies describes the peer research as using a 'conscious partiality' (1983, p. 123), when developing the reflective and critical ability of the researched. As Mies goes on to describe:

> The researcher takes the side of a certain group, partly identifies, and in a conscious process creates space for critical dialogues and reflection on both sides. This enables both research 'subjects' and 'objects' to become more aware of the power differences and dynamics involved, and of distortions of perceptions to be corrected on both sides.
>
> (Mies, 1983, p. 123)

In the Touch research there was a lot of discussion about whether it was ethical or collusive for male workers and peer researchers who embodied a certain type of maleness to which the researched related, to use this aspect of their 'peerness'. It was agreed that such contingent self-revelation was legitimate as leverage, but needed to be accompanied by a conscious intent to challenge and shake up the constructions of maleness in the researched life worlds, for it was damaging to them and others. Interestingly this idea came from the practitioners who had been employing conscious partiality for years as part of their relationship building – it just needed to be named.

One aspect of this that came to the fore in the Touch research was the idea of the 'near peer'. However, before examining this concept it is worth entering into a wider debate within peer research that the idea of near peer invokes - namely what is the nature of one's peerness. Implied in much of the literature (Cunningham & Diversi, 2012; Kilpatrick et al., 2007; Shier, 2001; Ward et al., 2005) is that one's peerness is alternatively on the basis of demographics – i.e. one's, race, age, gender, etc., or one's experience of the issue being researched or a combination of these (e.g. women who have been in prison wanting to speak to other women with experience of the criminal justice system) (Terry & Cardwell, 2016). However, as Thompson et al. (2015) note, the real question is which of these aspects of being a peer the researched will relate to enough to participate, and this can be quite nuanced.

We should also take account of literature that shows that on some issues participants may be *less* likely to talk to a peer. Simell (1921) notes that for more contested issues within a community, the participants may feel judged on their views by another member of the community and would prefer to talk to a stranger. Lundy and McGovern acknowledge that having researchers who were known to the participants and closely connected to the subject matter 'might have led to guarded responses' and an element of 'self-censorship' that led to only partial stories being told (2006, p. 58). Other authors have noted that for issues like gender (McLaughlin 2005) and local accent (McCartan et al., 2012) it can be detrimental, while others Oakley (1986) find the opposite. For France (2000, p. 22), the fact that peer researchers recognize these tensions in his research, and anticipated difficulties that may arise in the researcher/researched relationship shows how effective the peer research method is in 'developing peer researchers capable of thinking and undertaking research'.

Deciding how, when and where peers could be powerful or detrimental in a piece of research is contingent and contextual, and should be a part of the earlier, and ongoing, ethnopraxis of the research. One should also be clear about what the intent behind the peer is at any particular moment: is it to build trust, either personally or symbolically regarding the overall integrity of the project, is it to get data through their peerness, or to challenge what the person is saying through their peerness? Sometimes this challenge can also be symbolic.

Returning to the idea of the 'neer peer', in the Touch project we named this as, 'where workers and young people are purposely situated in peer relationships and environments close enough to build affinity and rapport, but sufficiently different so as to expand horizons on aspects of their identity, and the identity of the researched'. (Seal & Harris, 2016, p. 10). We challenged conventional community work which makes distinction, both in practice and in principle, between building bonding capital (that builds intergroup identity and pride) and bridging capital (that builds bonding between groups and across cultures).

We concurred with Leonard (2004) who contends that bonding capital, creating solidarity between community members with similarities, is often done at the expense of bridging capital, which aims to create mutual understanding between communities that are different. Too much bonding capital without bridging capital is in danger of reinforcing a sense of the other, and rendering the bridging capital as relatively shallow and contingent (Seal & Harris, 2016). To avoid tensions in either also underestimates community member's ability to function within liminal spaces, where there are tensions and contradictions, which is often where they live their lives quite successfully. In the Touch research we described the reactions of young people in their interactions with near peers within liminal spaces:

> Young people have neither totally different, nor totally parallel, experiences. They will simultaneously see similarities and differences in their peers, but in a way that, if skilfully managed, can create dynamism rather than conservatism.
>
> (Seal & Harris, 2016, p. 222)

We go on to discuss how these dynamics developed:

> Rather than reinforcing a static view of self and other, contact with other near peers begins to facilitate the shifts in identity that can be part of an evolving process of desistance from violence. Enough similarity and affinity with each other leads young people to feel safe enough to explore the differences. Enough difference means that their perceptions are challenged and the meanings they place on their lives, and the lives of others, can evolve . . . their pre-existing perceptions of difference and similarities with each other, as well as with the groups of young people they met from other partner projects, changed. Some of their pre-conceived ideas turned out to be false or more nuanced than previously perceived, as part of a creative dynamic triggered by

exposure to groups of people they would never have met had it not been for their involvement in the project.

(Seal & Harris, 2016, p. 222)

An interesting example from the Touch project illustrates how building bonding capital alone may not allow for change and being too close in cultures can mitigate against effective challenge. A woman worker of Pakistani origin expressed her frustration at trying to challenge some of the young people's closed views about certain aspects of Islam. When she tried they often closed her down, saying the subject was 'haram' (forbidden), and she should know this. She felt they could dismiss her view because she was too close, meaning they could construct her as not being 'properly' Muslim. However, encountering very different lived forms of Islam, such as those practised in Tunisia and Morocco, encountered on the research residential, could not be dismissed in the same way. Young people had to engage with a very different form and interpretation of Islam, and look at their own constructions of Islam in turn.

Bradford (2013), in evaluating our use of peers in the Touch project, saw that peer researchers had currency with the young people, but worried about the use of charisma, and whether the epiphanies that some peer researchers had, moments when they changed their lives, were common to all. However, he recognized the power of these epiphanies and the use of charisma if they were seen as contingent, useful in certain stages in the project, and in particular ways. For instance, one man in Bradford cultivated a strong relationship with me, commenting that he wanted to talk to someone outside his experience. This was his longest ever conversation with a white man, and his only conversation about Islam with any white man. However, importantly, he felt able to develop this relationship with me because one of the peer researchers respected me. Similarly, the peer researchers were 'blueprint selves' (Seal & Harris, 2016), rather than role models. Particularly in Graz and Germany the peer researchers were substantially older, from a very different culture and spoke different languages. The 'peerness' was about a certain experience of the street. A blueprint self (Seal & Harris, 2016) is more symbolic than a role model. The young person cannot follow the same path, or emulate that peers behaviour, however the can see in them a blueprint for change, the peer being a symbol that the change is possible, but the exact nature of the change will be theirs alone.

Peer research as an emancipatory practice

Similarly to claims mentioned in Chapter 1, peer research makes a third, over-arching claim – that it is empowering for the peer researchers. Kirby (1999) talks of the potential for involvement to improve the personal development of young people. There appears to be a general view that the research experience (as researchers) can increase the personal development of the researchers themselves and help them to gain knowledge, skills and confidence. Precht (1998) reports several benefits, such as improved confidence, development of new skills such as listening, understanding, inter-personal communication, etc. (see also Kirby, 1999). Hall and Hall (1996) talk in terms of opportunities for researchers to develop and exercise various personal transferable skills, such as oral communication, teamwork, motivation, initiative, leadership, organizing ability, etc. Garcia et al. (2013) note how it builds on the 'raw' abilities peer researchers already have and make them see their strengths and potential (Terry & Cardwell, 2016) including participating in civil society, critical thinking and social responsibility (de Winter & Noom, 2003); knowledge of services and interventions (Terry & Cardwell, 2016), ability to talk to new people (Coupland & Mayer, 2005), teamwork, and empathy for different cultures and experiences (Smith, 2010). Experience of peer research can help peer researchers build a CV (Sova, 2003) and possibly provides them with a professional reference (Harding et al., 2010). Others cite how their experiences as a peer researcher supports journeys of recovery and desistance from crime (Terry & Cardwell, 2016) and more generally that they can help people develop a positive identity (Clover, 2011), self-esteem and employability (Hayashi et al., 2012) and being a 'role model' for others, both in terms of research and treatment (Smith, 2010), although I do not find the term 'role model' helpful, preferring the idea of blueprint self – something I will return to again.

Beyond the personal, the whole process should be one which is consciousness-raising, whereby peer researchers not only learn new social and practical skills but also an awareness of the research issues (some of which impact upon them), and through this develop potential agency for individual and social change (Clarke, 2010; Cleaver, 2001; Fleming et al., 2009; Kilpatrick et al., 2007; Murray, 2006). Checkoway and Richards-Schuster (2003) establish ways in which peer researcher enact this potential. They note that it can be a legitimate way of developing knowledge for social action, can enable young people to exercise their political rights, allow them to share in the 'democratization of knowledge' and, prepare them to be active citizens and strengthen their social development. Various studies have found it to be empowering in terms of the aforementioned opportunity to be experts on their own lives (Wahab, 2003) and in offering that it offers a chance to connect with other people with similar experiences and goals (Terry & Cardwell, 2016) to engage researchers with wider society and potentially reverse profound social exclusion (Harding et al., 2010).

Perhaps most pertinently for this book several authors (Sova, 2003; Terry & Cardwell, 2016) note that when peer researchers are evaluating services that they have used, 'the process of working with these professionals in a different capacity may give people more confidence to deal with bureaucracy and agencies' (Terry & Cardwell, 2016, p. 26). It is for this reason that I think research as is one of the most effective methods for co-production. De Winter and Noom (2003) cite longitudinal studies show that people develop much better 'in a social atmosphere that invites them to actively participate – where they feel connected, wanted, welcome and necessary' (de Winter & Noom, 2003, p. 327). This sets the challenge for what peer participatory pedagogic research should be.

This pedagogy extends to all those within the project's remits, including researchers themselves. There can be benefits for wider community members as researchers, as reported by Dodson and Baker (1995). They reported that participants had learned valuable new skills, they became a confident and vocal group in terms of their own knowledge of research, and were able to critically comment upon other people's research, rather than taking it as fact. Peer research also benefits professionals, for example by exposing them to new viewpoints and explanatory theories (Fine and Torre, 2004). Fine and Torre (2004), having facilitated a prison-based project, found that they were obliged and honoured 'to join the . . . political struggle of prisoner's rights' (2004, p. 20). Clover (2011) discusses her 'explicit aim to better the lives of women' in her account of a feminist, arts based participatory process.

Conclusion: the need for support, training and effective, pedagogical critical spaces

Several authors note how the mutual identification that occurs between researchers and participants requires serious reflection on the vulnerable position this can create for researchers (Reinharz, 1992, p. 234). McDonagh (2000) talks about the vulnerable position that the researcher can be put in by self-revelation. Stanley and Wise (1983, p. 21) argue that this vulnerability is essential, as it is part of building trust with research participants. Key to effective peer research, therefore, is effective planning, training and support. There are several dimension to this, and section two of this book will go through them in more detail. Research training should cover similar ground to that provided to any researchers (Smith, 2010; Terry & Cardwell, 2016), and our experience is that, when taking a participatory approach, there is much positivist thinking to be undone. Given the emphasis on action and potential change, Garcia et al. (2013) suggest covering processes of policy change.

Several authors (Smith, 2010; Terry & Cardwell, 2016; Groundswell, 2014) suggest support for researchers in terms of the disclosures and trauma they will hear, particularly if these are reminders of their own experience and might be negative triggers for them. This can be quite nuanced. In one piece of research one of the peer researchers was very reluctant to work in an older person's homeless shelter. On reflection he realized that it was not so much that it reminded him of his own experiences, but it foreshadowed where he would have ended up if he had not changed things in his life. I have also seen peer researchers become exasperated if they are working with who people take a very different path from them – it takes time to learn that your experience is yours uniquely, and so is everyone else's. As an example of how to work with this, Groundswell (2014) explicitly sent two of its peer researcher's on a course in critical reflection 'designed to better equip the researchers to cope with [revisiting] many of the issues connected with their own episodes of homelessness' (Groundswell, 2014, 32).

In addition to training support, several authors (Ledden & Vickers, 2011; Garcia et al., 2013; Terry & Cardwell, 2016) suggest having training and facilitation around participation, including group work skills, confidence, self-esteem, and communication as well as providing emotional support, particularly where people are juggling multiple difficulties and problems, and are aware of the importance of working assertively and flexibly, keeping an open door for those participants who cycle in and out of the project; and of ensuring people are safe and well, not at risk of harm because of the project. Building on this, several authors (Clover, 2011; Hayashi et al., 2012; Terry & Cardwell, 2016) suggest building in extra time and flexibility to take account of absence, setbacks and personal commitments (e.g. Clover, 2011). A project needs to take account of the culture of the community to be worked with, as well as individual needs. Many communities discussed in this book have very different senses of time, which can mean fixed points are difficult for them to take account of. Also the research project is unlikely to be the only thing in a person's life, and in many ways represents one more thing to juggle, and this needs to be respected.

Perhaps some of the most difficult areas where support is needed is with an unsatisfying sense of injustice the peer researcher, and participants, may feel. In all likelihood the research will not change the world, and often as not it may not even change the service, at least not in the short run. This is the human side of Cooke and Kothari's (2001) criticism that participatory research promises too much. We will come back to this theme several times. Inequality can be demoralizing; I would suggest research projects have some acknowledgement of this. Fine and Torre have specific sessions 'so students can document inequity without losing their souls, spirits or their sense of hope' (Fine & Torre, 2004, p. 28). It is for this reason that Garcia et al. suggest having training on policy processes so peers can recognize the 'slowness of change and the many setbacks that can occur along the way' (Garcia et al., 2013, p. 25). Ultimately though, as we shall see, there is a balance between aspirational and realistic goals, and the negotiation of them is part of the process. Finally, an aspect of support that remains underdeveloped, but for the whole of the research process, is the need for liminal spaces to reflect upon the research process. We all need to become, and remain, meta reflectors, but this is itself a process – one which I shall try to articulate in the next chapter.

References

Alderson, P. (2001) 'Research by children: rights and methods.' *International Journal of Social Research Methodology: Theory and Practice*, 4(2): 139–153.

Archer, M. S. (2012) *The Reflexive Imperative in Late Modernity*. Cambridge: Cambridge University Press.

Behar, R. (1996) *The Vulnerable Observer: Anthropology That Breaks Your Heart*. Boston, MA: Beacon Press.

Benjamin, J. (1998) *Shadow of the Other: Intersubjectivity and Gender in Psychoanalysis*. London and New York: Routledge.

Beresford, P. (2016) *All Our Welfare: Towards Participatory Social Policy*. Bristol: Policy Press.

Bradford, S. (2013) *Touch: A Process Evaluation*. Birmingham: Newman University.

Bowles, G. & Duelli, R. (eds) (1983) *Theories of Women's Studies*. London: Routledge and Kegan Paul.

Burns, S. & Schubotz, D. (2009) 'Demonstrating the merits of the peer research process: a Northern Ireland case study.' *Field Methods*, 21(3): 309–326.

Cahn, E. (2004) *No More Throwaway People: The Co-production Imperative.* New York: Essential Books.

Caldas-Coulthard, C. R. & Coulthard, M. (1996) *Texts and practices: Readings in Critical Discourse Analysis.* London: Routledge.

Chambers, R. (2008) *Revolutions in Development Inquiry.* London: Earthscan.

Checkoway, B. & Richards-Schuster, K. (2003) 'Youth participation in community evaluation research.' *American Journal of Evaluation*, 24(1): 21–33.

Clark, A. (2005) 'Listening to young children: experts in their own lives.' *Adoption & Fostering*, 29(1): 45–56.

Clarke, T. (2010) 'On "being researched": why do people engage with qualitative research?' *Qualitative Research*, 10(4): 399–419.

Cleaver, F. (2001) 'Institutions, agency and the limitations of participatory approaches to development.' In B. Cooke & U. Kothari (eds) *Participation: The New Tyranny?* London: Zed Books, pp. 139–152.

Clover, D. (2011) 'Successes and challenges of feminist arts-based participatory methodologies with homeless/street-involved women in Victoria.' *Action Research*, 9(1): 12–26.

Cohen, L., Manion, L. & Morrison, K. (2000) *Research Methods in Education.* London: Falmer-Routledge.

Cooke, B. & Kothari, U. (2001) (eds) *Participation: The New tyranny?* London: Zed Books.

Coppock, V. (2011) 'Children as peer researchers: reflections on a journey of mutual discovery.' *Children & Society*, 25: 435–446.

Coupland, H. & Maher, L. (2005) 'Clients or colleagues? Reflections on the process of participatory-action research with young injection drug users.' *International Journal of Drug Policy*, 16(3): 191–198.

Cunningham, M. J. & Diversi, M. (2012) 'Aging out: youths' perspectives on foster care and the transition to independence.' *Qualitative Social Work*, 12(5): 587–602.

Decker, S. H. & Van Winkle, B. (1996) *Life in the Gang: Family, Friends, and Violence.* New York: Cambridge University Press.

Deutsch, M. (1958) 'Trust and suspicion.' *Journal of Conflict Resolution*, 2: 265–279.

Devotta, K., Woodhall-Melnik, J., Pedersen, C., Wendaferew, A., Dowbor, T. P., Guilcher, S. J. T., Hamilton-Wright, S., Ferentzy, P., Hwang, S. W. & Matheson F. L. (2016) 'Enriching qualitative research by engaging peer interviewers: a case study.' *Qualitative Research*, 16(6): 661–680.

de Winter, M. & Noom, M. (2003) 'Someone who treats you as an ordinary human being . . . homeless youth examine the quality of professional care.' *The British Journal of Social Work*, 33(3): 325–338.

Dodson, J. & Baker, J. (1995) *Time For Change: Local People Becoming Researchers.* London: Save the Children.

Du Bois, W. E. B. & Edwards, B. H. (1906) *The Souls of Black Folk.* Oxford: Oxford University Press.

Fairclough, N. & Wodak, R. (eds) (1997) *Critical Discourse Analysis. Discourse As Social Interaction.* Thousand Oaks, CA: Sage.

Fine, M. & Torre, M. E. (2006) 'Intimate details: participatory action research in prison.' *Action Research*, 4(3): 253–269.

Fine, M. & Torre, M. E. (2004) 'Re-membering exclusions: participatory action research in public institutions.' *Qualitative Research in Psychology*, 1(1): 15–37.

Fleming, J., Goodman, C. & Skinner, A. (2009) 'Experiences of peer evaluation of the Leicester Teenage Pregnancy Prevention Strategy.' *Children and Society*, 23(4): 279–290.

France, A. (2000) *Youth Researching Youth: The Triumph and Success Peer Research Project.* London: Josephy Rowntree Foundation.

Freire, P. (1972) *Pedagogy of the Oppressed.* London: Penguin.

Garcia, A. P., Minkler, M., Cardenas, Z., Grills, C. & Porter, C. (2013) 'Engaging homeless youth in community-based participatory research: a case study from Skid Row, Los Angeles.' *Health Promotion Practice*, 15(1): 18–27.

Glasser, B. & Strauss, A. (1967) *The Discovery of Grounded Theory.* New York: Aldine Publishing.

Gramsci, A. (1971) *Selections from the Prison Notebooks.* London: Lawrence & Wishart.

Griesel, R. D., Swart-Kruger, J. & Chawla, L. (2002) 'Children in South Africa can make a difference: an assessment of "growing up in cities".' *Childhood*, 9(1): 83–100.

Groundswell (2014) *The Escape Plan: Creating an Evidence Base of the Critical Success Factors That Have Enabled People to Successfully Move on From Homelessness.* London: Groundswell.

Hall, D. & Hall, I. (1996) *Practical Social Research: Project Work in the Community.* Basingstoke: Macmillan.

Harding, R., Whitfield, G. & Stillwell, N. (2010) 'Service users as peer research interviewers: why bother?' *Analysis and Debate in Social Policy*, 22: 317.

Hayashi, K., Fairbairn, N., Suwannawong, P., Kaplan, K., Wood, E. & Kerr, T (2012) 'Collective empowerment while creating knowledge: a description of a community-based participatory research project with drug users in Bangkok, Thailand.' *Substance Use & Misuse*, 47(5): 502–510.

Janis, I. L. (1982) *Groupthink: Psychological Studies of Policy Decisions and Fiascos.* Boston, MA: Houghton Mifflin.

Kaseniemi, E. (2001) 'Finnish teenagers and mobile communications: chatting and storytelling in text messages.' In A. Furlong & I. Guidikova (eds) *Transitions of Youth Citizenship in Europe.* Strasbourg, France: Council of Europe, pp. 157–180.

Kilpatrick, R., McCartan, C., McAlister, S. & McKeown, P. (2007) '"If I'm brutally honest research has never appealed to me . . .": the problems and successes of a peer research project.' *Educational Action Research*, 15(3): 351–369.

Kirby, P. (2004) *A Guide to Actively Involving Young People in Research: For Researchers, Research Commissioners, and Managers.* London: Involve.

Kirby, P. (1999) *Involving Young Researchers: How to Enable Young People to Design and Conduct Research.* York: Joseph Rowntree Foundation.

Kumar, S. (2002) *Methods for Community Participation: A Complete Guide for Practitioners.* New Delhi: Vistaar Publications.

Lather, P. (1986) 'Research as praxis.' *Harvard Educational Review*, 56(3): 257–277.

Lather, P. (1985) 'Empowering research methodologies.' Paper presented at the *Annual Meeting of the American Educational Research Association*, Chicago, IL, 31 March–4 April.

Ledden, L. & Vickers, S. (2011) *Alcohol – Young Women – Peer Research.* Cheshire: North West Regional Work Unit.

Leonard, M. (2004) 'Bonding and bridging social capital: reflections from Belfast.' *Sociology*, 38(5): 927–944.

Lucero, J. E. (2013) 'Trust as an ethical construct in community based participatory research partnerships.' Communication ETDs. Paper 43.

Lundy, P. & McGovern, M. (2006) 'The ethics of silence: action research, community "truth-telling" and post-conflict transition in the North of Ireland.' *Action Research*, 4(1): 49–64.

McCartan, C., Schubotz, D. & Murphy, J. (2012) 'The self-conscious researcher – post-modern perspectives of participatory research with young people.' *Forum Qualitative Sozialforschung / Forum: Qualitative Social Research*, 13(1): Art. 9.

McDonagh, R. (2000) 'Talking back.' In A. Byrne & R. Lentin (eds) *(Re)searching Women: Feminist Research Methodologies in the Social Sciences in Ireland.* Dublin: Institute of Public Administration, pp. 237–246.

McKnight, D., Cummings, L. & Chervany, N. (1998) 'Initial trust formation in new organizational relationships.' *The Academy of Management Review*, 23(3): 473–490.

McLaughlin, H. (2009) *Service User Research in Health and Social Care.* London: Sage.

McTaggart, R. (1996) 'Issues for participatory action researchers.' In O. Zuber-Skerritt (ed.) *New Directions in Action Research.* London: Falmer Press.

Mies, M. (1983) 'Towards a methodology for feminist research.' In G. Bowles & R. D. Klein (eds) *Theories of Women's Studies.* Boston, MA: Routledge Kegan Paul, pp. 117–139.

Mosse, D. (1994) 'Authority, gender and knowledge: theoretical reflections on the practice of participatory rural appraisal.' *Development and Change*, 25(3): 497–526.

Murray, C. (2006) 'Peer led focus groups and young people.' *Children and Society* 20(4): 273–286.

National Youth Agency (2010) *Young Researchers Network Toolkit.* Leicester: NYA.

Oakley, A. (1981) 'Interviewing women: a contradiction in terms.' In H. Roberts (ed.) *Doing Feminist Research.* London: Routledge and Kegan Paul, pp. 30–61.

Petty, J., Guijt, I., Scoones, I. & Whompson, J. (1995) *Participatory Learning and Action: A Trainer's Guide.* London: International Institute for Economic Development.

Precht, D. (1998) *The Paradise Project: Children''s Research on Tourism in Grenada.* Grenada: Save the Children.

Reinharz, S. (1992) *Feminist Research Methods in the Social Sciences.* Oxford: Oxford University Press.

Said, E. (1978) *Orientalism.* New York: Panthanon Books.

Seal, M. & Harris, P. (2016) *Responding to Youth Violence Through Youth Work.* Bristol: Policy Press.

Shier, H. (2001) 'Pathways to participation: openings, opportunities and obligations.' *Children and Society*, 15(2): 107–117.

Simmel, G. (1921) *Soziologie: Untersuchungen über die Formen der Vergesellschaftung.* Leipzig: Duncker & Humblot.

Smith, J. (2010) *Methodology Annex: Working with Young Homeless People as Co-researchers.* European Union Seventh Framework Programme.

Sova (2003) *Women into Work Report.* Sheffield: Sheffield Hallam and Sova. Available at: www4.shu.ac.uk/_assets/pdf/hccj-mm_report.pdf [accessed 10 May 2016].

Stanley, L. & Wise, S. (1983) 'Back into the personal or: our attempt to construct feminist research.' In G. Bowles & R. Duelli Klein (eds) *Theories of Women's Studies.* London: Routledge and Kegan Paul, pp. 20–60.

Terry, L. & Cardwell, V. (2016) *Refreshing Perspectives: Exploring the Application of Peer Research with Populations Facing Severe and Multiple Disadvantage.* London: Revolving Doors Agency.

Thompson, J., Lanchin, S. & Moxon, D. (2015) *Be Real With Me: Using Peer Research to Explore the Journeys of Young People Who Run Away From Home or Care.* Sandbach: Railway Children.

Tyler, P., Turner, T. & Mills, H. (2006) *Banardos Guide to Involving Young People in Research.* London: Banardos.

Wahab, S. (2003) 'Creating knowledge collaboratively with female sex workers: insights from a qualitative, feminist, and participatory study.' *Qualitative Inquiry*, 9(4): 625–642.

Ward, H., Skuse, T. & Munro, E. R. (2005) '"The best of times, the worst of times": young people's views of care and accommodation.' *Adoption and Fostering*, 29(1): 8–17.

Webber, S. S. (2008) 'Development of cognitive and affective trust in teams: a longitudinal study.' *Small Group Research*, 39(6): 746–769.

Winton, A. (2007) 'Using "participatory" methods with young people in contexts of violence: Reflections from Guatemala.' *Bulletin of Latin American Research*, 26(4): 497–515.

4 PPIR's key claim

Towards critical pedagogic reflective spaces

Introduction

As we have explored, participatory research (Chambers, 2010) criticises traditional research as 'privileging methods' in that it overemphasises the tools of research in a naïve belief that if we get them right at the outset they will mysteriously deliver the results we want. Chambers (2010) also critiques traditional epistemological stances as either separating the knower and the known, positing an objective world to be discovered, or an equally fruitless search for the authentic unheard 'voices', untainted by the research process. He says we should instead cultivate the attitudes and mindset of researchers, and their process of reflection, in order to enable them to select the right tools at the right time for the right context. However, he and others are remarkably silent on how we might do this, particularly with the process of reflection, and this will be the focus of this chapter.

Much of my claim so far has centred around the contribution of critical pedagogy. As we have noted, critical pedagogy, particularly in its Freirean formation, is not without its critics, particularly that it is not as liberatory as claimed (Taylor, 1993), and retains patriarchal qualities. These are also two of the central critiques of Cooke and Kothari about participatory research and so need to be addressed if we are to say that participatory research and co-production should draw on critical pedagogy more. To these ends, I continue my examination of the contribution of Rancière (1992, 2004), whose notion of radical equality has something to offer in ameliorating issues of power, and queer pedagogy, which can contribute to in a discussion around critical reflection.

I will do this within the context of outlining what critical reflective processes could look like drawing not only on critical pedagogy, but also youth and community work, particularly in its American existential form (Baizerman, 2001). My claim is that these spaces need to be liminal rather than safe and that all participants need to co-contain that liminality. These spaces should be characterized by inter-subjectivity, encounter, recognition, creativity and improvisation and that there is need for an emphasis on, and commitment to, the de-construction of power and the concept of knowledge and the cultivation of hope. The latter seeks to address the third critique of Cooke and Kothari (2001), the tyranny of action, and I draw on Archer (2010, 2012) to further theorise the interaction between structures and individual agency. But before this it seems important to re-examine the purpose of these critical reflective spaces.

The aim of critical reflective spaces

This was the subject of some discussion in the previous chapter. In practice these reflective sessions are where the stakeholders, including the facilitator and community members, learn about research and then conduct it. It is where decisions are made and where knowledge is created. Also, being mindful of Cooke and Kothari (2001), it is potentially where power plays out and the tyranny of participatory processes and groupthink (Janis, 1982) manifest. We need to ensure that our processes do not let this happen. From this stems a question of what kind of reflection we want in those spaces, and what kind of reflectors the actors involved need to become. Ultimately we want to create a space inhabited by the dedicated meta reflexives (Archer, 2012; Scrambler, 2013) mentioned in Chapter 1, able to reflect on themselves and others, see wider connections and step outside their own and others world views, while retaining a commitment to others and their communities. In order to do this we need the space to be one that enables people to move from being fractured reflexives, through being communicative and autonomous ones, to becoming those dedicated meta-reflexives.

However, there are potential dangers in this, as well as other ways of viewing the meta-reflective. In his publication *The Souls of Black Folk*, Du Bois (1906) explores the idea of double consciousness, seeing it as asense of always looking at one's self through the eyes of others in the mirror'. He was talking about when black slaves perceive themselves through their own culture and that of their oppressor. The oppressor, in contrast, only sees the other through their own perspective. He describes this kind of reflective ability as an existential crisis: identity is split into two parts, making it hard for an individual to have a single, unified identity. From this view the fractured reflexive may be closer to the meta reflexive, or the flip side of the meta reflexive – what happens when the meta reflexive burns out.

Rawls (2000), more recently, explains double consciousness in terms of her black students having contradictory interactional expectations placed on them. To fulfil the demands placed on them by white society, her black participants had to go against the expectations of their fellow black students. As a parallel danger, community members can get negative reaction when they return to their communities with accusations of having 'sold out', and lost their roots. However, Jason Orne in his article 'Queers in the line of fire: Goffman's stigma revisited' (2013) argues that there are two interpretations of double consciousness: one where different cultural orientations are in tension, and another of a positive socio-psychological lens through which people in marginalized positions view themselves and others. In this alternate usage, double consciousness is a mechanism through which marginalized people become be aware of the worldviews of those in positions of power, while holding their own opinions and drawing on their identities as resources to mediate those in power. Community members can see the perspective of the agencies who are meant to serve them, without internalizing this negatively or losing sight of their own community values.

Double consciousness is the dual lens that allows both of these understandings of a situation to co-occur within one individual. Orne also claims that having a double consciousness makes one stigma resistant (Siegel et al., 1998). He says a 'double consciousness allows participants to mobilize their bifurcated consciousness by anticipating and responding to potentially negative reaction.' (Orne, 2013, p. 230). They are stigma-resistant (Siegel et al., 1998), aware of discrimination, and its presence in the contexts in which they move. They are regularly put in the line of fire, from both management and other community members, but ultimately they 'see it for what it is', and reject it. We will return to the idea of stigma resistance as a concept for it is also useful, particularly in the idea of having liminal space and co-containing it.

Orne (2013) felt that Du Bois used both interpretations at different points, or at least understood both applications, but deployed double consciousness as a rhetorical device designed to engage the 'talented tenth' (Du Bois 1906) that he was trying to stir into political action. Another author, Black (2012) also sees double consciousness as a potentially positive metaphor – as something that we should aim to instil in others, including those with power. He uses the term multilateral double consciousness:

> Instead of black double consciousness being unilateral, it would be part of an equal negotiation where all parties share, explore, critique, and develop their views of themselves and others. This would mean that the imposition of identities would be replaced by the awareness and practice of mutual construction of identities. Double consciousness would change from a form of oppression of some to a form of dialogue and negotiation for all. Absence of double consciousness would change from a privilege for the dominant to a form of insight and shared inquiry into social formation of identities, on equal terms and with mutual dependency between all parties.
>
> (Black, 2012, p. 304).

That seems highly productive for what we are trying to achieve within co-production and participatory research for all stakeholders. Black's (2012) formulation also has an underpinning adherence to intersubjectivity and mutual negotiation, which seems part of our aim. Black's formulation also recognises that double consciousness can still cause tensions and distress, but that is a burden, or gift, to be shared. However, I think the term 'multilateral double consciousness' is confusing, not least what is multiple and what is double. It could imply that the sharing of meaning needs to be across multiple people, or everyone subject to the issue of concern. While an admirable ambition in participatory research there are instances where the double consciousness happens across only two people, or only across some people within a group. Alternatively, the multiplicity could apply to the perspectives rather than the people hold.

For this reason, I instead use the term 'intersubjective consciousness'. Intersubjectivity is, as Scheff states, conceptualised as 'the sharing of subjective states by two or more individuals' (Scheff et al., 2006, p. 172). Also the implication of intersubjectivity is about mutual meaning creating through 'the interplay of differently organized experiential worlds' (Stolorow et al., 2002, p. 2) a construction that seems entirely in keeping with co-production and participatory research. Perspectives involved in that meaning making could be binary or multiple (and certainly multi-layered), whatever the number of people. Finally, the term intersubjective also links well to Baizerman's (2001) idea of 'encounter', which as we shall see, is one of the motors for moving through different reflective states. I see this as a clarification of Black's (2012) vision, rather than an extension of it, and one that is conceptually clearer. Now we need to examine the nature of the spaces for reflection, and then the characteristics they will have for moving people through reflective states. Having established what kind of reflectors we want participatory researcher to become, we need to start unpicking what the conditions are for those reflective spaces that foster these reflexives.

Liminal rather than 'safe' spaces

Many authors call for reflective spaces to be safe (Berghold & Thomas, 2012; Baber & Murray, 2001; Galbreath, 2012; Terry & Cardwell, 2016). I would challenge this, and concur with Allen (2015) and others (Britzman, 2003; Schippert, 2006) that safe spaces are not possible, are a fantasy, and not necessarily desirable. As Allen (2015) says, 'a "truly" critical pedagogy might embrace a lack of "safety" as pedagogically productive, dislodging it from its negative connotations for learning' (2015, p. 767). These pedagogic spaces need to de-construct and reconstruct pedagogical power and knowledge, in line with critical pedagogy's ambitions, and I concur with pedagogues such as Talburt and Rasmussen (2010, p. 2) who call for 'spaces that reveal liberated subjects, liberated moments and political efficacy'. Similarly, Allen (2015) and Eliason and Elia (2009) maintain that in order to make our interventions meaningful we need to make the social construction of the group, including ourselves, apparent. We also need to 'teach each other how to look at the world from a critical perspective by pointing out the socially constructed nature of current events' (Allen, 2015, p. 749).

On a different tack, we need to ask where this desire for a safe space is coming from. Is it from community partners, who are often used to and can cope with unsafe and volatile situations, or somewhere else? As I discussed in my doctorate, one student critiqued the idea of safe spaces from both a queer and class-based perspective:

> I think the term safe space isn't helpful, it's one of those middle class counselly things, which is really about creating a safe space for them. In lots of ways there are no safe spaces for lgbt people, same as there aren't for many black people, apart from your home and I've had dog shit posted there before. It's what you do with those spaces that matters.

This person is demonstrating the aforementioned stigma resistance. This is not to say that they should have to suffer these things, but through them they had developed a resistance. These spaces are most effective when they are intersubjective, visceral, with an emphasis on encounter, working in the moment, and will need a fair amount of stigma resistance from its members to feel authentic. Land et al. (2014) talks about 'liminal' space – the spaces where pedagogy happens as new ideas and concepts and the boundaries of knowledge are encountered, engaged with and crossed (i.e. where pedagogy happens). However, this process is not linear, Cousin (2006, 2009) talks about liminal states thus: '(the) mastery of a threshold concept often involves messy journeys back, forth and across conceptual terrain' (2006, p. 142).

These spaces can be difficult and challenging, if the open expression of a community member's views and attitudes, however unpalatable they may be to others, is an important element of the educational process. I found in my doctoral research that reactions to oppression from professional educators were often characterised by guilt and hopelessness. Concurrently professional workers were far quicker to want to close down fractured and visceral reflections in the name of preserving 'safe space', than community members, who had much more natural resistance and consequent tolerance of such discussions. The wish to close down such potential 'breakthrough conversations' was borne from having an idealistic view of safe spaces and ultimately led to their abandonment. Safe spaces were often argued for from those in a position of privilege, rather than oppression, from someone who has developed double consciousness, but has not developed stigma resistance (Orne, 2013). There is still the need to protect people's physical, emotional and psychological safety, but this begs the questions of who holds and judges these spaces, and at what point, as safe or educational.

Co-containment of liminal spaces

Creating these spaces demands of participants an ability 'swim with', or be 'at ease' with, the troublesome tension, dissension and discomfort engendered by pedagogical exchanges. The threshold literature calls these 'holding environments for the toleration of confusion' (Cousin, 2006). Participants need to be able to 'contain' (Bion, 1961) the inner conflict and sometimes pain for both workers and community members, which can result from the disruption of worldviews and the deeply held values that reside therein. Authors such as Cousin (2006, 2009) saw the limits of critical pedagogy, with its emphasis on the rational, universal and humanist. It may leave community members stuck in liminal states because of its intolerance of the irrational, the affective and the contextual; we need to take account of this, and the spaces need to be able to hold the irrational, the unknowable, the affective and the contextual. With a commitment to an honest, but challenging, exploration of views and personal identities, raw, often previously hidden, emotions and projections need to be absorbed, detoxified and re articulated.

We should also not privilege the worker with the ability to contain these tensions, as this firstly perpetuates inequality and a dependency relationship, and is secondly not possible. As noted workers may have developed double consciousness, but have often not developed stigma resistance (Orne, 2013). As a result, in other research I have conducted, the worker viewed a space as visceral and oppressive, when it is actually at the point of being productive, and the community members are actually fine and used to functionig at higher thresholds of volatility. Interrupting and reconstructing our understanding of research, co-production and the subject under review necessitates the development of intersubjective consciousness's and this can only be done through a collective pedagogy, where people hold each other to account for the fine lines between containment, oppression, retreat and necessary stigma resistance. The ability to contain spaces should certainly be present within the worker, but not them alone. We need to have faith that community members also have the resilience and emotional intelligence to do this, although, as with cognitive intelligence, we may need to work on their will to exercise it.

Characteristics of reflective spaces: an emphasis on inter-subjectivity, encounter and recognition

In order to move through different reflexive states, stakeholders will need to have mechanism for recognizing, confronting and moving on from how they currently reflect. In addition to critical pedagogy, existential concepts may be useful in critical reflection. There is an emphasis on the development of agency, encounter and mutual meaning making. Key ideas include the relativity of experience, intersubjectivity, the importance of trying to understand the perspective and 'life world' of others (Noddings, 1984) and being 'present' in the moment with people within an 'encounter' (Buber, 1923, 1958). This seems highly relevant to the idea of developing an intersubjective consciousness.

If we are to embrace such ideas, all stakeholders, including community members, should be encouraged to think critically at a time when they are intrinsically motivated to do so, with workers and other community members, and under their gaze. This gaze means that the experience is in its nature intersubjective, drawing on individual experience, but epistemologically 'performed' within a more collective context with a focus on exploring the 'inter-subjective, dialogical and dialectic processes at work' (Harris & Mac an Ghail, 2015). This emphasis on intersubjectivity explains the aforementioned emphasis on existential notions of encounter, and intersubjective notions of recognition (Benjamin: 1998, Butler: 1990), combined with elements of hooks's (1994) engaged pedagogue.

This is partly achieved by bringing theory into the visceral, embodied experience of co-production and research groups and by working to bring tacit, sometimes unconscious processes into a learnable, theoretical framework (Harris, Mac an Ghail & Heywood, 2017), recognizing the performativity of this (Butler, 1990). Emphasizing thinking about the immediate environment mitigates against the temptation for workers to bring preconceived activities from a de-contextualised repertoire to that encounter, thereby casting community members in the role of passive receptor and 'objectified other' rather than potent co-creators. We will expand on the skill of working in the moment later. Conceptually, Baizerman (2001) summed up well this process meaning making, saying it is about

> developing the skills necessary to pierce one's taken-for-granted, ordinary, mundane life so that one becomes aware of how the ordinary is constructed and how one is implicated constructing one's own reality . . . awareness of how one's biography pre-forms the present gives the worker the possibility of seeing in the moment its manifold possibilities, not simply what is there. Done well, all of this slows down the instantaneous process of seeing and making meaning. Once slowed, the worker (and community member) can 'control' how she makes sense, and, in this way, come to be accountable to herself.
>
> (Baizerman, 2001, p. 1)

Later Baizerman (2001) noted that central to this encounter is a duty on workers to aid community members to understand and escape their biographies and their common sense notions, in a way that is akin to the countering of hegemony and development of conscientization highlighted earlier. Important here though, the stress is laid on how people have agency, to become free to create their own meanings and flourish, echoing humanist and Aristotelian concerns. Baizerman argues that we must learn to uncouple perception (how we see the immediate), apperception (how this perception relates to the past) and biography (how we make sense of ones past). Through understanding the tendency to conflate these three, we can stop looking at the chronology of our lives, and begin to look at them as a series of experiences 'in, but also outside, of time' (Seal & Harris, 2016, p. 132). For Baizerman, it is the meaning that people put on their experiences that is important, not the events themselves, as we have no control over the events, but do have control of the meaning we place on them. In this way while being a fractured, communicative or autonomous reflective may have been a sensible strategy in particular circumstances, one can move on from it, and develop the kind of reflection needed for co-production and participatory research.

As noted, Baizerman (2001) has some powerful things to say about 'normalcy', and how and why workers and researchers have to de-construct it in the conversations we have with community members. For him people often have a powerful belief in normalcy, and in the permanent nature of their personal trouble and problems. This can range from certain views on themselves, the nature of research, their relationship with authority, or that the issues under consideration are impossible to move forwards, as is the goal of creating a co-productive culture in an agency. For him *the normalcy assumption must be treated as a failed hypothesis.* I am reminded of those community members I have worked with who say they just want to be normal, or homeless people who say they just want a house, with a wife/husband, a job, loving family etc., not realizing that this ideal is largely fantasy and, when it does exist, is no guarantee of happiness. I think again this is powerful in our work with community members, to help them see that they are not their problems; their problems do not define them. This is also a reminder that one of the key characteristics of communicative and autonomous reflectors is a hegemony of the normal.

This overall approach is also an important step in breaking down perceptions about the other; mutual recognition starts to lead to the breakdown of power as we realise the humanity in all of us, and that no one experience should be privileged. Workers and community members should be encouraged to be open about their biographies including discussion of professional challenges within their own practice and experience, but also personal reflections on experiences as members of privileged hegemonic or marginalised and oppressed groups. Important within this is that community members of other stakeholders, including workers, develop 'mutual recognition'. Jessica Benjamin, in her theory of intersubjectivity, describes this as, 'a relationship of mutual recognition [is] a relation in which each person experiences the other as a "like subject," another mind who can be "felt with," yet has a distinct, separate center of feeling and perception.' Intersubjectivity is 'the process by which we become able to grasp the other as having a separate yet similar mind' (1998, p. 34). Mutual recognition involves seeing the other as a subject with an equivalent centre of experience. However, this is not enough to defuse power – it needs to be a dominant characteristic of critical reflective spaces.

An emphasis on and commitment to de-construction of power and the concept of knowledge and democratic decision-making

> [T]he rhetoric which announced the importance of dialogue, engagement, and equality, and denounced silence, massification and oppression, did not match in practice the subliminal messages and modes of a Banking System of education. Albeit benign, Freire's approach differs only in degree, but not in kind, from the system which he so eloquently criticizes.
>
> (Taylor, 1993, p. 148)

As Taylor (1993) indicates, Freire's concept of conscientization, while central to critical pedagogy, and, I argue, co-production and participatory research, is not immune from criticism, we would be neglectful to ignore the potentially patriarchal and authoritarian nature of conscientization and particularly of concepts like 'false consciousness'. There are several critiques of Freire's project's authoritarian tendencies (Elias & Merriam, 1980; Illich, 1974; Zachariah, 1986) and they need to be dealt with in turn. First, Freire, at least in *Pedagogy of the Oppressed*, has binary rigid views of the oppressor, oppressed and the emancipated (Ellias & Merriam, 1980).

This is all the more nuanced when looking at research and co-production, although all too often I have seen them falling into such divisions, with the community partners as the oppressed, the agency who commissions the work or the more ephemeral 'government' as the oppressor and the professional researcher or co-production worker/facilitator as the emancipated. If it is an agency's front line workers, they may be constructed as being part of the oppressed, or more often as the oppressor. While we shall see from the case studies that sometimes these divisions can be all too real, with workers actively sabotaging the research (see Chapter 12), to construct this as inevitable seems to leave little room for agency.

It can also exacerbate things. This divisional perspective has the oppressor knowing they are oppressing and consciously finding ways to create false consciousness in the oppressed. The oppressed may have an inkling they are oppressed, but separated from praxis; they are not able to articulate the nature of this oppression. It is for the liberated pedagogue/facilitator/researcher to unlock this within the oppressed. The notion of false consciousness is even more binary. It is not clear whether the entire consciousness is false of the oppressed, or aspects of it. Either way it is the liberated pedagogue who determines false consciousness's false nature, and when the liberation has occurred. Zachariah (1986) finds such a view deeply patronising, and simply wrong:

> Do ordinary men and women need to be conscientized before they recognize that they lead desperate, oppressed lives marked by hunger, disease, and the denial of dignity? They know the score and do not need middle class do-gooders to tell them. They acquiesce in their oppression because they have no other choice.
>
> (Zachariah, 1986, p. 123)

In the research we will describe, most community members and clients were very aware of their own oppression and could often apply sophisticated analysis of how services meant to serve them were often there to oppress or hold them back; it was what to do about it, and whether there was any point in trying, that was their primary concern. Such a construction also fails to take account of more recent debates centred around intersectionality (Crenshaw, 1989; Collins, 1998) and Kriarchy (Fiorenza, 2001) whereby we all have vectors of multiple oppression and privilege. We need to examine these interactions, and how we impose our own privilege, while condemning others for their exercise of it. For instance, within agencies most of the front line workers are often women, and the managers tend to be male. We need to consider what the gender balance of the co-production/ research team is, and what impact that may have. Although Freire's later work acknowledges the absence of colour, it is still underdeveloped.

A second criticism that stems from these binary constructions is that 'conscientization' is not as democratic as it propounds (Ellias & Merriam, 1980; Illich, 1974). As we have said, in this schema it is for the worker/researcher to determine when a consciousness is false, and how. While the stated process of conscientization has democratic intentions, it remains for the worker/researcher to find the generative themes, the codifications that will have resonance. The worker/ researcher determines when the oppressed have seen their lived lives anew. This presents a real challenge to the worker/researcher of not falling into a modified banking approach to participatory research, whereby the outside facilitator reveals to the oppressed the true nature of their oppression. Illich (1974) was scathing of Freire, calling his approach neo-colonial, describing the finding and codifying of generative themes and the whole process as 'professionally planned and administered rituals that have as their purpose the internalization of a religious or secular ideology' (Illich, 1974). The resonance with Cooke and Kothari's (2000) criticism of the tyranny of participatory methods are notable. Even though Freire is careful to note that the selection of the educational and research problems to be considered should be a shared process, there is still a privileged role for the educator, who validates this selection. This necessitates a fixing of the roles of oppressed and liberator, with the pedagogue unlocking the consciousness of the oppressed.

Third, there is a philosophical issue with Freire's pedagogy in that it necessitates a change in the consciousness of the community members, but not the professional worker/researcher. While Freire, in all his works, says that learning should be mutual experience, it is only for the oppressed or community member that a perceptual change is necessary. While most workers and researchers will cry that they learn from community members, it is a question of degree. There is a danger that the learning for the worker or researcher becomes purely contextual, understanding the nuances of how a universal oppression operates, and the potential methods for countering it within the particular community or culture they are working with. As Galloway (2012) notes, equality is never achieved, as was Freire's intent: the distinction between educator and educated, and researcher and researched does not dissolve.

Even when planning action there will always be a discursive pedagogical element, as different tactics and approaches to co-production and research are discussed and decided upon. The issues of power and the binary of liberator/oppressed is preserved. Even if we assume it is possible to reach Freirian state of genuine co-production, a fourth criticism comes into play. It is not clear how someone moves from a false consciousness to an emancipated one, or from a dependant relationship to one of equality and liberation, or how the judgement that this transition has taken place is made, and by whom. Furthermore, if conscientization, of necessity, needs to be brought about by a professional worker from the outside, where the task of the worker is to make visible that which is hidden from everyday view, such an approach creates a dependency between emancipators and emancipated and it is, again, unclear how and when it will dissolve – equality will always be one step away.

There is a need to actively deconstruct notions of power and knowledge. We assume equal intelligence with community members, and seek out answers and perspectives with them, deconstructing power, existing knowledge and the process of knowledge creation. Professional researcher's pedagogical practice should centre on acting on community members will. Evoking Bourdieu's (1990) notions of 'habitus' and 'doxa', community members many not value intellectual cognitive thought and challenging hegemonous assumptions: it is the will to do this that we act upon. We start to do this by breaking down notions of the spaces where learning takes place, hence the emphasis on queer pedagogy, challenging who is the learner and the learned, the nature of pedagogical relationships and who has the right to create of knowledge. Participants in the research in this book consistently thought that the creation of knowledge is a process of co creation needed to be emphasized from the begging of the programme and integrated throughout. Professional researchers should not privilege their own intelligence and insights, recognizing them to be inherently partial and contingent.

As we have noted, Rancière, akin to Zachariah (1986), views community members as inherently capable of learning and developing intellect. However, they may not believe they have the intellect, or have lost the will to use it, often in the face of seemingly monolithic social forces or the prioritizing of short term material survival that grinding poverty breeds. Rancière thought that many forms of pedagogy were designed to keep people ignorant, or at least make them dependent on others for their acquisition of knowledge. In his book *The Ignorant Schoolmaster* he gives an account of a teacher, Jacotot, who is tasked with teaching a group of Dutch students who speak no French, while he speaks no Dutch. He obtains a book which had a dual translation and, with the group, they teach each other how to speak their respective languages. In the process he questions his own role: the students had learnt without his instruction, and he pondered whether his instruction was needed at all and whether there was a role for him – it was not about knowledge transfer.

Expanding on the implications of this idea, Rancière asks us to imagine what the social world would be like if we assumed a radical equality of intelligence. The pedagogue or researcher should act under the assumption that we are all intelligent enough to understand the world, and that, given access to resources, we can discern the knowledge that will enable this understanding. In one step Rancière sidesteps the authoritarian tendencies of Freire, whereby it is the educator who identifies 'teachable moments' and validates which themes are generative. He says that everyone is capable of articulating and analysing their experience and creating metaphors that others will be able to understand.

Galloway (2012), takes this further saying that as well as actively not transmitting knowledge, the researcher should actively deconstruct the view that the teacher has the knowledge, and question the deficit relationship between 'teacher' and 'student', 'researcher' and 'researched', 'community member' and 'co-production worker'. If there is a difference, it is not that the teacher knows more or understands better, it is simply that the teacher knows they are intelligent and how to construct an argument. They may have more facts at their fingertips, but this is not better knowledge, just broader. While they may know about research processes and approaches, they do not necessarily know what to apply in a particular situation.

As we noted in Chapter 1, the role of the participatory researcher is twofold. First, to act on the students will, their self-belief and efficacy, the will to engage and challenge themselves and others, and to learn. Second, it is to attend to the content of what argument people are creating, but only in terms of logic and internal consistency, or access to resources, but not the content of those resources. For Rancière, like Zachariah, there are no great revelatory moments, for the oppressed know they are oppressed, but have given up trying to impact on things, or do not believe they are intelligent enough to truly understand their situation and how to move it forwards. The process is a slow deconstruction and reconstruction of such positions, as the oppressed and the pedagogue create knowledge together.

There are signifiers of success. Discovering new language is of particular importance in developing a critical reflective sensibility (Harris, Heywood & Mac ah Ghail, 2017). In 'Higher education, de-centred subjectivities and the emergence of a pedagogical self among Black and Muslim students' students celebrated that they were now able to 'name past and current experiences and imbue them with meanings and reflexively to articulate self-representations to themselves and others' (Harris, Heywood & Mac ah Ghail, 2017, p. 323). Community members in the research in this article similarly valued this, but also the recognition that they could be an active participant in the creation of this new language and new conceptual frameworks to name the world. One community member in the Touch project recounted the crossing of a threshold when they were told that they could create their own theory to explain phenomena. A different participant describes crossing a threshold within the probation project when they believed that they had the right and knowledge to be able to come to some conclusions, and could then defend them with confidence.

Privileging spontaneity and working in the moment

As noted in Chapter 2, participatory research has recognized the need to work and reflect in the moment bit has not given enough attention to the process. It does not really seem to feature in the co-production literature significantly if at all. Neelands, looking at the use of drama and particularly improvisatory drama, sees something more genuine about those spontaneous 'in-life' moments, both in authenticity and in a conversation's ability to allow all parties to transcend social constraints, i.e. to show palpably that we have agency.

> To be spontaneous requires the (worker) to imagine and respond to the immediate in ways that are authentic and existential. It is a crucible for the creative exploration of the centrality of the social context in determining human agency and capacity. To be authentic, (workers) must bring what they collectively know about human behaviour to a newly created situation which requires their verbal and physical responses. These responses, shaped by prior experience, must be truthful to the situation – to the social and cultural conventions and codes that determine the context. Improvisation flexes the muscles of a (youth worker's) potential to act on and within the constraints or structure of the imagined situation. It provides the direct lived experience of the tension between social and cultural structures and the capacity for human action. The given circumstances of the improvisation determine the authenticity of what can be said and done.
>
> (Neelands, 2011, p. 171)

As Harris notes (Seal & Harris, 2016, p. 32) improvisation is employed as a metaphor in formal education settings (Sorenson & Coombs, 2007), psychotherapy

(Keeney, 1990), organization science (Pasmore, 1998) and in youth and community work where Tony Jeffs and Mark Smith in *Informal Education, Democracy and Learning* (2005) briefly employ jazz as a metaphor to illustrate the power of improvised youth work practice:

> [M]uch as musicians learn to respond to each other to create an intelligible performance, so informal educators must draw out the contribution of others whilst simultaneously making their own . . . it is a delicate balance but one which good informal educators, like good jazz musicians, seek to maintain. Both jazz musicians and informal educators are improvisers.
>
> (Jeffs & Smith, 2005, p. 127)

Schon also employs jazz improvisation as a metaphor for reflection in action, stressing the way in which the jazz player is heavily influenced by his/her environment:

> Listening to one another, listening to themselves, they feel where the music is going and adjust their playing accordingly. A figure announced by one performer will be taken up by another, elaborated, turned into a new melody. Each player makes on-line inventions and responds to surprises triggered by the inventions of the other players . . . when good jazz musicians improvise together they . . . display reflection-in –action . . .
>
> (Schon, 1983, p. 55)

He acknowledges that jazz improvisation is underpinned by deep theoretical knowledge:

> [T]he collective process of musical invention is organized around an underlying structure. There is a common schema of meter, melody, and harmonic development that gives the piece a predictable order. In addition each player has at the ready a repertoire of musical figures around which he can weave musical variations as the opportunity arizes. Improvisation consists in varying, combining, and recombining a set of figures within a schema that gives coherence to the whole piece. As the musicians feel the directions in which the music is developing, they make new sense of it. They reflect-in-action on the music they are collectively making- though not of course in the medium of words'
>
> (Schon, 1983, p. 55)

However, can improvisation be taught? Harris thinks it can and cites Peters (2009) who argues for teachers of improvisation in any context to focus on bringing what may be in the realms of a facilitator's unconscious competence, 'back under a degree of critical, reflective control and recognize that in fact improvisation often involves the re-marking, revising or reconfiguring of existing familiar ideas' (Harris, 2014, p. 32). For Harris, while a researcher or co-production worker (and ultimately community members themselves) cannot prepare for unknown situation, they can develop a predisposition to 'act in a certain manner regarding unknown events' (Harris, 2014, p. 32).

This idea has precedent. Dewey called this habit, 'an acquired predisposition to ways or modes of response' (Dewey, 1933, p. 42); it also has links to Aristotle's concept of 'hexis' and Pierre Bourdieu's concept of 'habitus' (Bourdieu, 1997). The individual biographies of all practitioners, their past experiences and values will clearly have an impact on how they approach uncertainty, their disposition towards learning and ultimately their ability improvise. Harris describes the culture and disposition of jazz musicians well:

> A culture exists, which actively seeks the unfamiliar musical situation to avoid habitual thinking. Regulation and control are viewed as restricting interplay. Retrospective sense making is preferred to attempts to plan for anticipated outcomes, an approach mirrored in improvisational approaches to therapy, 'where the score or script comes into play after the performance rather than before'.
>
> (Harris, 2014)

He talks about even when we are playing, a familiar melody (substitute any session on research methods) we should '[strive] to interpret the melody as if performing it for the first time' (originally quoted by Lee Konitz, in *Berliner*, p. 67). He also cites Chuck Israel describing music and how one can make the familiar unfamiliar, and incorporate something within one's repertoire into something new – an excellent exposition of how Schon (1983) describes reflection in action:

> [A]n essential ingredient in learning to be a musician is the ability to recognise a parallel case when confronted with one. If things remind you of other pieces when you approach a new piece you generally catalogue them very quickly so that you can draw upon your accumulated knowledge (originally quoted by Chuck Israel, in *Berliner*, p. 78).

Harris considers that elements of the approach to teaching musical improvisation within jazz education 'could be adapted to the teaching of improvisation to co-production and participatory research practitioners' (Harris, 2014, p. 32).

Cultivating hope and a future orientation

In Chapter 2 we noted the danger within participatory research of a tyranny of action whereby participatory research promises more than it can deliver. We also noted how Hickey and Mohan (2004) said we should be more pessimistic about what research can achieve. However, such structural pessimism can have its own impact if not handled positively. In the Touch project we found that many young people, who had been subject to empowering interventions from youth workers, and were pessimistic about structural change, had developed a knowing hopelessness that was far worse:

> Structural pessimism abandoned the young people in their state of hopelessness, rather than reinvigorating their sense of personal agency. This sense of hopelessness was often exacerbated, rather than alleviated, by worker responses. As a result of youth workers highlighting structural oppression, some young people had developed a 'knowing' hopelessness, an informed sense of powerlessness, not one borne of ignorance of their potential or chances, but one that stemmed from knowledge of the limited nature of such chances. Young people were prone to turn this hopelessness on themselves or their communities, become depressed, or lapse into conspiracy theories.
>
> (Seal & Harris, 2016, p. 123)

The aforementioned emphasis on existentialism and developing critical reflection may go some way towards ameliorating this; as Baizerman emphasizes, experience of critical reflective spaces should be

> a facilitating process in which an individual penetrates his taken-for-granted reality and, by so doing, comes to understand how reality for her is constructed. Thus are extended the possibilities of finding moments of (for) choice and, in this, for extending and living her freedom. Youthwork is a process of creating the opportunities for a youth to choose more often about more things in her everyday life and in this way more thoroughly construct herself. Choice is a freedom-in-action . . . 'Why?' does not matter; what is and what emerges does. Life is forward and is to be lived together, worker and youth, from 'right now' to 'next minute'.
>
> (Baizerman, 2001, p. 1)

Bradford (2013), in his recommendations for the Touch project, outlines four levels that a project can look for 'action' on: the participants, the individual service, local policy, and strategy and national/international strategy. This broadly concurs with Reid et al. (2006) who go onto make links between the levels, but identify the danger of people becoming disillusioned at each level. There is an interaction between personal empowerment and structural change. A sense of personal empowerment increases if you affect the service you are within. Conversely, you can also lose sight of your personal empowerment if affecting others or 'policy' is the only goal.

It is important that discussion about these levels and the dynamics between them is active in the research. In many ways these debates goes back to the age-old discussion about structure and agency (Archer, 2010, 2012; Giddens, 1984). Archer accused approaches she calls 'methodological individualism' that favours agency, of 'upward conflation' in that they deny the impact, and constraints, of society. She equally criticizes 'methodological holism', that sees structure as paramount, for downward conflation, denying the impact that individual agency has. She is also critical of attempts to conflate structure and agency, particularly Giddens' concept of structuration. Giddens (1984) structuration theory sees structure and agency as inseparable and mutually informing. For Archer, while this is an attempt to allow for both, in reducing them to each other, it renders them unanalysable.

As touched on in Chapter 2, Archer (2010, 2012) sees agency and structure as distinct entities. She does not deny that there is an interaction, but separating them allows for their interaction to be understood, something she calls the 'morphogenetic approach'. As noted before, we need to recognize that there is a temporal delay between agential actions and structural change. I have found this useful in that many of the constructions management and community members had of each other were distinctly products of local, and national histories, and permeated debates. For Archer (2010, 2012), how these agents then react to their current conditioning will, over time, change these social and cultural structures, which will set the conditions for future social actors. I have again found this useful and have community members, who, while they would like their actions to change their own material and cultural conditions, recognize that their labours may not come to fruition during their lifetime with the project, or even their community (Seal, 2009).

Being distinct, and operating in different temporal spheres, makes it possible to unpick structure and agency analytically. First, we need to isolate and analyse how structural and/or cultural factors provide a context of action for agents. It is then possible to investigate how those factors shape the subsequent interactions of agents and how those interactions in turn reproduce or transform the initial context. Through doing so, argues Archer, it is possible to give empirical accounts of how structural and agential phenomena interlink *over time* rather than merely stating their theoretical interdependence. We will give examples of this happening and being put to use in Chapters 11 and 13.

The Touch project found that there is potency is symbolic violence, symbolic power, and symbolic resistance, and this metaphor extends to the participatory methodological approach. In between all of these stages of action there are symbolic acts and achievement that give people hope. Reid et al. (2006) talk about the need for hope and that some actions, while not actualized now, remain hopes for broader actions in the future. Sometimes giving people a glimpse of possibilities, be that taking over a public space even for an evening, or being received positively by policy makers, even if the changes are ultimately diluted to the point of disappearing subsequently, are powerful symbols. Indeed, participating in research and seeing that you have a legitimate claim to power can be immensely powerful symbolically. To give a concrete example:

One young woman in London demonstrated how through the use of visual symbolic representation it was possible to refuse to be determined by the social terrain in which she lived. When asked to visually represent the community and area in which she lived, she drew a large faeces-coloured mass, which she said represented how she felt she was viewed by wider society.

However, what she inscribed within the image demonstrated her decision to reject this. 'This is a piece of shit [points to a green, brownish mess] and it says, "Your opinion of me doesn't define who I am."' In part, she felt her relationship with youth workers had played a role in bringing her to a point where, in her insistence on individual free will and dignity, she was beginning to resist the structural forces that weighed so heavily on her life chances.

(Seal & Harris, 2016, p. 126)

Conclusion

I hope that this chapter has outlined the key characteristics and concerns of a potential critical reflective space, and in doing so has addressed both a gap in the literature and some of the key criticisms of participatory research and co-production. Perhaps most importantly, as we shall see in the case study chapters, all these debates need to be overt, foregrounded and lived. I remember huge debates in research groups about whether our actions were realistic, selling out, too pushy or not pushy enough, and whether our approach was 'proper' research if we did not have a control group. I felt gladdened when a participant turned to me and said he was disappointed to find out he knew something better than I, the academic, did (we then discussed why he was disappointed). I remember my own sense of shame over my surprise at the speed with which some participants picked up interviewing techniques, but of course they were used to selective self-revelation with particular aims in mind – they lived this through the services designed for their use.

References

Allen, L. (2015) 'Queer pedagogy and the limits of thought: teaching sexualities at university.' *Higher Education Research & Development*, 34(4): 763–775.

Archer, M. S. (2012) *The Reflexive Imperative in Late Modernity.* Cambridge: Cambridge University Press.

Archer, M. S. (2010) *Conversations About Reflexivity.* London and New York: Routledge.

Baber, K. & Murray, C. (2001) 'A postmodern feminist approach to teaching human sexuality.' *Family Relations*, 50(1): 23–33.

Baizerman, M. (2001) 'Why train youth workers?' CYC On-line: *Reading for Child and Youth Care Workers*, 31. Available at: www.cyc-net.org/cyc-online/cycol-0801-baizerman.html [accessed 28 February 2018].

Benjamin, J. (1998) *Shadow of the Other: Intersubjectivity and Gender in Psychoanalysis.* London and New York: Routledge.

Berghold, J. & Thomas, S. (2012) 'Participatory research methods: a methodological approach in motion.' *Forum Qualitative Sozialforschung/Forum: Qualitative Social Research* [S.l.], v. 13, n. 1, January 2012.

Bion, W. R. (1961) *Experiences in Groups.* London: Tavistock Publications.

Black, M. E. (2012) 'Meanings and typologies of Duboisian Double Consciousness within 20th century United States racial dynamics.' Paper 87. Available at: https//:scholarworks.umb.edu [retrieved 2 July 2016].

Bourdieu, P. (1997) *Outline of a Theory of Practice.* London: Cambridge University Press.

Bourdieu, P. (1990) *The Logic of Practice.* Stanford, CA: Stanford University Press.

Britzman, D. (2003) *After-education: Anna Freud, Melanie Klein and Psychoanalytic Histories of Learning*. New York: State University of New York Press.

Buber, M. (1958) *Paths in Utopia*. 2nd edition. Translated by R. F. C. Hull. Syracuse, NY: Syracuse University Press.

Buber, M. (1923) *I and Thou*. Edinburgh: T&T Clark.

Butler, J. (1990) *Gender Trouble*. New York: Routledge.

Chambers, R. (2010) *Provocations for Development*. Rugby: Practical Action Publishing.

Collins, P. H. (1998) 'Toward a new vision: race, class, and gender as categories of analysis and connection.' In R. F. Levine (ed.) *Social Class as Stratification: Classic Statements and Theoretical Debates*, Lanham, MA: Rowman and Littlefield, pp. 231–247.

Cooke, B. & Kothari, U. (2001) (eds) *Participation: The New Tyranny?* London: Zed.

Cousin, G. (2009) *Researching Learning in Higher Education*. New York: Routledge.

Cousin, G. (2006) 'Threshold concepts, troublesome knowledge and emotional capital.' In J. Meyer & R. Land (eds) *Overcoming Barriers to Student Understanding: Threshold Concepts and Troublesome Knowledge*. London: Routledge, pp. 134–147.

Crenshaw, K. (1989) 'Demarginalizing the intersection of race and sex: a black feminist critique of antidiscrimination doctrine, feminist theory and antiracist politics.' Chicago, IL: University of Chicago Legal Forum, pp. 139–167.

Dewey, J. (1933) *How We Think. A Restatement of the Relation of Reflective Thinking to the Educative Process*. Boston, MA: D. C. Heath.

Du Bois, W. E. B. & Edwards, B. H. (1906) *The Souls of Black Folk*. Oxford: Oxford University Press.

Elias, J. L. & Merriam, S. (1980) *Philosophical Foundations of Adult Education*. Malabar, FL: Krieger.

Eliason, M. & Elia, J. (2009) 'Collaborations across difference: Coming Out as a "Queer" Research Team.' In V. Clarke & V. Braun (eds) 'Coming Out in Higher Education,' *Lesbian and Gay Psychology Review Special Edition* 10(1): British Psychological Society, 23–32.

Fiorenza, S. E. (2001) *Wisdom Ways, Feminist Bible Interpretations*. New York: Orbis Books.

Freire, P. (1971) *Pedagogy of the Oppressed*. London: Penguin.

Galbreath, B. (2012) 'An argument for teaching a human sexuality course within the context of a Women and Gender Studies program.' *American Journal of Sexuality Education*, 7(1): 62–77.

Galloway, S. (2012) 'Reconsidering emancipatory education: staging a conversation between Paulo Freire and Jacques Rancière.' *Educational Theory*, 62: 163–184.

Giddens, A. (1984) *The Constitution of Society, Outline of the Theory of Structuration*. Cambridge: Polity Press.

Harris, P. (2014) 'The youth worker as jazz improviser: foregrounding education "in the moment" within the professional development of youth workers.' *Professional Development in Education*, 40(4): 654–668.

Harris, P., Haywood, C. & Mac an Ghaill, M. (2017) 'Higher education, de-centred subjectivities and the emergence of a pedagogical self among Black and Muslim students.' *Race Ethnicity and Education*, 20(3): 358–371.

Hickey, S. & Mohan, G. (2004) *Participation: From Tyranny to Transformation*. London and New York: Zed Books.

hooks, b. (1994) *Teaching to Transgress. Education as the Practice of Freedom*. London: Routledge.

Illich, I. (1974) *Disabling Professions*. London: Penguin.

Israel, B. A., Schultz, A. J., Parker, E. A. & Becker, A. B. (1998) 'Review of community-based research: assessing partnership approaches to improve health.' *Annual Review of Public Health*, 19: 173–202.

Janis, I. L. (1982). *Groupthink: Psychological Studies of Policy Decisions and Fiascoes*. 2nd edition. New York: Houghton Mifflin.

Jeffs, T. & Smith, M. K. (2005) *Informal Education: Conversation, Democracy and Learning*. Ticknall: Education Now.

Keeney, B. (1990) *Improvisational Therapy*. London: Guilford Press.

Land, R., Rattray, J. & Vivian, P. (2014) 'Learning in the liminal space: a semiotic approach to threshold concepts.' *Higher Education*, 67(2): 199–217.

Neelands, J. (2011) 'Drama as creative learning.' In J. Sefton-Green, et al. (eds) *Routledge International Handbook of Creative Learning*. Abingdon: Routledge, pp. 168–177.

Noddings, N. (1984) *Caring: A Feminine Approach to Ethics and Moral Education*. Berkeley, CA: University of California Press.

Orne, J. (2013) 'Queers in the line of fire: Goffman's stigma revisited.' *Sociological Quarterly*, 54(2): 229–253.

Pasmore, W. (1998) 'Organizing for jazz.' *Organization Science*, 9(5): 562–568.

Peters, G. (2009) *The Philosophy of Improvisation*. Chicago, IL: University of Chicago Press.

Rancière, J. (2004) 'Introducing disagreement.' *Angelaki: Journal of the Theoretical Humanities*, 9(3): 3–9.

Rancière, J. (1992) *The Ignorant Schoolmaster: Five Lessons in Intellectual Emancipation*. Stanford, CA: Stanford University Press.

Rawls, A. W. (2000) '"Race" as an interaction order phenomenon: WEB Du Bois's "Double Consciousness" thesis revisited.' *Sociological Theory*, 18(2): 241–274.

Reid, C., Tom, A. & Frisby, W. (2006) 'Finding the "action" in feminist participatory action research.' *Action Research*, 4(3): pp. 315–332.

Scheff, T., Phillips, B. S. & Kincaid, H. (2006) *Goffman Unbound!: A New Paradigm for Social* Science (Advancing the Sociological Imagination). Oxon and New York: Paradigm Publishers.

Schippert, C. (2006) 'Critical projection and queer performativity: self-revelation in teaching/learning otherness. Review of Education.' *Pedagogy and Cultural Studies*, 28(3/4): 281–295.

Schon, D. A. (1983) *The Reflective Practitioner: How Professionals Think in Action*. New York: Basic Books.

Scrambler, G. (2013) 'Resistance in unjust times: Archer, structured agency and the sociology of health inequalities.' *Sociology*, 47(1): 142–156.

Seal, M. (2009) *Not About Us Without Us: Client Involvement In Social Housing*. Lyme Regis: Russell House Publishing.

Seal, M. & Harris, P. (2016) *Responding to Youth Violence Through Youth Work*. Bristol: Policy Press.

Siegel, K., Lune, H. & Meyer, I. H. (1998) 'Stigma management among gay/bisexual men with HIV/AIDS.' *Qualitative Sociology*, 21(1): 3–24.

Sorenson, N. & Coombs, S. (2007) 'Towards an improvisation based pedagogy: using a four-phase framework for teacher development to identify individual staff training needs.' International Professional Development Association, conference in Belfast, 30 November to 1 December. Available at: http://www.leeds.ac.uk/educol/documents/167987.pdf [accessed 16 February 2018].

Stolorow, R. D., Atwood, G. E. & Orange, D. M. (2002) *Worlds of Experience: Interweaving Philosophical and Clinical Dimensions in Psychoanalysis*. New York: Basic Books.

Talburt, S. & Rasmussen, M. (2010) '"After queer" tendencies in queer research.' *International Journal of Qualitative Studies in Education*, 23(1): 1–14.

Taylor, P. (1993) *The Texts of Paulo Freire*. Buckingham: Open University Press.

Zachariah, M. (1986) *Revolution Through Reform*. Praeger: New York.

Part 2

Participatory Pedagogic Impact Research

Towards a process

5   Meaningful organizational impact

Winning stakeholders over to the process

Drawing on practical experience this chapter looks at how to sell the concept of co-production and participative research to all stakeholders. It will examine what needs to be in place for a participatory research project to have a chance of making an impact on the overall organizational culture, particularly stakeholders' mindsets towards research and community partner co-production. In doing so it warns against falling into what I, and others (Seal, 2005; Skyrme, 1999), have called elsewhere the 'fallacy of information' which is the self-deception that if stakeholders just knew how good a thing participatory research and co-production is, they would come on board. They might say they embrace the ideas – and even mean it – but other factors came come into play and sabotage the process, including unconsciously. The arguments for co-production and participatory research have been well rehearsed earlier in the book and elsewhere. The challenge is finding an organization that is in the right place to hear them.

Introduction

It may help here to discuss a project where everything that could go wrong did. I was brought in to embed evidence-based practice (Dickinson, 2001) within a new service initiative for young people. This was around the time of the coining of the term NEET (not in education, employment or training) when the government realized that a substantial number of people were 'slipping through the net' and not 'engaging' in ways that it was felt they ought. This was a top down initiative that was once countrywide (Smith, 2000, 2007). As Smith (2000, 2007) notes, its premise was based, ironically, on two non evidence-based governmental perceptions. The first was why people were NEET. The government did not entertain that perhaps young people were NEET because there were no decent jobs; and that training and education did not lead to jobs any more, had been cut, or farmed out to private companies and dumbed down. The government instead assumed that young people were not motivated, and/or had been mollycoddled, and it was they who needed to change (Smith, 2000, 2007). This was the underlying premise of the service. It took a carrot and stick approach, where young people were both compelled to engage (benefit laws were changed to ensure this) and were to be given the right advice and support to make the best of this, hence the new service.

The second perception was about existing services for young people (Smith, 2000, 2007). There was a perception that the careers service needed to be more young people friendly, and youth and community work a little less so, or rather that it needed to give advice 'properly', especially careers advice. There was also the 'round table communication deception' (Seal, 2005) which assumes that having multiple agencies involved with one young person is inefficient – i.e. that what was needed was for agencies to communicate better, often round a table, and identify one of them to be the keyworker to co-ordinate services and build a coherent plan. What this does not anticipate is the level of organizational defensiveness of many young people's services (Seal, 2005) with many assuming that they already had young people at their centre of their planning. As Jeffs and Smith (2002) also note, this view of multi-agency working ignores the agency young people already employ. Young people often only got what they needed through their own strategic management of the agencies input. Multi-agency approaches, whereby all agencies work out a package of support between them, represents a net loss for them.

I have gone into some detail on this because it was an initiative that was fairly doomed from the start. The new service was top down and rejected by most agencies, who had been corralled into multi-agency partnerships, and had some of their budgets diverted into it (Smith, 2000, 2007). To then try and embed evidence-based practice into the partnership would have been difficult under any circumstances. As one stakeholder commented, 'are we going to apply evidence-based practice to this mess then?' – the research project was an initiative borne of necessity rather than commitment. In my first planning meeting the chief executive said that they 'had to do something about evidence-based practice' and asked if I could come up with a 'toolkit' to do this. Evidence-based practice was popular with government at the time (Catlan, 2002; Dickinson, 2001). It was a medical model that was being grafted on unquestioningly onto any social intervention (Smith, 2000, 2007). However, like co-production and participatory research, it had potential to be meaningful. I countered that evidence-based practice was not about doing a couple of small scale evaluations and then saying this was the best model; it was about embedding a culture of research and evaluation that could continually develop and evolve current best practice. We needed to embed a culture across the partnership to do this and then develop infrastructure to allow for research to be conducted on an on-going basis. After some discussion the chief executive reluctantly agreed and I went away to develop a project proposal to these ends.

In the original proposal I suggested a series of five-day courses spread across different agencies and stakeholders to develop an understanding of evidence-based practice and to start to embed a culture around it – this being the bare minimum of what I thought it would take to make this process meaningful. This was cut to two days supplemented by a paper I produced to be read beforehand, which I never saw any indication of having been read by anyone, including the chief executive. The two-day workshops were changed by the steering group to a dedicated operational group meeting in each area, which would only be attended by middle management. This, in all but one case, became an item on the existing agenda of around 45 minutes, which was often then cut down again, in one case to 10 minutes. As you can imagine, no culture change happened around evidence-based practice; in fact only some middle managers got to hear that the project was happening at all.

We conducted a pilot piece of participatory research, which had a small impact for those concerned and produced some interesting results. The proposed all-stakeholder conference looking at the implications of the results and how to further embed evidence-based practice became a dedicated high level board meeting with only service leads attending, which then became an item on the agenda of their next general board meeting. They asked me to reduce the final 30-page report (as agreed) to a two-page executive summary that 'could be read in two tube stops on the way to the meeting'. I was asked if I could minimize the stuff about doing further research, as they did not have the budget, and concentrate on what needed to change. In the presentation the chief executive asked what had happened to his original idea of a toolkit.

While a woeful tale, it certainly was a learning curve for me in what is needed for a project to even have the possibility of having meaningful impact. I had succumbed to the fallacy of information. The project was a good idea, and everyone genuinely agreed to it. I also think that no one deliberately sabotaged it, although some definitely undermined it. However, other factors came into play that meant it unravelled. There was not a partnership culture, in that particular time and place, that would have allowed it to succeed, whatever different stakeholders intentions were. This example highlighted the importance for me of taking into account both the external and internal factors that impact on the organization or initiative that is interested in developing a co-production/participatory research project. Building on previous work (Seal, 2009) I think that there are a number of characteristics of what will make for successful engagement of an organization and its stakeholders:

1) That you have taken account of the external factors on the organization.
2) It is a learning organization; overall it has more enhancing features than inhibiting ones for co-production and participatory research.
3) That you have access to and are allowed to cultivate a champion with all stakeholders, from community members to senior management.
4) That there are processes whereby all stakeholders can develop a meaningful understanding of co-production and participatory research.
5) That the aims of the project highlight and dovetail with stakeholder concerns and that the project has a focus that threads through, illuminates and finds common ground between the concerns of stakeholders.

Taking account of external factors

Perhaps a first consideration is whether the organization has chosen to take part in the project. While perhaps an ideal situation, I think it makes a real difference if they have. Even if the decision to participate has only really been exercised by senior management, it gives researchers leverage when you encounter cynicism from others in the organization. It also means that you can motivate those lower down the hierarchy with the carrot of making senior management accountable. If the organization is only engaging in the project because they have been told to by government or external forces, then achieving buy in becomes all the more difficult, as the detailed example just given demonstrates.

There are many models for considering external factors that impact on organizations, known by acronyms such as PEST (political, economic, social and technological), PESTEL or PESTLE (which adds legal and environmental factors), SLEPT (which adds legal factors), STEEPLE and STEEPLED (which adds ethics and demographic factors), and DESTEP (which adds demographic and ecological factors). I like SPELIT, which stands for Social, Political, Economic, Legal, Intercultural and Technological – although the E can also stand for environmental, ecological or even ethical. Of definite relevance to the previous case study were legal, political and intercultural factors. Politically, as said, the new service was not well received by any existing stakeholders, was seen as top down, and a product of the prevailing ideology at Westminster. Legally the aforementioned young people's service was never made statutory and was only an 'initiative'. The government at the time throwing out a number of initiatives and seeing which ones prevailed (Smith, 2002). Culturally the new service clashed with many existing organizational and service cultures, as did evidence-based practice which was seen as tainted with the new young people's service and the prevailing governmental regime. The prevailing culture was to ride out the initiative and have as little damage done to the core cultures and services as possible. It also had a very hierarchical culture and structure (Smith, 2002b).

The danger of schemas such as SPELIT is that there are always going to be political, legal and cultural issues, and it can cause pessimism about the chances of a project having an impact. The fundamental question is whether these factors are too strong or make the service too fragmented, to allow an impact on the organization and its stakeholders, or whether the project would be hijacked or undermined by some of the stakeholders to a negative end. As an example of success in the face of such problems, we have our project with probation services. The project was initiated at a time when probation services were undergoing privatization. In some ways it was the worst possible time to engage as staff motivation was at an all-time low and suspicion and reluctance to take on new initiatives was at an all-time high. However, underneath this all stakeholders had a commitment to the core principles of the probation service, although very different views of how to actualize them, and these core principles could be related to the aims of co-production and participatory research. As Beth Coyne will describe in Chapter 12, the project was able to have a discernible impact. While there was sabotage from some stakeholders, it could be identified and mediated, at least to a degree.

The learning organization: inhibiting and enhancing factors

Even if the organization and senior management buy into the idea of participatory research and co-production project planners need to know whether this is likely to succeed in reality. It is, as we have noted several times, easy to claim principles and a belief in such things. One way of viewing this is to try to assess to degree to which the organization is a learning one. I have previously examined different models of what constitutes a learning organization (Anderson, 1997; Argyris, Putnam & McLain, 1985; Senge, 1994; Smith, 2001a & b) and identified inhibiting and enhancing models, with dimensions of control, protectionism, views about evidence and research, views on history, views on dissent, 'holy cows', staff relationships, openness on information sharing and public or private debate. Table 5.1 is a refined version of that previous work (Seal, 2005, 2009).

Table 5.1 Different models of what constitutes a learning organization

Factor	Inhibiting model	Enhancing model
Control	*The organization wants to control the environment and task of co-production and participatory research.* The staff and management groups spend a long time defining participation and research, foreseeing barriers without talking to the community members.	*The organization is open to co-production and research and the form it could take* – even to the point of people admitting that they do not know where to start – people experiment with venues and ideas, and talk to and involve community members from the outset.
Protectionism	*The organization 'protects' itself and others.* Many ideas for co-production and research are quashed for reasons of risk, health and safety, or being divisive – before consulting community members. Professional boundaries are often invoked.	*The organization takes risks.* Ideas from community members are entertained, and then risk and health and safety factors are considered. The excuse of 'setting people up to fail' and boundary concerns are not invoked.
View on evidence and research	*Unqualified and covert attributions and evaluations are made* – e.g. that community members are unmotivated or will not engage unless they get something out of the situation, without evidence beyond 'I know my community'. This equally applies to managers – e.g. the managers are only doing this for X reason, or I cannot imagine a worker doing that.	*Attributions are only made with evidence.* Generally claims are made, but where they are they are evidenced and checked out with the people they concern. Similarly this applies to workers' and managers' perceptions about each other, and people are not disturbed by negative views on them by others.
View on history	*History is either used as a reason for not doing something or as something to get past* – e.g. let's not talk about the past; that's over. We want clients to concentrate on the positive. Where history is invoked it is as a reason for why ideas will not work.	*People are keen to learn from the past and see history as important.* Initially people concentrate on the past, but in a positive sense, people want to learn from it rather than just raking over old coals; it is something to learnt from.

(continued)

Table 5.1 Different models of what constitutes a learning organization *(continued)*

Factor	Inhibiting model	Enhancing model
View on dissent	*There is an emphasis on the need for unity.* Managers place great emphasis on unquestioning loyalty and dissent is discouraged. Workers aren't 'burdened' with (and don't seek) decision-making, but are expected to respect decisions and concentrate on their implementation.	*Loyalty is seen as something to be earned.* Dissent and contribution are encouraged. Views are sought at all stages of decision-making, formally and informally. Many decisions are devolved to workers
Holy cows	*The agency has many 'holy cows', both overt and covert.* These can be ideas (i.e. that clients just want a service) to parts of the project (e.g. the drop in service must stay). There are often histories associated with them. Workers and clients often only know about covert holy cows when they question them.	*The organization regularly questions its fundamentals* both in terms of its ideas and what services it delivers. The organization develops both formal and informal mechanisms for doing this. Social events and annual away days (and not just when there are crises) are features of the organization. Open view of what research is and could be.
Staff relationships	*There are defensive relationships between staff* – i.e. staff report feeling demoralized or powerless within the organization. Conversely managers deride staff as sabotaging efforts or 'resisting'. Resentments about this are played out in private and public.	*Relationship are characterized by respect.* Staff may argue, but have respect for each other. Conflicts are played out in the open, without maintenance of a 'united front'. Clients are able to criticize all parties. Formal structures exist to bring people together.
Public/private debate	*Little public testing of ideas.* Initiatives are very much tried out in private, with people not wanting the findings, even if they are generalized and may be of use to others, to be made public, or conducted in public.	*Ideas and findings are open to all* agencies are keen for others to learn from their experiences and take the view that airing their difficulties is a sign of strength rather than weakness

I have noted before (Seal, 2009) that in reality it is unlikely that any organization will display all the characteristics of one model. The lives of organizations are far more fluid and idiosyncratic than that (Smith, 2001b; Senge, 1994). I noted previously (Seal, 2009) that it is more useful to look at agencies' learning abilities as a continuum from being inhibiting of learning to being enhancing of it. However, sometimes a binary is useful and if there are more enhancing factors in the organization then it would seem worth pursuing it; if there are more inhabiting factors then unless you are convinced that the project itself will transform the

organization, then it is probably not worth pursuing. As for assessing the organization, it would be good to get the relevant information early on, although there is
a danger that it may paint a picture of how the organization works in theory, rather
than in practice (Argyris & Schön, 1974). I think building in some assessment into
the information, training sessions on co-production and participatory research,
with a break to assess the situation, is in order. People's reactions to training on
these, in my experience, normally elicits how people think and the culture they
embody quite quickly.

That you have access to and are allowed to cultivate a champion with all stakeholders

As you will see below, I am a great believer in the Champions model (Seal, 2009)
as a method embedding a new idea within an organization.

> Co-production and participatory research needs champions, people with a
> passion for it, knowledge of it and, importantly, time to promote it. Crucially
> they are needed at all levels of the organisation and preferably in all its
> projects. This way the ideas behind it can achieve critical mass, rather than
> relying on a few committed individuals who inevitably burn out.
>
> (Seal, 2009, p. 56)

The end point is a criticism of a tendency to appoint a sole dedicated worker to a
project. While it is attractive to have someone dedicated, this person is often low in
status, does not have real power and control and cannot impact on the whole culture
easily. As I noted in 2009 'they often end up feeling token and resentful, and become
marginalised and burnt out, having been blamed when the resistance and lack of
responsibility of others have stalled a service users' initiative' (Seal, 2009, p. 56). A
dedicated person as well as a system of champions is even better, but a dedicated
person alone is no substitute for champions.

This brings me to the question of governance. Having day-to-day contact within
the base of operations, at a level where decision can be made, is invaluable for
a project. Similarly the active involvement of champions in the operation of the
project embeds co-production well. A steering group that meets throughout
the project is invaluable, and needs representation from all stakeholders, with a
balance between having enough senior management to enact change, but not so
many as to intimidate other stakeholders. Terms of reference and ground rules are
useful, as long as they do not fall into the previously mentioned traps of such
conventions stifling thinking and re-inscribing existing power relationships – there
needs to be a commitment to 'think differently' and set aside traditional notions
of power relations, apart from where it can allow for structural obstacles to
be overcome. These steering groups should meet regularly enough to see the
unfolding of the project and ameliorate any issues encountered. As we will discuss
in Chapter 12, this will include being a part of the selection of issues to be
researched, as a way of bringing all stakeholders together, having meaningful

impact and it becoming a pedagogic experience for all. The steering group will also really come into its fore when looking at, and formulating the research recommendations and looking at dissemination.

That all stakeholders can develop a meaningful understanding of co-production and participatory research

As we can see from the new young people's service example, if we do not train people and develop an understanding of co-production and research there will likely be negative consequences. I recommend a project gives at least five days to developing these understandings, but I know this may not be realistic. On the other hand, reducing this stage to a 10-minute presentation to a select group – as happened in the detailed example at the beginning of this chapter – is meaningless. It is also true that many people are not won over until they see changes happening and have some of their perceptions challenged in reality rather through theory or on a course. I think this is particularly true of perceptual barriers which the holders see as 'truths', such beliefs about clients not being motivated unless the action directly benefits them.

My experiences have shown me that people do not need to sit through a mini version of an undergraduate course to understand research or co-production. It is as much about undoing what people think research and co-production is, and how it relates to their jobs. Key questions for developing understanding of co-production and research include these:

1) How and why should clients/community members be involved in decision-making/have their views represented?
2) How do you think power flows and decisions are made in the organization?
3) How and why should clients/community members be involved in research?
4) What do you think are the elements of legitimate research?
5) What are the barriers for clients/community members being involved in research and co-production?
6) What are the barriers for your stakeholder being involved in research and co-production?
7) How can research and co-production involving clients and community members help you in your job?
8) What research do you think should be conducted? How should the service change for the better?

These questions should make for an iterative process: while the first few questions may get stock answers, once they are seen in the light of the third question they can take a different turn. Several authors (Wilcox, 1995; Lukes, 1974; Brandon et al., 1980) note how workers' sabotage of co-production is based on a kind of jealousy that clients are being listened to when they are not. This is operating on a model of power as finite, where if community members and clients get more power, they get less. We need to show how power need not operate in this way

(Lukes, 1974), and that clients and community members becoming empowered can lead to workers also being listened to more (Friere, 1972; Seal, 2009).

Taking the example of the fourth question, as with clients and community members, other stakeholders may well, when discussing research, talk about their cynicism about statistics, or the need for control groups and remaining objective and independent. This positivist assumption needs to be undone. Similarly, I have met many workers, and managers, who see co-production as an add-on, or even a distraction, from their key roles, rather than something fundamental to achieving goals. The links to stakeholders' concerns need to be made. Many workers see raising people's self-esteem, self-belief and self-efficacy as a key, if difficult, part of their job, similar to developing resilience and autonomy and taking responsibility (Seal, 2009). Pointing out that participating in an involvement project such as research and/or co-production is the best way of achieving these things (Bryant, 2001; Carpenter & Sbarani, 1997; Edgar et al., 1999; Godfrey et al., 2003; Welsh Assembly, 2004) can be a light bulb moment for people.

That the aims of the project highlight and dovetail with stakeholder concerns and that the project has a focus that threads through, illuminates and finds common ground between the concerns of stakeholders

> It was wrong to assume that man would pursue morality on a level higher than his day-to-day living demanded; it was a disservice to the future to separate morality from man's daily desires and elevate it to a plane of altruism and self-sacrifice. The fact is that it is not man's 'better nature' but his self-interest that demands that he be his brother's keeper.
>
> (Alinsky, 1971, p. 23)

> Healthy self interest is one of the marks of integrity or wholeness in a person. It is the source of the initiative, creativity, and drive of human beings who are fully alive . . . To live is to be among people, to have interests. Human beings are interpersonal beings, relational selves.
>
> (Chambers with Cowan, 2004, p. 25)

This characteristic is based on a community organizing principle of cultivating and harnessing people's different self-interests (Alinsky, 1971, Chambers & Cowan, 2004), and is a departure from much of the existing literature on participatory research and co-production. The central idea that Chamber and Alinsky express is that everyone has self-interests, and that this is both all right and a key to developing mutual self-interest. In formulating the idea of self-interest Alinsky rails against both selflessness, or altruism, and selfishness. Selfishness is wanting the best just for yourself, and is purely living in the world as it is. Self-interest takes account of, and often includes, the mutual interests of the stakeholder group you belong to, and is a bridge to the world as it should be. As well as immediate material needs, it will include things like belonging, community and solidarity, not in an idealistic way, but in a concrete lived experience. He believed that all stake-holders have these self-interests and if organizers can find issues that speak to the self-interests of all of the stakeholders, it becomes mutual, and is more likely to be winnable.

He makes a distinction between the world-as-it-is and the world-as-it-should-be, saying that we should work in the world as it is, but seek a bridge and link to the world as it should be. For Alinsky (1971), too many radicals only operate in the world as it should be, and too many cynics stay in the world as it is. Alinsky rejects organizing around altruism, both in our own motivations, and certainly in expecting it of those in power. He felt that many on the left, and those advocating for communities, were expected to be selfless, and in turn to expect self-sacrifice from others. They worked as though they were already in the world as it should be. He felt that this was a negating force and not sustainable and he had many tales of figures who self-sacrificed to little end. Alinsky also felt that appeals to those with power should similarly not just expect them to be overly altruistic and change for moral reasons without any gain.

This resonates with me. I ran a project where stakeholders, workers, clients and management had a remarkably negative, but similar, perception of each other. All stakeholders felt that they were not listened to, that other stakeholders were the true barriers to change, and that yet other stakeholders only looked after themselves and were not to be trusted – the accusation of selfishness, rather than self-interest, in others, is notable here. An educative intervention was needed on the distinctions between selfishness, self-interest and self-sacrifice. Through these educative sessions we discerned common positive threads or interests that could be drawn out – all wanted to be heard more because they felt they had something to say that would make the service better. They all could see that there was a need to change and they were prepared to be a part of this, and they all recognized that mutual trust had to get better (even if they placed the blame for all this with others). They all also had mutual self interest in the service getting better: clients would get a better service, workers would have an easier and less frustrating job, and management would run a service that was more efficient. The mutual aims they developed for the project were for everyone to be heard more by the other stakeholders (with a corollary that the least powerful in the organization, the client, closely followed by the workers, would be heard proportionally more), that it should make an aspect of the project better, and that is should result in more mutual trust. They also (eventually) agreed that they would not try and apportion blame for the situation.

We will come back to the idea of mutual self-interest when looking at how we identify the issues to be researched, and again in how a research project develops recommendations, as similar principles apply. Suffice to say that to establish self-interest there is an idealistic dimension as well as a self-orientation one. Chambers and Cowan (2004) says that we need to go back to people's motivations for being in, or engaging with, a project and help them step back from the everyday politics, gripes and mutual blame gaming. Beth Coyne will explore in more detail how in one of the probation projects it was the question of why people got involved in the service in the first place that both liberated people from rehearsed scripts and allowed them to start seeing each other in different lights. Clients were generally surprised to hear that workers often got involved because they wanted to help or make a difference, and workers were surprised to hear that managers had not always been managers, and that their motivations were remarkably similar, as were their frustrations.

Conclusion

Getting organizations and stakeholders to embrace the power of co-production and participatory research takes time and the right balance of factors. It also means, at times, saying no to undertake a project. One would need to be very clear in these cases that it is not about the organization's intent and genuine motivations and desire to engage; rather, it's that other factors are going to make a project difficult. However, going back to the new young people's service example, sometimes it is just not going to work, within a particular culture, and in a particular time and place, and we need to be brave enough to say so. I have only done this a couple of times in my career, and both organizations were not happy with my decision. In time one organization came back to me and said that on reflection, it had been the right decision, but they had changed their culture and now felt they were ready – I took the project on. The other asked me to tender for another research project a year after the previous one had collapsed. Nothing had changed – I did not take it on.

References

Alinsky, S. (1971) *Rules for Radicals: A Pragmatic Primer for Realistic Radicals*. New York: Vintage Books.

Anderson, L. (1997) *Argyris and Schön's Theory on Congruence and Learning*. Available at: http://www.scu.edu.au/schools/sawd/arr/argyris.html.

Argyris, C. & Schön, D. (1974) *Theory In Practice: Increasing Professional Effectiveness*. San Francisco, CA: Jossey-Bass.

Argyris, C., Putnam, R. & McLain Smith, D. (1985) *Action Science: Concepts, Methods, and Skills for Research and Intervention*. San Francisco, CA: Jossey-Bass.

Brandon, D., Wells, K., Francis, C. & Ramsey, E. (1980) *The Survivors: A Study of Homeless Young Newcomers to London and the Responses Made to Them*. London: Routledge and Kegan Paul.

Bryant, M. (2001) *Introduction to User Involvement*. London: The Sainsbury Centre for Mental Health.

Carpenter, J. & Sbarani, S. (1997) *Choice, Information and Dignity: Involving Users and Carers in Care Management in Mental Health*. Bristol: Policy Press.

Catan, L. (2002) 'Making research useful: experiments from the Economic and Social Research Council's Youth Research Programme.' *Youth and Society*, 76: 1–14.

Chambers, E. with Cowan, M. (2004) *Roots for Radicals: Organizing for Power, Action and Justice*. New York: Continuum.

Dickinson, P. (2001) *Lessons Learned from the Connexions Pilots*. DfES Research Report No. 308.

Edgar, B., Doherty, J. & Mina-Coull, A. (1999) *Services for Homeless People: Innovation and Change in the European Union*. Bristol: Policy Press.

Freire, P. (1972) *Pedagogy of the Oppressed*. London: Penguin.

Godfrey, M., Callaghan, G., Johnson, L. & Waddington, E. (2003) *A Guide to User Involvement for Organisations Providing Housing Related Support Services*. London: ODPM.

Jeffs, T. & Smith, M. K. (2002) 'Individualisation and youth work.' *Youth and Society*, 76: 39–65.

Lukes, S. (1974) *Power: A Radical View*. London: Macmillan.

Seal, M. (2017) *Trade Union Education: Transforming the World*. Oxford: Workable Books, New Internationalist.

Seal, M. (2009) *Not About Us Without Us: Client Involvement In Social Housing*. Lyme Regis: Russell House Publishing.

Seal, M. (2005) *Resettling Homeless People: Theory and Practice*. Lyme Regis: Russell House Publishing.

Senge, P. (1994) *The Fifth Discipline – The Art and Practice of the Learning Organisation*. London: Century Business.

Skyrme, D. (1999) *Knowledge Networking: Creating the Collaborative Enterprise*. Oxford: Butterworth Heinemann.

Smith, M. K. (2000, 2007) 'The Connexions Service in England.' *The Encyclopaedia of Informal Education*. Available at: www.infed.org [accessed 12 December 2017].

Smith, M. K. (2002a) 'From youth work to youth development: the new government framework for English youth services.' *Youth and Society*, 79: 46–59.

Smith, M. K. (2002b) 'Transforming youth work – resourcing excellent youth services. A critique.' *The Encyclopaedia of Informal Education, Informal Education Homepage*. Available at: www.infed.org/youthwork/transforming_youth_work_2.htm [accessed 20 February 2018].

Smith, M. K. (2001a) 'Chris Argyris: theories of action, double-loop learning and organizational learning.' *The Encyclopedia of Informal Education*. Available at: www.infed.org/thinkers/argyris.htm [accessed 20 February 2018].

Smith, M. K. (2001b) 'Peter Senge and the learning organization.' *The Encyclopedia of Informal Education*. Available at: www.infed.org/thinkers/senge.htm [accessed 20 February 2018].

Welsh Assembly (2004) *Consulting with Homeless People: An Advice Note Issued by the Welsh Assembly Government*. Cardiff: Welsh Assembly.

Wilcox, D. (1995) *Community Participation and Empowerment: Putting Theory Into Practice*. London: Partnership Press.

6 Ethical considerations in PPIR

Negotiating power and position

Ethics within participatory research can be considered either as a minefield or an illumination of the conceptual contradictions within research ethics. It exemplifies how ethics has been constructed with positivist science in mind, and through a lens of western ethics (Berghold & Thomas, 2012; Dentith et al., 2012). Certainly there are issues to consider. Informed consent becomes interesting when the methodology is something to be negotiated and the focus of the research is something that will shift and evolve. Similarly, the ability of the approach to change people and open up taboo subjects might make research participants vulnerable within their community or existentially challenge them and their values and belief systems. However, as Dentith et al. (2012) note, it depends on how these ethical issues are framed and contextualized. Should the focus of issues be on the individual and the impact of the research on them in the moment, and what counterweight can be given to the consciousness raising impact of successful participatory research? This chapter will examine the ethics of pedagogic participatory research in general, and how to approach ethics for a specific project in a pedagogic and participatory way.

Introduction

As stated, currently many ethical procedures for research tacitly are designed with positivist approaches in mind (Mertens & Ginsberg, 2009). They assume that, similar to one's methodology and methods being designed beforehand, our ethical procedures can also be mapped out a priori. At the same time ethical procedures, particular in the academy, normally take a deontological approach (Pérez-Pinar & Ayerbe, 2017; Schaffer, 2009) with the establishment of rules and guidelines for ethical research from which one needs to justify deviation. These guidelines are often determined centrally by national bodies such as the British Educational Research Association or the British Psychological Society. None of these are a good fit for participatory research. We therefore call for a re-examination, or at least re-orientation, of the philosophical basis of participatory research ethics. Within participatory research we need to see ethics, and their amelioration, as a dynamic between researchers and researched, rather than something that we do a priori. While our research needs to be mindful of ethical principles and guidelines, it also needs to consider who these guidelines are benefitting at any point, and develop a framework for making ethical judgements as the research evolves. Research should unsettle and occasionally disturb, and in doing so take risks, but it should not humiliate and undermine. This is the tension to be explored.

We noted in Chapter 3 some of the particular ethical issues of using peers in participatory research, from looking after them, mediating their reactions to what they hear, and how the tales they hear resonate with their own experience. However, as Terry and Cardwell (2016) note, we also need to work with community members' reactions to seeing and living oppression, and their sense of injustice about inaction as a result of the research. Chapter 4 illustrated the importance on cultivating a sense of hope and a future orientation in research participants, and of seeing the importance of symbolic and small changes. I think these are all ethical concerns that we need to give attention to.

Looking more widely several participatory authors (CSJCA & NCCPE, 2012; Fine & Torre, 2004; Terry & Cardwell, 2016) note that universities' ethical procedures are not set up for participatory research and construct it as problematic. These authors challenge such constructions (CSJCA & NCCPE, 2012; Fine & Torre, 2004; Yanar et al., 2016) and instead say that participatory research is inherently more ethical than most research in that it gives due attention paid to power relationships, is more egalitarian and democratic in approach, that it is based on respect for, and partnership with, community members, and that continuous reflexivity makes one more mindful of *emergent* ethical issues. Banks (2011) and Banks et al. (2013) highlight the ethical challenges that are often unique to, or certainly prevalent in, participatory research including the difficulties and power relationship in developing and maintaining partnerships, difficulties in maintaining anonymity and confidentiality, protection from harm, questions of rights and democratic representation and the blurred boundaries between researcher and researched. All are worth exploring, but I will concentrate on the first three and try to outline a framework that incorporates the others.

Ameliorating, partnership, collaboration and power

Banks et al. (2013) highlight from the literature examples where there are ethical issues in tackling the mismatch between different timelines and expectations of community organizations, funders and academics (Love, 2011). It is worth considering whose interest gives way to whose, how shifts are advocated for, and by whom. Simone Helleren, in Chapter 11, will talk about the phenomenon of 'investor pester', where funders will want to have a say, or even just be involved with a project, and sometimes not appropriately. As we discussed in Chapter 2, many community members are not involved in the genesis of the project, its broad parameters or even its broad topic. Any more than this, then I would suggest that its claim to be a participatory project starts to become untenable. This means that the timescales and broad parameters are often pre-determined. Where possible it is best to try to build in the scope to accommodate changes, which will have a discernable impact on community members' feeling of ownership.

In the Probation project (Chapter 12) for example, we extended the life of the project considerably. We also made changes to the way that people got expenses. It was highly motivating for community members to see that their views had changed factors like timescales.

Dodson & Baker (1995) found that closer research relationships also bring greater potential for exploitation, going on to say that the proximity required by true collaboration can at the same time place participants in situations where they are susceptible to being manipulated, betrayed, and exploited (Behar, 1993; Lal, 1996; Stacey, 1991; Wasserfal, 1993). Dodson et al. (2007) say that we should establish criteria for trustworthiness. I would agree, but reiterate that what these criteria are, should be co-created, and originate from what understanding and theories in use community members already have around trust. I also hope that the nature of the critical reflection session described in chapter four will ameliorate some of risks inherent in these power dimensions.

Ponic & Frisby (2010) say we need to take account of the fact that co-researchers may experience moments of inclusion and exclusion in the research process. While true, I think the power and nature of inclusion and exclusion are highly nuanced. For example, one participant I worked with was asked to come and be a co-presenter at a conference. Later we managed to secure funding for an additional participant, but the first participant felt that this diminished his contribution because he had never been singled out for anything before. One could argue that he needed to work this through, and he did, but the incident also made me aware of my privileged position. I, as someone with little need for affirmation, vary from this experience. The group understood and appreciated his position and thought it would be good for him to do the conference alone, which he did. What constitutes inclusion and exclusion are shifting and highly contextualized, and we need to develop an understanding of them that works from participants' own understandings of them. Also, bearing in mind Archer's (2012) morphogenetic approach, as a group of researchers we need to understand when, and if, our feeling of inclusion and exclusions are a playing out of old battles and positions, or a true representation of the moment and how we then work with it.

Anonymity and confidentiality

Hang on, so you are saying that you want to have our voices heard, but also that we need to try and make them confidential. Don't hide it, I wanna be heard, that's why I'm here, and If people do not want to be identified then do they have the courage of their convictions about what they are saying?

A research participant in the criminal justice system

Banks et al. (2013) make valid points about the importance of confidentiality and anonymity in community-based participatory research. Peer researchers may feel exposed if wide dissemination within their community is planned, and that there will be matters that some representatives of a community or group do not wish to be revealed. However, the above comment, from a research participant, was thought provoking and there are several layers to it that need to be unpacked. In other work (Seal, 2005, 2009) I have talked about the cultural relativity of confidentiality – it can be seen as an extension of individualism and the neo-liberalist project, a western and neo-colonial imposition and be associated with the atomization of community. This community member felt that it was only with secrets, and ones where one has not consulted with others about their accuracy or revelation, that one would not want something to be revealed. If a piece of research is truly participative then the community and the individual would have been involved intimately in the production of the data.

As the quote implies, anonymity without responsibility, can have implications for the validity of data. If you have no chance of being identified, then you can say what you like and present a version of yourself, and your community, that you or they want to present to the world – again without comeback. It seems to be a question of where one places the emphasis of one's ethics. What I liked about the above quote was its questioning the privileging of confidentiality and anonymity as inherently ethical, and as defining the starting point that we may, reluctantly, depart from. Should data be published that, while it safeguards the individual, damages a community that does not agree with its accuracy, or the publishing of it, in the first place?

On a philosophical level, some of the ethical debates on issues such as confidentiality and anonymity need to be contextualized with the different underpinning ethical paradigms. There are traditionally three basic ethical approaches. The first are de-ontological approaches, whereby we have rules for how we conduct ethics in research – e.g. that we remain anonymous and maintain confidentiality. Second is utilitarianism, where we weight up the common good in terms of an ethical decision, such as breaking an individual's, or group's confidentiality if it benefits the group overall. Third is virtue ethics, whereby we try and cultivate a sense of ethics in the research team in the hope that whatever decision is made, including in the moment, is a virtuous one.

As we noted in the introduction, traditionally ethical procedures have taken a de-ontological approach. However, even here it is nuanced. It depends on whose values we are adhering to and building our framework around. Following the aforementioned principles of ethno-praxis, we should work with participants to uncover and make explicit a community's own ethical framework, which will include differently constructed, and occasionally inverted, principles. As participatory researchers and critical pedagogue, we will not accept the community's ethical framework unconditionally, as with all frameworks it will be partial, potential contradictory and oppressive, and equally subject to dominating hegemonic forces, from above and within. However, in terms of power, for participatory researchers it should be our starting point, rather than an imposed framework for ethics, underpinned by outside concerns, from which we then need to justify deviation. The projects undertaken for this book often found frameworks did exist, and, interestingly, mapped across and simultaneously drew upon all of the ethical paradigms mentioned, though not always evenly and consciously.

To give an example, in the probation project described in Chapter 12, confidentiality, particularly between peer researchers and others on probation, had to be very sensitively handled as it was associated with 'grassing'. However, this was less about confidentiality being broken, and more about the integrity of what was done with the information. These participants commonly expressed indifference as to what happened to the information, or if people knew its origin as long as it made some difference. This put a different kind of pressure on the research team, and particularly the peer researchers, and their framework drew more heavily on utilitarianism (was it making a difference to others?) and virtue ethics (were the team making the right judgements about this?). The question becomes whether ethics can work across these different paradigmical positions.

Certainly they are all differently problematic when held in isolation. We have discussed the limitations of a priori rule based codes of conduct, even if they are developed within the community's own framework, particularly their inability to take account of situations as they unfold. Many authors have cited the danger of holding a utilitarian position in isolation (Howe & Moses, 1999; Macintyre, 1984), and cite famous biomedical examples such as the Tuskegee study of the progression of untreated syphilis in African-American men (Jones, 1992) where the men were not told of life-saving cures that could save their lives, social research such as Milligram's (1974) studies of obedience where people were tricked into thinking they had inflicted pain and even death on others, and the Tearoom research with gay men (Humphreys, 1970) which involved identification and deception issues. One of the main criticisms of virtue ethics is that there is no single common set of universal virtues (Fröding, 2013; Hursthouse, 1999). Authors such as Macintyre (1984) argue that the virtues should stem from what a community views as virtuous, and this certainly chimes with the ethnographic approach advocated there. Another criticism is that it does not guide the virtuous person at all in terms of their acts, and could therefore lead to relative judgements of the virtuous nature of the Tearoom, Miligram and Tuskegee research referred to.

It seems that a participatory ethical framework would need to be able to incorporate elements of all these paradigms. The question then becomes whether this is possible. Previously, but in relation to making ethical decisions as a youth and community worker, I have argued that it is.

Is it possible to maintain all three of these perspectives, but acknowledge their tensions? – I think it is. We can say that we will uphold some universal ethical positions, but that we will be mindful of the majority, who are often the young people and communities we are fighting for anyway, particularly when, following Habermas's principles of idea speech situations, our work involves powerful minorities who cannot, will not, or should not, engage in our conversations. In those situations, we have to employ different tactics, such as an Alinskian approach, at least in the short term, which go against our universal principles. The decisions about when we will do this, to whom, when and why is mediated by cultivating ethical, virtuous reflective workers.

(Seal & Frost, 2014, p. 156)

It is important to acknowledge that we can combine, but hold in tension, these different paradigms on research. I am also making a separate point within this paragraph about protection from harm, another common principal of ethical research that I will now discuss.

Protection from harm

Protection of the rights of research participants is high on the agenda of most research ethical guidelines (Banks et al., 2013; Terry & Cardwell, 2016). We talked in the peer research chapter how this can mean giving training, support and supervision for researchers both in terms of what the research might invoke and in holding their frustrations and sense of powerlessness when change cannot happen. We have also acknowledged that the reflective research spaces will not always be safe, and will at times be irrational, on the edge and visceral. However, returning to safety eventually, by working through these emotions, is the ultimate goal.

There is still the question of to whom this protection extends to, and whether it is equitable across stakeholders. An example might be appropriate here. In the probation project (Chapter 12) the group wanted to research the reception experience of those subject to protection as within the group this had not been positive, and the pilot had also shown it to be a pertinent issue. Initially the research group wanted to observe reception covertly in terms of how quickly people were seen and their treatment. The group rightly pointed out that if the reception knew they were being observed they would change their behavior to be seen in a good light. We discussed the ethics of this, with its use of deception and the vulnerable position that it would put the receptionists in.

The group, again rightly, pointed out that those waiting in reception were also suffering and, it could be argued, to a greater degree, getting breached due to phone calls not being put through, and misrepresentations of whether they had turned up for appointments – the group also pointed out that those on probation were very powerless in this situation. This was a utilitarian dilemma indeed. However, we also agreed that receptionists were not in an organizationally a powerful position themselves, were often caught between workers and those on probation, and could be made scapegoats for being at the pinch-point of wider structural issues. We decided not to undertake the observation approach, but did still research people's experiences of probation. We were also careful in the research to not target the receptionists themselves, but concentrated on wider structural issues, particularly in our recommendations.

At the morning launch of the report (which took place for some stakeholders in the morning and others in the afternoon) a senior worker was present who had consistently objected to the research in principle ('These are people who are being punished and we are protecting the public from; why should we ask them their views on the service?' was one of her comments). She had not participated and had been party to some of the sabotaging tactics that Beth will talk about in Chapter 12. At the launch she made a speech objecting to the focus on reception saying it was a personal attack, selectively focusing and exaggerating what was said in a way that was very distorted. She directed this speech towards one of the more volatile, or passionate, members of the research group, who responded in turn, making the argument previously mentioned that this was an important issue that could not be ignored. In the break the rest of the group mildly chastised the more passionate member of the group for rising to the bait. One of them said, and this stuck with me, that 'we should not stoop to their level'. This crystalized for me how the protection of stakeholders cannot be equal. This worker was blatantly abusing their power and the researchers were aware of the inequity of the situation and yet still appealed to one other to maintain the moral high ground. I made a formal complaint.

On another occasion a worker, who had participated on the basis of anonymity, revealed their own blatant abuses of power and negative views about those being researched, with some enjoyment. My view was that the worker was abusing the spirit of anonymity deliberately and that the damage being done to clients had to be addressed – I broke his confidentiality and reported him. Interestingly other workers, on hearing about this, still participated in the research, saying this person's actions indeed had to be reported. As I said previously a Habermasian (1984) view of the ideal speech situation would say that sometimes those in power who refuse to engage, or deliberately sabotage, and from a position of power, should not be afforded protection.

Informed consent

An aspect of this is informed consent. Simply put, this is the principle that people give consent to an involvement in the research process in an informed way, and can remove their consent at any stage. The difficulty with participatory research is that it is not evident from the outset exactly what people are giving their consent to. At the beginning it is often just a topic, and sometimes not even that. The focus, methodology and dissemination strategy will all evolve. In some ways the participatory research process ameliorates this because it is a continual process of negotiation. However, there are issues when participants who were involved early on, and give usable data, disappear and then the focus and/or approach evolves. Banks et al. (2013) also give instances where people's circumstances, perspective or understanding changes, such that they want to change their contribution, or nuances of it. Banks et al. (2013) note that informed consent in participatory research is not just an individual thing; consent may need to be obtained across the community and include those who, while not direct suppliers of data, are nevertheless effected by its release and/or have a view on it. Jamshidi et al. (2014) call this 'consensus consent' and note its parameters as personal information, privacy, anonymity, ownership of data and research achievements, share of knowledge and knowledge translation, sustainability, and maintenance of developed relationships. In Chapter 13, Simone Helleren will cover how in the Escape Plan research we made extensive use of focus groups in the shaping of the data interpretation that seemed to honour this process.

Issues of ownership and recognition

Equally important is the question of who owns the data and can make use of it. I will quote Banks' et al. (2013) thinking on this, as it is both summative and succinct.

> When research is a collaboration between several people or partner organisations, it is important to be clear who 'owns' any data, new knowledge or collaborative outputs that have been produced. 'Ownership' in this context means the right to use it and pass it on. If it is jointly owned, then it is important to decide what rights each partner has to use the data to inform their work or produce publications and whether the permission of all partners is required. Sometimes a funder may control the use of data and findings, and all parties need to be clear about the implications of this from the outset. It is particularly important that recognition is given to new knowledge made by communities and that when appropriate they receive financial rewards and have the right to own and use it.
>
> (Banks et al., 2013, p. 10)

Publication choices can be difficult. The academic, or professional researcher's reputation would mean the article, or book, is more likely to be accepted. I have always found community members to be fairly accepting of the expediency of this. Personally I have always made a point of going through the potential angles articles could make and conferences where papers can be delivered and been honest about how and why they can be strategically important, including expectations from my own institution as to where to publish. Difficult decisions may need to be made such as approaching a more prestigious academic publisher who will charge more and therefore be less accessible to activists and community members, or to go with a cheaper, less prestigious publisher. In a previous book, *Not About Us Without Us* (2009), I managed to reach and agreement with the publishers (Russell House Publishing) to extend the photocopying and distribution regulations in favour of activists and community members.

Practical example of putting ethics into practice

When training community members become researchers I normally dedicate a good couple of days to ethics, spread out across a number of sessions. Community members may often have extensive experience of being subject to interventions, treatment, policies and events that they would consider unethical, and it is not hard to uncover and articulate their ethical frameworks. All too often they have been subject to unethical research themselves, to the degree that many communities may suffer from research fatigue (Terry & Cardwell, 2016), and have developed a cynicism about research, based on direct experience – this needs to be worked through. Similarly, a lot of community members will have fears borne through experience of inappropriate information sharing – countering these is not as simple as assuring others about confidentiality and anonymity.

I think many of the standard ethical case studies mentioned, the Miligram experiment, the Tearoom study etc., are good starters to open up debate with community members. However, as noted, most community members have their own tales to tell. Similarly, when we start to consider the ethics of particular approaches, community members often have an innate understanding of the issues. For instance, most community members are used to being interviewed, and their knowledge about the fear that interviews bring can be drawn out and made into ethical guidelines. Issues about being recorded or filmed are also very familiar to people. An interesting debate was held in both the Escape Plan research and the probation projects, directly related to the relative power of the stakeholders. A distinction was made between different stakeholders' rights as individuals and whether the role they were holding should impact on this.

For example, in the probation research it was agreed that the workers should not be given the interview questions beforehand, because they would then be more likely to say what they thought we wanted to hear, or be evasive. They would also be interviewed in structured way so that the interviewer retained some control and power in the situation. Conversely, community members would be given the areas to be covered and questions beforehand, and interviewed in a semi-structured way, precisely because it would give them some sense of control and power. The chief executive was asked questions that were deliberately meant to get them to break out of corporate speak and humanize the discourse and challenge the power differential. A question such as 'Why did you get into this in the first place?' is an example of this, but also one that is not trying to demean the interviewee.

Therefore, ethical consideration should also be given to the settings for research, and interviewees' expectations of research processes, with an aim to redress issue of power. Such considerations could be extended to a consideration of the quality and diversity of the responses a piece of research will elicit – an ethical issue in itself. To work through an example, some years ago I was brought in to undertake a large consultation for a London borough with different homeless stakeholders. Previous consultations had had a limited and muted response. On enquiry we found that the consultations had been held in the ornate and intimidating town hall and some of the porters had not let the homeless people in. The structure of the consultations were in a format that was familiar to counsellors and council officers, and all the speaking had been in public. The participatory research, and dissemination, in contrast, were held in settings familiar to community members, in formats they knew and through advocates they felt comfortable with. The council members wanted to meet with them face to face. There was good intention behind this as they wanted to humanize themselves and the service. However, the councillors did not realize the strength of association the group had with officialdom, such that an honest conversation would not happen – an intermediator, a peer researcher, was needed.

In another setting the young people deliberately set the consultation up with a format and structure that would be unfamiliar to councillors – councillors were made to sit in a circle, there was no agenda, and only first names were used.

This was partly to make councillors aware of the power dynamic they had set up on previous occasions, and to slightly wrong foot them so that they got potentially more honest answers from them. As Saul Alinsky says (1971), always stay within the experience of your community and outside of the experience of those in power.

Conclusion

As we noted in Chapter 2, while we need to make our research goals and recommendations realistic, we also want to push the boundaries and balance of power in favour of the oppressed. We have to remember whose ethics considerations are to be privileged. This can mean making those in power, even if they commissioned the research, feel uncomfortable rather than safe, and even if they agree with the recommendations there is still work to be done to create tension such that they cannot afford to ignore them – this again may mean that they do not feel 'safe'. I will come back to the idea of tension within the selection of research issues and the development of recommendation chapters. We have outlined that research needs to be rooted in the communities' own understanding of research, and be able to respond to the shifts of the research approach and focus. A list of positivist a priori principles therefore seems superfluous. However, I would refer the reader to the excellent work by Banks et al. (2012) www.dur.ac.uk/resources/beacon/CBPREthicsGuidewebNovember20121.pdf who give us some starting principles on how to undertake a piece of research, such as building an ethical framework in the way described – as is Jamshidi et al.'s (2014) excellent systematic review on the subject.

References

Alinsky, S. (1971) *Rules for Radicals: A Pragmatic Primer for Realistic Radicals*. New York: Vintage Books.

Archer, M. S. (2012) *The Reflexive Imperative in Late Modernity.* Cambridge: Cambridge University Press.

Banks, S. (2011) 'Ethics in an age of austerity: social work and the evolving new public management.' *Journal of Social Intervention: Theory and Practice*, 20(2): 5–23.

Banks, S. Armstrong, A., Carter, K., Graham, H., Hayward, P., Henry, A., Holland, T., Holmes, C., Lee, A., McNulty, A., Moore, N., Nayling, N., Stokoe, A. & Strachan, A. (2013) 'Everyday ethics in community-based participatory research.' *Contemporary Social Science*, 8(3): 263–277.

Behar, R. (1993) *Translated Woman: Crossing the Border with Esperanza's Story.* Boston, MA: Beacon.

Bergold, J. & Thomas, S. (2012) 'Participatory research methods: a methodological approach in motion [110 paragraphs].' *Forum Qualitative Sozialforschung/Forum: Qualitative Social Research*, 13 (1): Art. 30.

Centre for Social Justice and Community Action (CSJCA) and National Co-ordinating Centre for Public Engagement (NCCPE) (2012) *Community-based Participatory Research: A Guide to Ethical Principles and Practice*. Durham: Durham University.

Dentith, A. M., Measor, L. & O'Malley, M. (2012) 'The research imagination amid dilemmas of engaging young people in critical participatory work.' *Forum Qualitative Sozialforschung/Forum: Qualitative Social Research*, 13(1): Art. 17.

Dodson, J. & Baker, J. (1995) *Time For Change: Local People Becoming Researchers.* London: Save the Children.

Fine, M. & Torre, M. W. (2004) 'Re-membering exclusions: participatory action research in public institutions.' *Qualitative Research in Psychology*, 1(1): 15–37.

Fröding, B. (2013) 'Critique of virtue ethics.' In *Virtue Ethics and Human Enhancement.* Dordrecht: Springer.

Habermas, J. (1984) *The Theory of Communicative Action* (Volume 1). Cambridge: Polity Press.

Howe, K. R. & Moses, M. S. (1999) 'Ethics in educational research.' *Review of Research in Education*, 24: 21–59.

Humphreys, L. (1970) *Tearoom Trade.* London: Duckworth Overlook.

Hursthouse, R. (1999) *On Virtue Ethics.* Oxford: Oxford University Press.

Jamshidi, E., Morasae, E. K., Shahandeh, K., Majdzadeh, R., Seydali, E., Aramesh, K. & Abknar, N. L. (2014) 'Ethical considerations of community-based participatory research: contextual underpinnings for developing countries.' *International Journal of Preventive Medicine*, 5(10): 1328–1336. Available at: https://www.ncbi.nlm.nih.gov/pmc/articles/PMC4223954/ [accessed 21 February 2018].

Jones, J. (1992) *Bad Blood: The Tuskegee Syphilis Experiment.* London, Free Press.

Lal, J. (1996) 'Situating locations: the politics of self, identity, and other in living and writing the text.' In D. Wolf (ed.) *Feminist Dilemmas in Fieldwork.* Boulder, CO: Westview, pp. 185–214.

Love, K. (2011) 'Little known but powerful approach to applied research: community-based participatory research.' *Geriatric Nursing*, 32(1): 52–54.

Macintyre, A. (1984) *After Virtue.* Notre Dame, IN: University of Notre Dame Press.

Mertens, M. D. & Ginsberg, P. E. (2009) *The Handbook of Social Research Ethics.* London: Sage.

Milligram, S. (1974) *Obedience to Authority: An Experimental View.* New York and London: Harper and Row.

Pérez Pinar, M. & Ayerbe, L. (2017) 'Virtue ethics of clinical research.' *Perspectives in Clinical Research*, 8(2): 103–104.

Ponic, P. & Frisby, W. (2010) 'Unpacking assumptions about inclusion in community based health promotion: perspectives of women living in poverty.' *Qualitative Health Research*, 20(11): 1519–1531.

Schaffer, J. (2009) 'On what grounds what.' In D. Manley, D. J. Chalmers & R. Wasserman (eds) *Metametaphysics: New Essays on the Foundations of Ontology.* Oxford: Oxford University Press, pp. 347–383.

Seal, M. (2009) *Not About Us Without Us: Client Involvement In Social Housing.* Lyme Regis: Russell House Publishing.

Seal, M. (2008) 'Saul Alinsky, community organizing and rules for radicals.' *The Encyclopedia of Informal Education.* Available at: http://infed.org/mobi/saul-alinsky-community-organizing-and-rules-for-radicals/ [accessed 20 February 2018].

Seal, M. (2005) *Resettling Homeless People: Theory and Practice.* Lyme Regis: Russell House Publishing.

Seal, M. & Frost, S. (2014) *Philosophy in Youth and Community Work.* Lyme Regis: Russell House Publishing.

Stacey, J. (1991) 'Can there by a feminist ethnography?' In D. Patai & S. B. Gluck (eds) *Women's Words: The Feminist Practice of Oral History*. New York: Routledge, pp. 111–119.

Terry, L. & Cardwell, V. (2016) *Refreshing Perspectives: Exploring the Application of Peer Research With Populations Facing Severe and Multiple Disadvantage*. London: Revolving Doors Agency.

Wasserfall, R. R. (1993) 'Reflexivity, feminism, and difference.' *Qualitative Sociology*, 15(1): 150–168.

Yanar, Z. M., Fazli, M., Rahman, J. & Farthing, R. (2016) 'Research ethics committees and participatory action research with young people: the politics of voice.' *Journal of Empirical Research on Human Research Ethics*, 11(2): 122–128.

7 Defining your terrain

Community member and issue identification

Introduction

In this chapter I examine how community partners and research themes are to be identified and explored. In doing this we feel that any judgements about demographics should be taken after recruitment rather than at the start of the project and the emphasis should be on strategies for when representation becomes problematic rather than trying to adhere to some mythical ideal representative sample that is never applied to other stakeholders, such as managers. Tentative criteria for becoming a researcher are discussed, as well as different ways that we can access and recruit potential researchers. A pertinent discussion is also held about the degree to which a member of service user communities should have distance from their issues before becoming a researcher or whether it is legitimate to use being a researcher as part of a therapeutic approach. A concurrent discussion is had on looking at the skills a team needs overall and not underestimating the transferability of skills many communities have developed in roles not always associated as skills based, including by community members themselves.

The second part of the chapter examines criteria for identifying research themes, and seeks to combine elements of critical pedagogy, participatory research and community organizing in doing this. A stance is taken on the degree to which we should be utopian and idealistic in our research goals, or pragmatic in identifying our research themes. Using the community organizing metaphor that effective research themes are located in the space and tension between the world as it is and the world as it should be, as Ed Chambers (Chambers with Cowan, 2004, p. 65) would say this means 'acting in the world now on behalf of the world as it should be'.

Identifying community partners

As discussed in Chapter 5, a sign that an organization is inhibiting rather than enabling of co-production, is that they engage in protracted discussion about who the community is and what the constitution of those involved needs to be to be representative – criteria that are mysteriously seldom applied to the staff, and almost never the senior management team. The demographics of community members are not a consideration to be ignored, but over-focusing on it can be a distraction and a sign of avoidance. I have discussed elsewhere (Seal, 2009) how you should 'start with what you have and build from there'. This is not to say that you ignore issues of representation and demographics, it is about where you start. To these ends I propose two criteria about judging representativeness. First, that the judgement should not be on how representative you are to start with, but how representative you are at the end. Second, when considering participatory research groups' demographics, we should not ask what at its ideal constitution should be, but when its demographic constitution becomes a problem. In the Escape Plan research (Chapter 11) and the probation research (Chapter 12) we established when biased representations of gender, race, age, etc., would start to become un-representative, both in terms of the research team, and in the selection of participants. In one probation case, four of the peer researchers were men and there was only one woman, and the professional facilitators were a man and a woman. That said, the group agreed that the strength of the two women ameliorated the situation, as they were not afraid to challenge the male researchers. However, had one of the women left it was agreed that this would have become a problem.

Criteria for community participants

Aside from saying that community partners should come from the community being researched, and citing demographic considerations, the literature is surprisingly sparse on the subject of criteria for community partners in participatory research. I have also found few 'person specifications' for participatory or community researchers. Interestingly there are a plethora of person specifications for peer researchers. Based on a sample of 20, and combined with the few participatory researcher person specifications, I identified several common themes. Participants needed to:

- be prepared to work together as a team
- be prepared to give their ideas and share experiences
- be able to stand back from their own experiences and appreciate the experiences of others
- commit to the whole duration of the project
- be punctual and reliable
- be willing to learn and could listen to, and take account of, the ideas of others
- be able to communicate, and use their experiences in a way that enables others to give their opinions
- analyse information and make connections between ideas
- be committed to diversity and equal opportunities.

Some of these are standard for any researchers, although commitment and time-keeping need to be measured against the flexibility needed to take account of the complexity of some community members lives (Terry & Cardwell, 2016). The criteria about researchers use of their experiences are much more specific and play to the nature of participatory research. I do not think literacy is essential, although analytical ability is. If all the researchers have literacy issues it may cause difficulties, particularly with data analysis, but I have run courses without relying on written materials and people have still successfully engaged. How we assess these criteria will vary according to recruitment processes. I have used formal interviews, although many community members find these intimidating, or have negative associations with interviews from experience of the benefits or criminal justice systems, etc. Group discussions can be a very good way of assessing these criteria, and many community members are used to group discussions, to different degrees, and may have more positive associations with them, particularly where they have benefitted from therapeutic groups.

This leads to a pertinent discussion about the degree to which community members of certain communities, particularly service users of social care organizations, need to have worked through their 'issues' before becoming a researcher. There are practical and emotional dimensions to this, such as whether on-going issues will render a person unable to engage effectively with the research process. Those still with issues may also, as we have discussed before, be too close to them to be able to stand back from them, and they may act as a negative trigger for them. While contested, systematic literature reviews tend to say that 'wounded healers', as Jung termed them, with support, can aid others while working through their own issues (Conchar & Repper, 2014). There is also some evidence that they are better placed to do so, being a model that people can still carry their issues while functioning well and aiding others (Conchar and Repper, 2014). I have detailed before (Seal, 2007, 2009) how some organizations, such as in the homeless sector, used to have rules barring people from returning as workers, volunteers and certainly not researchers, for two years. This arbitrary period does not take into account how some people can manage the issues, and others will not be able to even after two years. The priority and key is to evaluate how well an individual is managing these tensions, and this needs careful assessment and on-going support. For these reasons I think participatory researchers need supervision, as do all researchers, but in a form that is sensitive to the issues.

However, certain groups might be more ready at particular points. For example, some years ago I was involved in doing a client involvement audit of a major homeless charity. In the initial crisis phase, often when people were coming off the streets, potential participants were more interested in meeting their immediate needs. In second stage, often hostel accommodation, people did want to get involved, primarily in making their own environment better, for themselves and others. Residents' groups and activities within these projects were often their focus. Interestingly it was assumed that people in the final stage housing would be the hardest to engage as their focus would be turning towards, and gearing up for, their lives beyond the homeless system. However, it was this group that was the most interested in getting involved, not in order to have a say on their immediate environment, but to directly give support to others, to give back, and it was from their group that peer and participatory researchers were drawn.

Another dimension is whether research participants should see the process of engaging in research as therapy. We noted in the Chapter 1 that co-production, of which research is a form, is personally beneficial increasing self-belief, self-efficacy and developing skills. In the Escape Plan research detailed in Chapter 11, where we researched positive critical factors in entrenched rough sleepers escaping homelessness, engaging in group work, volunteering, giving back and engaging with peer and co-production were all major factors in breaking a rough sleeping cycle. Beth Coyne in Chapter 12, will discuss an example of this where people leaving the project for employment was the major source of attrition for the group. here is, of course, a balance to be struck between people meeting their own needs and fulfilling the objectives of the research project, but these are not mutually exclusive.

On a team level it is important to conduct a skills inventory of what is needed to conduct a research project, and match it against what skills are in the research team. This can be important to break down barriers, and the facilitators can show anything that is lacking and which attributes will therefore need to be sought in recruitment. Table 7.1 is an example of an inventory used on the probation project.

I think these can be broken down further as research skills constitute a broad area, and communication skills can be at different levels, both written and oral. Creative skills such as drama, music, film, art and new media should not be forgotten. These can lead to very interesting research and dissemination techniques, as we shall see. Such mapping is also useful at the end of the project because community members can use it to evaluate how effective the project was for them and how far they have moved. It is important to note that many community members, particularly those from marginalized communities, will not necessarily see or acknowledge the skills they already posses (Seal, 2005, 2006, 2009), having been subject to negative reinforcement about the illegitimacy of many of the roles they have undertaken. Exercises can show the transferable skills that can be gained from marginalized and demonized roles such as being a survivor of the mental health and/or criminal justice systems, being an ex-drug

Table 7.1 Inventory used on the probation project

Skills area	Self score
I am confident in research skills	1
I have experience conducting research	4
I feel comfortable running groups	2
I have excellent communication skills	5
I can put people at ease	3
I can encourage people to tell me what they think	4
I can interpret data	7
I can write reports	3
I can give presentations	4
I can work in a team	2
I understand confidentiality	5
I can plan and organize a project	6
I can work with different stakeholders	4
I can explain complex ideas simply	7

Table 7.2 Skills required by graduates based on surveys undertaken by Microsoft, Target Jobs, the BBC, Prospects, etc.

1	Verbal communication	Able to express your ideas clearly and confidently in speech
2	Teamwork	Work confidently within a group
3	Commercial awareness	Understand the commercial realities affecting the organization
4	Analysing and investigating	Gather information systematically to establish facts and principles; problem solving
5	Initiative/ self-motivation	Able to act on initiative, identify opportunities and be proactive in putting forward ideas and solutions
6	Drive	Determination to get things done; make things happen and constantly looking for better ways of doing things
7	Written communication	Able to express yourself clearly in writing
8	Planning and organizing	Able to plan activities and carry them through effectively
9	Flexibility	Adapt successfully to changing situations and environments
10	Time management	Manage time effectively, prioritizing tasks and able to work to deadlines

user, or single parent, or having lived on benefits; often it can take work to elicit these from people but nevertheless the skills are there and are transferable. It is also important to outline the skills that the community member should gain from the project. In Coyne and Seal's (2016) report on developing peer research in probation they note the skills required by graduates based on surveys undertaken by Microsoft, Target Jobs, the BBC, Prospects, etc., include those listed in Table 7.2.

Accessing potential researchers

Any approach to sourcing community members will need to be multifaceted and evolutionary. In much of the research detailed in Part 3, access to communities was brokered through agencies. However, this can prove both difficult and unrepresentative for a number of reasons. Some agencies will be directly discriminatory and choose people so as to show them in a good light (Coyne & Seal, 2016). We also found in all of the research that those who label community members and clients as unmotivated and unlikely to engage, are, unsurprisingly, also those who will not find potential participants. Less insidiously agencies will often choose those who are already the most engaged, and indeed a project needs high levels of sustained engagement from at least some participants to be effective. However, those who are already engaged are not always the most representative. Anthropology has a history of relying on such 'key informants', and the dangers of doing so are well documented (Cohen et al., 2000; Patton, 2014). While not always a reliable source for unbiased information, they can be useful for accessing others. The key informant structure can also be applied to workers.

Even in organizations where levels of cynicism and negative constructions of community members and their motives are high, there are normally individual workers who do not buy into them, and these are the ones to approach. Snowball sampling is acknowledged as being useful with hidden populations which are difficult for researchers to access (Salganik & Heckathorn, 2004), and for including people in the survey that we would not have known otherwise (Goodman, 1961). Both these authors also note that there are dangers of validity for snowball sampling in that you are recruiting more participants like those already recruited. However, in my view it depends on what question you are asking, and what kind of community you are trying to reach. I have always found key informants receptive when you explain that you are seeking to cast your net wider. Obviously they will have inherent bias in who they know, but this is true of any source – thus the importance of a multifaceted approach.

In Chapter 12, services ran drop in session so we accessed potential participants directly as part of that. This approach relies on participants taking a leap of faith, particularly in terms of trust, because they do not know you. You are largely relying on the 'proxy trust' (Seal & Harris, 2016) via the project, if it was they who referred the person, or on the faith of the individual, and we have previously discussed how for many, trust is not something they extend easily. In the Commissioning Together project initial efforts did not work at all. On reflection we had concentrated our efforts on building relationship with managerial stakeholders, and relied on workers, with whom we had no direct contact, to recruit participants who had little knowledge or investment in the project. Participants were also expected to travel to a council venue some distance away, which they either had no knowledge of or already had negative associations with. A different approach was needed. We talked to the commissioners about the range of projects that they supported. One of the most popular was a sports-based project, so one of the team went and joined in the projects activities, got to know people and built relationships from there. He did not pretend to be a client, and was overt about what he was doing, and people were accepting of this.

In almost all of the research detailed in Part 3, we used a multitude of these techniques. To give an example, in the Escape Plan we recruited through people we already knew (the organization being a self-help NGO for people who were homeless and ex-homeless), through agencies we knew and then a snowball sample from those we interviewed. We then supplemented this with an advert in the *Big Issue* to attract people outside of these circles and who might either still be *Big Issue* sellers or readers, who may have broken out of the circle of rough sleeping some time ago.

Choosing issues: the world as it is and the world as it should be

In the world as it is, man moves primarily because of self-interest. Organizing should target winnable, immediate, concrete changes.

(Alinsky, 1971, p. 43)

To illustrate this, I will start with an anecdote. During the Commissioning Together research my colleague came to me a little perturbed. He had been at a conference for others who were also undertaking research projects, under the same funding regime. As we shall describe, we had been action orientated in our choosing of issues, choosing things that had the potential to change, and also taking into account other stakeholder interests. By contrast, another research team had spoken only to community members, as the most powerless, and built from there. They criticized my colleague for allowing the wants and desires of the community to be compromised and that for re-inscribing existing power relationships. They had also started with visioning exercises from the community, asking community members to imagine what the future could be, without any restrictions. In consequence the vision presented to commissioners was quite utopian. While appreciative most of what was being asked for was not within the commissioner's power to enact and little was changed as a result. That researcher felt that while practical things had not really changed, the most important thing was that the community member had had a chance to dream, and the commissioners had seen a vision of a different world. The workers hoped that the anger and frustration of community members when their vision was not acted upon would spur social action and might also shake some of the commissioners out of their complacency. This is a distinct vision of how to conduct research and develop themes. It is also not the approach that this book advocates.

Despite that, we need to explore this approach more, as it has a distinct tradition with principles to be respected. It has most recently been articulated by Levitas (2013) as utopianism which he sees as 'a critical tool for exposing the limitations of current policy discourses . . . [promoting] genuinely holistic thinking about possible futures . . . The core of utopia is the desire for being otherwise, individually and collectively' (Levitas, 2013, xi). This is to be admired as it can help a community escape its own restricting habitus (Bourdieu, 1997) formed by dominating hegemony forces (Gramsci, 1971). Another tradition that uses similar a similar device is Trotsky's concept of transitional demands/programme (Trotsky, 1938). Rather than seeking demands that are possible within the existing economic and political regime, we deliberately ask for things that we know cannot be achieved within it – the theory being that this exposes structural flaws and shows the only solution as being a complete overhaul of the system. It also exposes the vested interest in the old system of those in power and points to revolution as the only solution.

I think Utopianism in participatory research fails on a number of levels. Theoretically, going back to Chapter 4's discussion about the problem of conscientization, the Utopian/transition demand vision re-inscribes a view of community members as those who need 'awakening' and 'liberating mentally'. This kind of thinking is also present, as discussed before in Freire (1972), Gramsci (1971) and Bourdieu's (1997) work. Alternatively, we take a Rancierian (1992) view on this: the real issue is not people's awareness of their own oppression, but their will and hope of achieving any change, and consequent lack of vision of how to go forwards. A Utopian/transitional demand vision reinforces this sense of hopelessness, apart from an all or nothing commitment to the revolution, but with little vision of how to enact it, apart from reliance on more experienced cadre.

Alinsky (1971) would call this, as discussed before, a rhetorical radical position, and he was critical of the lack of programmes that emerges from such as approach. Speaking of the radicalism of the 1960s, which had echoes of the Utopian approach (Levitas, 2013), in the introduction to his book, *Rules for Radicals*, Alinsky said: '[T]hey have no illusions about the system, but plenty of illusions about the way to change our world. It is to this point that I have written this book' (Alinsky, 1971, xiii). He made a distinction, which was then refined by Chambers (with Cowan) in *Roots for Radicals* (2004), between the 'world as it is', and 'the world as it should be', saying:

> As an organizer I start from where the world is, as it is, not as I would like it to be. That we accept the world as it is does not in any sense weaken our desire to change it into what we believe it should be – it is necessary to begin where the world is if we are going to change it to what we think it should be. That means working in the system.
>
> (Alinsky, 1971, xix)

This does not preclude holding visioning exercises to explore what the radical version of change could look like. Such activities can motivate people, and clarify for them, and us, where they have been susceptible to the limitations placed on them by themselves and others (we are, after all, all subject to this to varying degrees). However, the point is then to relate it back to what is possible in the here and now, and understanding how it relates to the radical vision. Then, if successful, we can celebrate the achievement of something that contributes to moving towards the world as it should be, even when the achievement is symbolic, as it builds, rather than crushes, one's sense of hope. Even if on a fundamental level the radical vision is not possible within the system as it is, we are starting to build that all-important bridge towards the world as it should be.

In *Roots for Radicals*, Chambers (with Cowan, 2004) is quite clear that community organizers, and the communities they work with, live in the place in between the world-as-it-is and the world-as-it-should-be. He criticizes those who live entirely in the world as it is as accepting of a 'received culture of materialism' and those who reside too much in the world as it should be as having 'impotent idealism'. He also makes an interesting comparison between the world-as-it-is and its concerns with self-interest, power, change and imagination, contrasted with the world-as-it-should-be and its parallel concerns with self-sacrifice, love, unity and harmony and hope. He feels to be effective a broad-based organization needs to ride the tensions between these two positions in the issues it works with and how it works with them. It is the tensions between these differing concerns that give us the energy and drive to carry on. He quotes Berdyayev (1937) in saying that overall there is a tension between being and becoming and that we are always in the process of becoming, because the world as it should be is similarly always in a process of becoming.

Conclusion: criteria for choosing research themes

In keeping with the themes of this book I wish to combine elements of community organizing, participatory research and critical pedagogy in coming up with a schema for identifying research themes. The participatory literature is remarkably scant on the subject beyond saying that it needs to come from the community and be rooted in their concerns. Chamber's work (2004) talks about the conditions that need to exist for these genuine concerns to emerge and the skills needed for facilitators to enable this process, and we have gone into some detail about this in Chapter 4. Other guides and materials (Petty et al., 1995) detail exercises and tools for gaining an understanding of a community's needs. This concurs with Cooke and Kothari's criticism that much participatory research has not really explored impact, particularly not in the selection of issues to work on. The main source I found for discerning issues beyond this comes from a Foundation for Sustainable Development Toolkit (UNESCO, 2017), which makes an attempt in this direction.

The schema I have used for community organizing is from Chapter 5 ('The practice of public life: research, action, and evaluation') in Chambers and Cowan's (2004) book *Roots For Radicals*. In this chapter they make a distinction between choosing 'issues' and 'problems'. Chambers broadly describe 'problems' as things that require structural societal change and, while important, are rarely something that an action can change. He sees 'issues' as things that manifest from the problem and have consequences for people, and change can be achieved on a local scale, and he sees community organizers as concerned with 'issues'. This seems a departure from his earlier position, as it is coming down quite firmly on the side of working in the world as it is. For this reason, I have incorporated some of his thinking from an earlier chapter (Chapter 1, Chambers with Cowan, 2004) about straddling the tensions between the world as it is and the world as it should be, specifically hope, imagination, power and love, and unity. I have also brought in our previous emphasis, discussed in Chapter 4, on the importance of the community organizing concept of developing mutual self-interest.

From critical pedagogy I have focused on the aforementioned criteria for generative themes as develop by Freire (1972) and further developed by Aliakbari and Faraji (2011). These should be: 1) a galvanizing force for the community, something about which there is passion and feeling; 2) they should have tensions and contradictions within them – things that do not add up, that need to be worked through and have a potential to create new ideas that resolve these tensions; 3) they should open up discussion about, and relate to, wider social issues; and 4) they should have the potential for action, meaning that something concrete can be done about them.

A cross comparison of their schemas looks like the one shown in Table 7.3.

The only criteria where there is cross over across all three is *policy and wider impact* – whereby highlighting or addressing these issues should have the potential to make a significant impact on policy. It should also open up discussion about, and relate to, wider social issues. Within community organizing Chambers and Cowan (2004) recommend that we need, even from the outset, to conduct a

Table 7.3 Cross comparison of schemas

Participatory research (based on UNESCO's Foundation for Sustainable Development, 2017)	**Critical pedagogy** (based on generative themes (Freire, 1972)	**Community organizing** (based on Chambers, with Cowan 2004)
Fit with existing efforts Will addressing this issue build upon existing efforts in the community?	Themes should be a galvanizing force for the community, something about which there is passion and feeling.	
Relationship to other problems Will addressing this particular issue also have a positive effect on other issues of concern?		Do the issues develop and build on all stakeholders' self-interest?
Local expertise Do we have expertise within our partnership to assist in the efforts?		
Capacity Does capacity exist within organizations to address this problem	Themes must have the potential for action, meaning that something concrete can be done about them.	Do we have a winnable issue here? Is it immediate enough?
Feasibility - Are there funds available to address this problem (with particular attention given to funding resources within the community)?		Will leaders mobilize their followers around the issue?
Policy impact Will addressing this problem have the potential to make a significant impact on policy?	Themes should open up discussion about, and relate to, wider social issues.	Who are the key decision makers, who will oppose us and what is their strength?
Synergy - Is this an issue that everyone can rally around so that your combined efforts will have more of an impact than if individual partners focused separately on the problems?		Do we have a sufficient number of leader with followers who feel the issue is in their interest? Who are our allies? Will they help? Do they need to be talked to?
		Will the action build the capacity of community participants?
	Theme must have tensions and contradictions within them: things that do not add up, that need to be worked through and have a potential to create new ideas that resolve these tensions.	

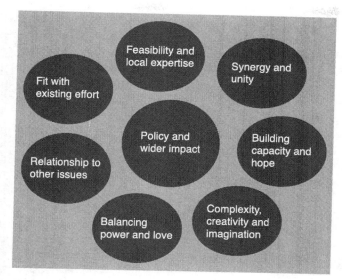

Figure 7.1 Policy and wider impact

power analysis by asking questions to identify the key decision makers, our opponents and their strength, our mutual self-interests, our allies, and whether they will help. I would then recommend three more criteria that broadly fit into concerns with the world as it is, and then four that bridge the world as it is and the world as it should be, which acknowledge the tensions between them and attempt to make them into a creative force (see Figure 7.1).

I will take the criteria in turn. First, will the research theme *fit with existing efforts* – i.e. will addressing this theme build upon existing efforts and concerns in the community? Second, building on the previous criteria, what is the *relationship to other issues of concern* – i.e. will addressing this particular issue also have a positive effect on another issue of concern and will it build upon and highlight mutual self-interest? Third, and practically, is *feasibility and local expertise* – i.e. do we have expertise and capacity across stakeholders to research and then carry through the changes needed? Are there funds, and other resources, available to address this problem, with particular attention given to resources within the community?

The fourth criterion, and the first bridging criterion, is whether the research creates *synergy and unity*. It needs to be an issue that everyone can rally around so that their combined efforts will have more of an impact than if individual partners focused separately on the problems. Fifth is *balancing power and love*. The research theme should explore, address or highlight issues of power inequity, while at the same time building mutual understanding across stakeholders, humanizing each other, to each other. A sixth criteria is *building capacity and hope* – will researching and addressing the research theme build the capacity of community participants to do, and want to do, further research and push the boundaries and tensions further? Concurrently, will working on this research theme give all stakeholders a sense of hope about the future, without descending into idealism, and instead enabling them to identify a path to create new knowledge that goes beyond the pragmatic and immediate?

The seventh and final criterion is very much taken from critical pedagogy, criteria for a generative theme. It is whether the research theme has *complexity, creativity and imagination*. Within this criterion lie several ideas. First, does the research theme have tensions and contradictions within it – things that do not add up, that need to be worked through? This is not to preclude simple answers, such as in the probation project where one recommendation was to allow people on probation a say in how reception was decorated. However, contained within this theme are deeper issues, in this case democracy, ownership and power.

To give another example, on the same project we considered the question of 'what makes for a good relationship between a probation officer and an offender'. This seemed simple enough but brought up huge issues contradictions and tensions in the massive differences of interpretations of concepts like professional boundaries, care and respect, and even what makes for a good relationship with anyone. Different accounts highlighted gulfs between people's behavior and self-belief, perceived motivations and lived experience, which then went deeper into issues of identity and validation for both workers and clients. What such depth gives is positive potential to create new ideas that stretch our imagination and gives us vision for the future that resolves or at least ameliorates these tensions and highlights, and may even give us a way into, wider personal and structural issues.

References

Aliakbari, M. & Faraji, E. (2011) *Basic Principles of Critical Pedagogy.* Paper presented at 2nd International Conference on Humanities, Historical and Social Sciences, IPEDR vol. 17.

Alinsky, S. (1971) *Rules for Radicals: A Pragmatic Primer for Realistic Radicals.* New York: Vintage Books.

Berdyaev, N. (1937) *The Destiny of Man* (translated from the Russian by Duddington Natalie). London: The Centenary Press.

Bourdieu, P. (1997) *Outline of a Theory of Practice.* London: Cambridge University Press.

Chambers, E. with Cowan, M. (2004) *Roots for Radicals: Organizing for Power, Action and Justice.* New York: Continuum.

Cohen, L., Manion, L. & Morrison, K. (2000) *Research Methods in Education.* London: Falmer-Routledge.

Conchar, C. & Repper, J. (2014) '"Walking wounded or wounded healer?" Does personal experience of mental health problems help or hinder mental health practice? A review of the literature.' *Mental Health and Social Inclusion*, 18(1): 35–38.

Cooke, B. & Kothari, U. (2001) (eds) *Participation: The New Tyranny?* London: Zed.

Coyne, B. & Seal, M. (2016) *Running a Peer Research Project With Offenders in the Community.* London: Revolving Doors Agency.

Freire, P. (1972) *Pedagogy of the Oppressed.* London: Penguin.

Goodman, L. A. (1961) 'Snowball sampling.' *Annual of Mathematical Statistics*, 32(1): 148–170.

Gramsci, A. (1971) *Selections From the Prison Notebooks*. London: Lawrence & Wishart.

Levitas, R. (2013) *Utopia as Method: The Imaginary Reconstitution of Society*. London: Palgrave Macmillan.

Patton, P. (2014) *Qualitative Research and Evaluation*. London: Sage.

Petty, J., Guijt, I., Scoones, I. & Whompson, J. (1995) *Participatory Learning and Action: A Trainer's Guide*. London: International Institute for Economic Development.

Rancière, J. (1992) *The Ignorant Schoolmaster: Five Lessons in Intellectual Emancipation*. Stanford, CA: Stanford University Press.

Salganik, J. M. and Heckathorn, D. D. (2004) 'Sampling and estimation in hidden populations using respondent-driven sampling.' *Sociological Methodology*, 34: 193–239.

Seal, M. (2009) *Not About Us Without Us: Client Involvement In Social Housing*. Lyme Regis: Russell House Publishing.

Seal, M. (2007) *Working in the Homeless Sector: Worker Perspectives*. London: YMCA George Williams College Occasional Paper.

Seal, M. (2006) *Working With Homeless People: A Training Manual*. Lyme Regis: Russell House Publishing.

Seal, M. (2005) *Resettling Homeless People: Theory and Practice*. Lyme Regis: Russell House Publishing.

Seal, M. & Harris, P. (2016) *Responding to Youth Violence Through Youth Work*. Bristol: Policy Press.

Terry, L. & Cardwell, V. (2016) *Refreshing Perspectives: Exploring the Application of Peer Research With Populations Facing Severe and Multiple Disadvantage*. London: Revolving Doors Agency.

Trotsky, L. (1938) *The Death Agony of Capitalism and the Tasks of the Fourth International*. Paris: Pathfinder Press.

UNESCO (2017) Foundation for Sustainable Development Toolkit. London: UNESCO.

8   Methodology in action

Transforming participant knowledge

Introduction

All too often within research the methodology and resultant methods are chosen because a researcher has a particular interest or expertise in that approach. Alternatively, particularly in health and social care research, over-familiar tools such as interviews and focus groups are used, and in particular ways, forgetting that community partners may have prior associations with such approaches, through key working and group work. In PPIR we ground the approach in the medium(s) that are familiar to those being researched, which includes the researcher's experience. PPIR methods are often creative, but are deliberately not exotic – they are grounded in means by which the researched express themselves.

The tyranny of methods

In some ways the methods used in participatory research should be no different from those used in any research; it is the process by which they are determined and mediated that is participatory (Danieli & Woodhams, 2005; Lynch, 2000; McDonagh, 2000; Pain & Francis, 2003). However, this assumes that research is neutral. In her ground-breaking book *Decolonising Methodologies: Research and Indigenous Peoples* (1999) Linda Smith eloquently questions the whole basis of traditional research which rests on the western tradition of classifying and representing the other, and instead calls for the embracing of local and indigenous ways of knowing as the basis for research. She also talks about the cynicism of community members towards research as they recognize its colonial nature. This means that we may have a culture of distrust of research to overcome with community members, and many community members display 'research fatigue' (Terry & Cardwell, 2016). However, in many of the research projects in this book community members have concurrently internalized the positivist models of research they reject, seeing only those as it as what legitimate 'proper' research.

We therefore need to unearth and take as our starting point the ways in which our community members have previously learnt and come to know things. Many participatory research approaches and guides have exercises aimed at eliciting community approaches and indigenous knowledge. In doing this, and in keeping with participatory research's origins in critical pedagogy (which in its Freirian guise was very much concerned with literacy) often used approaches that emphasize the visual, and other creative ways of conducting research which do not rely on the written word (Chambers, 2008; Petty et al., 1995). A wide range of participatory methods is in use, many drawn from developing world contexts and adapted to new needs and settings. These have been categorized by Pretty et al. (1995) into four main classes: 1) group and team dynamics (all our reflective meetings were recorded and had minutes which were used to accent the research findings); 2) sampling; 3) interviewing and dialogue; and 4) visualization and diagramming. Other methods include community surveys and a range of audio-visual techniques including storytelling, popular theatre, songs and photovoice. Lists of such approaches are numerous, but are remarkably similar. The typology outline in Table 8.1 is one of many and is fairly comprehensive (Beazley & Ennew, 2006).

While they are all positive approaches and clearly aimed at getting the perspective of community members, a worry is that by applying a patented 'technique', this becomes a substitute for engaging with, deconstructing and decolonizing

Table 8.1 Summary of the use of some widely used 'participatory methods'

Method	Process	Issues explored
Social mapping	Participants in a group draw a visual map of the houses, important institutions (village head, doctors, midwives, hospitals) and places people congregate – shops, mosque, church, river, etc. – transport hubs, in the community	Importance of institutions in the community Where health services are, including traditional midwives Where children, single, pregnant women, old people live, etc. Where and how people spend their time Location and availability of transport
Resource mapping	Participants draw a visual map of where they go to get the important resources in their community	Where water pumps, wells, rivers are Wetland resources (Mekong Delta) Where wood, fish, grass, thatch for roofs is collected Location of gardens, crops, animals
Mobility mapping	Participants individually draw a visual map of where they go everyday/week/ month/in the past year, etc.	Mobility of men, women and children in rural and urban areas. Where they go to work, school, look for resources, for leisure and entertainment, for health seeking practices, to hang out/ sleep (street children)
Body mapping	Participants individually or in a group draw the outline of a body and mark places on it when asked specific questions	To ascertain maternal health issues Issues of sexual abuse; where young people have been touched/abused Corporal punishment; where children have been hit

(continued)

Table 8.1 Summary of the use of some widely used 'participatory methods' *(continued)*

Method	Process	Issues explored
Social network diagrams	Participants are individually asked to answer questions that allow a facilitator to draw a map of the social networks participants are engaged in	Questions asked of street children included who do you go to when you are lonely? When you are hungry? When you are scared? When you have a secret? When you need some money? When you are tired? When you have money and want to have fun, etc.?
Matrix ranking and scoring	Participants in a group list items during a guided brainstorming session, and then rank them in importance and frequency	Severity and frequency of disease Types of food eaten in a community Health seeking preferences
Seasonal and social calendars	Participants in a group draw events that happen during different seasons of the year	Wet, dry seasons; cycles of migration; cycles of religious events; work patterns; when people are rich, when poor; when people are sick
Time transects	Participants individually draw how they spend their time on a time-line or in a pie chart that is divided into 24 hours	How people spend their time Time as a factor related to seeking services Time for being involved in work activities Time spent looking for food/resources
Causal flow analysis	Participants in a group draw a diagram of what causes certain problems or situations	Community perceptions of causes of infant and maternal mortality Reasons for going on the street (street children) Reasons for migrating for work
Focus group discussions	Participants discuss a topic in a group, facilitated by a researcher with a record taken by a note taker	Identification of community priorities Good for establishing questions for a questionnaire

(Beazley & Ennew, 2006, pp. 194–195)

people's cynicism, fear, and internalization of received notions about research. We are in danger of imposing a new orthodoxy of 'methods' that have worked before and this is one element of Cooke and Kothari (2001) and other authors' (Cleaver, 2001) criticism of participatory methods tyranny of method. Indeed one of the ironic things about participatory research is that there is a plethora of approaches that have fine distinctions between them and yet make claims for distinctiveness. These include Participatory Action Research (PAR), Participatory Leaning and Action (PLA), Participatory Rural and Rapid Appraisal (PRA) and Community Based Participatory Research (CBPR). The literature is also full of reviews of particular, often patented, techniques from Geographical Information Systems to photovoice. These are interesting techniques and are often useful - indeed Nika Balomenou looks at the use of photovoice in Chapter 15. However, as stated, it is concerning when the details of the technique becomes the focus, with naïve assumptions about their transferability to another culture, rather than engaging in the hard process of finding of the particular ways of knowing of a given community.

I recently came across an example of this technique-first approach when I met with a funder about a potential research project. We were looking at those labelled with complex needs – constructions of the complexity in their lives (although we found that the complexity label was a projection from agencies because they did not fit in neatly with their funding streams – they felt their needs were actually quite simple). The funder had heard about a new 'participatory' approach using videos, where people catalogued their lives and could build vlogs that other could interact with, etc. He was excited about this and wanted to fund a participatory research project that used it. I replied that this might be possible, but it would need to come from the participants, or at least be compatible with their natural ways of learning. He did not fund us, instead funding a piece of research that did want to use this new technique. Another time I heard a paper examining the use of 'yarning' (Walker et al., 2014), 'a conversational process that involves the sharing of stories and the development of knowledge that prioritizes indigenous ways of communicating, in that it is culturally prescribed, cooperative, and respectful' (p. 1216). While very interesting, I was somewhat puzzled when the presenter went on to say that we should adapt the technique for use with other communities. For me the point is that each community will have its own cultural equivalent to yarning, if we take the time to unearth it.

The nature of local ways of knowing and eliciting them

In one sense the creating of research tools based on community members' ways of knowing is a matter of applying anthropological and ethnographic approaches, which we call ethnopraxis, towards epistemological as well as empirical concerns. I do not intend to expand on ethnographic techniques in detail here, as most research books have well rounded discussion of their techniques and limitations. Suffice to say that ethnographies tend to focus on describing the culture of a group, or a subgroup, in a very detailed and complex manner. It involves engaging in extensive fieldwork where data collection is mainly by participant observation, formal and informal interviews, exploring the significance of symbols, artifacts and many other sources of data. The researcher looks for patterns of the group's behavior, ideas and beliefs expressed through language or other activities in ethnography; the emphasis is on what is available, what is normal, what people do, what they say, and how they work (Draper, 2015). In our case we should look for patterns in the ways that communities and people know and learn by examining their interactions 'in ordinary settings and discern pervasive patterns such as life cycles, events, and cultural themes' (Hammersley & Atkinson, 2007, pp. 94–95).

Concurrently with participatory research there is an emphasis on reflexivity, 'to explore the ways in which [the] researcher's involvement with a particular study influences, acts upon and informs such research' (Nightingale & Cromby, 1999, p. 228). This is also called the 'anthropological gaze' (Stoller, 1992), whereby one observes a specific human interaction, extracts and widens it into the framework of a social phenomenon, while simultaneously abstracting oneself from the process. It is not therefore surprising that one of the major criticisms of ethnographic approaches is that this is not achievable, particularly as an individual (Stoller, 1992), and why we suggest that this reflexivity is done collectively as part of the research process.

Also, as many ethnographic authors note (Geertz, 1973; Gluckman, 1961), ethnography takes time, and one of the criticisms and realisms of participatory approaches is that they do not build in the time that is needed to find out local ways of knowing (Smith, 1999). This is one of the arguments for involving peers. One example, detailed quite extensively earlier, but worth repeating, is in the building of trust, for without some degree of trust one will never be able to get past the distrust and cynicism Smith (1999) describes, and start to elicit and utilize meaningful ways of knowing.

Many toolkits and guides (e.g. Petty et al., 1995) give trust-building and group-building exercises and, while useful, they are undoubtedly conceptually euro-centric (Smith, 1999). We detailed before how peer researchers can be useful in building 'proxy' trust, but they can also be useful in unearthing conceptions of trust, and in identifying who the gatekeeper for such trust might be. For example, in the Touch research we were working with a group of young people in Bradford. After some interactions with the group I had identified one loud member as a key informant whom the others seemed to turn to. The peer researcher had identified someone quite different. Having had experience of this community, as well as the dynamic of groups involved in illegal activities within this community, the peer researcher saw the louder individual as the lieutenant, and the key gatekeeper was in fact very quiet, but the louder person was deferring to him non-verbally.

The true gatekeeper was also aware that the peer researcher had noted this dynamic and let him know this, again non-verbally. In a cigarette break the true gatekeeper asked what the project was really about and why the peer researcher was involved. The peer researcher explained his understanding of the project, his motivation for involvement and a little of his history. In this way they established a number of mutual acquaintances, which gave the peer researcher some proxy trust. This personal connection was important as without it trust would never have been forthcoming in this cultural milieu.

Depending on the context, there are many different types of peers, and sometimes they can be workers in care organizations or researchers themselves. I have worked in, and been a client of, a number of services. I have also been involved with developing and advocating client voices through a number of NGOs for over 20 years. While I would not make a claim to know *what* clients think, I have sometimes developed a sense of *how* they think. I utilized this in the probation research. I knew that there is often a large gulf between how workers and management think and that clients are quite used to a reassuring spiel that they receive, but rarely believe. Clients were used to being spoken to in a highly codified language by workers.

I was explaining the probation project to a number of the potential researchers, and giving the motivations the management had given me for their involvement –

which were of course all benevolent. I remember one of the group was very cynical and said that he had heard it all before. He asked if I really believed it, because he didn't. I answered that they were making all the right noises, but of course it could all be bullshit, and they were simply doing it to look good, but if we didn't try it would never change, and at least I would guarantee that if it ended up being bullshit I would use what position I had to make sure people knew it. Later on the cynic said that this was the moment when he decided to give it a go. I had shown I was not naive, was prepare to break the normal code and to make myself vulnerable and stand up, if needed – all elements of trust building that I had learnt were a part of the cultural make-up of the criminal justice system.

Co-creating ways of knowing

There is also a danger of simply re-enforcing community practices or ways of knowing if we perceive them as static and somehow immune from received hegemonies. We should not orientalize people's ways of knowing, and as with any critical project, challenge is needed. Again within the Touch research several groups of young people in London and Austria had rapping as a point of commonality and felt that creating rhymes should be their way of expressing how they felt about violence. One of the peer researchers was an experienced producer and worked within them on their rhymes. Initially their work was quite misogynist, sensationalist about violence, focused on postcode disputes. The peer researcher challenged them about whether this was truly reflective of the world they inhabited, and even if they were being derivative, following what commercial Hip-Hop had become. He then introduced them to earlier, more reflective and politically challenging, 'old skool' Hip-Hop, and together they reflected on why and how modern Hip-Hop has taken a very different turn. He ran several workshops getting them to hone and developed their writing skills. As illustrated below the final set of lyrics were consequently very different.

> That's my way, you don't know my life
> depressive times and aggressive tears
> that's my way – this is my life
> these are my tears which rain outside
>   (Magreb 186, 'My Way'/'Mein Weg')

> One for the grinders, demand, suppliers
> One for my riders, one for the lifers
> Nine to fivers, all the skivers
> One for the ones that hate and don't like us
> One for the mums that stand strong
> And older brothers that man up when Dad's gone
> We ain't lying fam, you must've got your facts wrong
> It's real life, more than a rap song
>   (Chasers, 'One For')

It would also seem dangerous to see ways of knowing as monolithic within any one community. In the Escape Plan research, in trying to identify the critical incidents that had led participants out of rough sleeping, the core group suggested wider participants create a timeline of their journeys through homelessness. Procedurally we used an adapted form of the 'Critical Incident Technique' (Flanagan, 1954) used in a major study by Macknee and Mervyn (2002) on the subjects' transitions from homelessness. In the Macknee and Mervyn study (2002) participants were asked to recall specific events that they believed facilitated or hindered them leaving the streets. After a participant had recalled an event that either helped or hindered the transition, the researcher repeated the process by asking him/her to think about other events that helped or hindered the transition. This process was continued until the participant could not recall any other events. Their average length of the interview was 90 minutes.

However, when we piloted this approach we found participants took a variety of nuanced approaches to their timeline. Some people started with the key incidents; others recalled events sequentially. Others thought about the events, and recalled them visually, while others started with their feelings when things went well, and associated these incidents with songs and or other events. Many found the process difficult to get started, and if they took the critical incident approach literally, it produced gaps. People's learning styles seemed to be a factor here, echoing ideas of visual, kinaesthetic and aural learning styles (Bandler & Grinder, 1981, 1988; Bandura, 1977). Piloting also found gender differences. Unless prompted, some people, particularly men, did not talk about people who were significant, only events. It depended on how people conceptualized the term 'significant events'. With this in mind we developed different versions of a script to use with people.

People are also multi-layered and we should not take the context and culture that we encounter them within as necessarily definitive. People sometimes need permission to go beyond these contexts and reveal other aspects of themselves, or to make the connection with this as a form of research. I worked with a group of young people to develop and research their interests and then present this to a group of local government councillors. We had originally met this group of young people on the street playing football and had used the medium of sport to engage them and then conduct the research. We held sports and team activities, with discussions and explorations of their lives, and arising needs, in between sessions. They decided that they wanted sports facilities, complemented by youth work to help them developmentally. We went to an event to present their perspectives to the local councillors. This was held in the local town hall. We arrived early, and were waiting in the main hall which had a stage at the end of it. The group spontaneously went behind the stage, drew the curtains, and after a few minutes came out and did an impromptu play. We remarked in surprise that we did not realize this was one of their talents or interests. They replied that we had never asked, and only seemed to want to talk about sports.

I learnt from this that building in exercises and discussion from the outset to illustrate the potential breadth of research is one way of developing a wider, more expansive culture around research. In the probation research we asked people to draw a picture of an animal and/or a form of transport that represented their relationship with probation. Everyone did this, although some responded to it with more enthusiasm than others. Those who had taken to it said they went into far more depth than they would have with words. We logged their artistic and creative ability as something they had skills in, and that they could develop more visual research techniques to use with others later. An exercise with a similar theme asked them to relate a good and bad experience of probation, another to list down all the good and bad points about probation. There two exercises revealed those that were more kinaesthetic or verbal, respectively, in their thinking, and that they had skills in this that we could also utilize.

This shows that sometimes permission comes from having a selection of activities to choose from, especially when creativity is required, and then allowing people to choose, something Richard Campbell will explore in greater detail in Chapter 13. It can be hard to start with a blank canvas, but even a little input can give people permission to take ideas further. I remember asking a group of masters' students to explore how they came to be at university, and what had been significant about their journey to date. They were given mapping, storytelling, drama, song, 'found objects' or something else (whereby they used, and asked other to use, objects that could be found in the university to express their journeys). The 'found object' group found a globe and invited people to identify their home, and then where they were in their university journey in relation to that. A young woman of African descent, who had apparently never spoken before, instantly broke into song, and then talked about her homesickness contrasted with her desire to study, and feeling of freedom and loneliness inherent in this. Another group did body sculpts (not on the list, but something of common interest to two in the group), and invited the group to translate and interpret the different sculpts that they did of their journeys, in turn prompting other to talk about their journeys.

However, as I have talked about elsewhere, some communities (Seal, 2005, 2006), particularly those who are marginalized, may not see their ways of learning as 'legitimate', or simply see their ways of knowing as just surviving, and not as having transferability. Rancière (2007) says that the facilitator's role is again one of working with people's will and self-belief, and helping them to become critical:

Human animals are distant animals who communicate through the forest of signs. The distance the ignoramus has to cover is not the gulf between her ignorance and the schoolmaster's knowledge. It is simply the path from which she already knows to what she does not yet know, but which she can learn just as she has learnt the rest; which she can learn not in order to occupy the position of the scholar, but so as better to practice the art of translating, of putting her experience into words and her words to the test; of translating her intellectual adventures for others and counter-translating the translations of their own adventures which they present to her.

(Rancière, 2007, p. 98)

One way of creating this epistemological and psychological gap is to expand the aforementioned skills inventory. I asked a group of ex-drug users how they found out the right information to get what drugs they needed when they moved to a new city. They described highly elaborate, but highly efficient, methods of networking, negotiating, working out other people's needs, who was gatekeeper of the inform-ation, and ways of accessing resources and people. There was a highly codified way of working out the accuracy of information, and of ascertaining what the cost of good information would be. These transaction and networking skills and approaches were highly transferable. They were very highly useful in gaining access to participants, and of verifying the accuracy of information. They were also incorporated into the research tools themselves, with the use of informal interviews, focused group discussion and information sharing that built on how knowledge was naturally shared and built within the communities.

I worked with another group of people with histories of accessing mental health services exploring the levels of complexity in their lives (complex needs being a label that had been attached to the group, when in fact we found, as stated before, that the complexity lay in the systems that were not designed to respond to their needs). We explored participants' lived lives and strategies for survival in the mental health system, cataloguing how information was found out and the skills they had developed in doing this. We found that they had developed highly sophisticated participant observation skills from observing psychiatrists, doctors and nursing staff, and other clients, in order to assess the volatility of the ward, and how to get the most out of their interactions with staff, particularly those who were diagnosing them. When examining the levels of complexity within people's lives, the subject under study, we used these skills of observation, self-observation and mapping complex systems to use as a research method. As a theoretical framework symbolic interactionism was readily understood and had resonance with the group, and so became the basis for our analysis.

In another project we found that those with experience of the criminal justice system were very used to interviewing, and being interviewed. Their observational skills were also highly attuned, as were their group skills, from both engaging in the many therapy groups they had been expected to engage with over the years, and for surviving, assessing, and getting what they needed on prison wings. The research group made highly skilled group workers, focus group facilitators and interviewers. They were particularly good at conducting unstructured interviews and could hold in their heads the schemas of information they were looking for, while at the same time asking open questions and gently steering people back to their agenda if they went off topic. In the research we made extensive use of the waiting room as an interview space. Clients were used to spending long periods of time and it was a place where ideas were discussed, away from the direct gaze of the probation service. Private rooms, in contrast, were not safe spaces but spaces associated with being interrogated. Public cafes were another good source of information and clients and interviewers were highly skilled in only revealing what they wanted to in such interviews, taking away the need for traditional 'confidential' spaces.

Many young people I have worked with have often been adept at the uses of the internet and other digital sources as ways finding out and passing on information, making short shrift of literature and policy reviews and quick to create, and assess, shared knowledge through wikis. They also use social media as ways of knowing and creating knowledge, from creating and sharing encoded information about events and their views of them to creating profiles, through collating demographic information about people, things and phenomena of interest to them. We worked with a group of young people who developed an app which allowed them to blog, catalogue and rate their interactions with the police directly after it happened, and their phones allowed us to trace their exact geographical location and time. On another project we worked with young people to create films on their cameras, and make use of selfies creatively in building profiles and gaining access to potential research subjects. Once they had the knowledge, they wanted, indeed took, the freedom to create films in the way that made sense to them. The only boundary set for them was a requirement to demonstrate how these films were genuine and authentic, and did not big up problems or try to portray themselves in a particular light – the young people agreed to these parameters, and gave excellent accounts as to why the data they had gathered was reliable. We will come back to this process in the next chapter, as such accounts became a way of validating data.

Conclusion: valuing existing ethnopraxis

Some readers might be disappointed that this chapter does not give a series of tools and techniques that can be used in participatory research. This is because that would be the wrong place to start. We need to take the time to find out from participants their ways of knowing and being, and build our research framework from there. Positively the work is already happening. Community members, and those who have worked with them, and advocated for them, have often had to collect data for years to sustain the meagre resources they are given. In the Touch project (Chapter 13) we worked with youth and community workers who had worked within communities, sometimes for up to 30 years, and knew their lives and ways of knowing and being intimately. What we need to do is to help community member and community workers realize the depth of knowledge they have and that it is, indeed, research. Occasionally it might need to be framed differently, honed and accounted for, but the work has often been done and normally quite rigorously. Linda Smith (1999) realized this, seeing one of the first tasks as enabling workers to realize that they are already ethno-practitioners developing ethno-praxis.

> They search and record, they select and interpret, they organize and re-present, they make claims on the basis of what they assemble. This is research. The processes they use can also be called methodologies. The specific tools they use to gain information can also be called methods. Everything they are trying to do is informed by a theory, regardless of whether they can talk about that theory explicitly.
>
> (Smith, 1999, p. 17)

Once we have this knowledge, and have a group of researchers who, by default, are versed and skilled in unearthing this knowledge, we will create something remarkable. The remarkable also resides not in the exotic, but in the ordinary, the everyday, and in taking this ordinariness from the mundane to something rich and powerful with its roots in how people understand things and create their own knowledge. This may well mean we use techniques that are different, inversions of traditional approaches. It also may mean that we use things that are quite traditional. In the probation project one of the groups used very traditional interviews, questionnaires and focus groups, but this is what stemmed from their ways of knowing things – it was how we got there that is important.

References

Bandler, R. & Grinder, J. (1988) *Frogs Into Princes: Neuro Linguistic Programming.* Santa Cruz, CA: NLP Comprehensive.

Bandler, R. & Grinder, J. (1981) *Reframing: Neuro-Linguistic Programming and the Transformation of Meaning.* Santa Cruz, CA: NLP Comprehensive.

Bandura, A. (1977) *Social Learning Theory.* Englewood Cliffs, NJ: Prentice Hall.

Beazley, H. & Ennew, J. (2006) 'Participatory methods and approaches: tackling the two tyrannies.' In V. Desai & R. B. Potter (eds) *Doing Development Research.* London: Sage Publications, pp. 189–199.

Chambers, R. (2010) *Provocations for Development.* Rugby: Practical Action Publishing.

Chambers, R. (2008) *Revolutions in Development Inquiry.* London: Earthscan.

Cleaver, F. (2001) 'Institutions, agency and the limitations of participatory approaches to development.' In B. Cooke & U. Kothari (eds) *Participation: The New Tyranny?* London: Zed Books, pp. 139–152.

Cooke, B. & Kothari, U. (2001) (eds) *Participation: The New Tyranny?* London: Zed.

Danieli, A. & Woodhams, C. (2005) 'Emancipatory research methodology and disability: a critique.' *International Journal of Social Research Methodology,* 8: 281–296.

Draper, J. (2015) 'Ethnography: principles, practice and potential.' *Nursing Standard,* 29(36): 36–41.

Geertz, C. (1973) *The Interpretation of Cultures.* New York: Basic Books.

Gluckman, M. (1961) 'Ethnographic data in British social anthropology.' *The Sociological Review,* 9(1): 5–17.

Hammersley, M. & Atkinson, P. (2007) *Ethnography: Principles in Practice.* 3rd edition. London: Routledge.

Lynch, K. (2000) 'The role of emancipatory research in the academy.' In A. Byrne & L. Lentin (eds) *(Re)searching Women: Feminist Research Methodologies in the Social Sciences in Ireland.* Dublin: Institute of Public Administration, pp. 73–104.

McDonagh, R. (2000) 'Talking back.' In A. Byrne & L. Lentin (eds) *(Re)searching Women: Feminist Research Methodologies in the Social Sciences in Ireland.* Dublin: Institute of Public Administration, pp. 237–246.

MacKnee, C. M. & Mervyn, J. (2002) 'Critical incidents that facilitate homeless people's transition off the streets.' *Journal of Social Distress and the Homeless,* 11: 293–306.

Nightingale, D. J. & Cromby, J. (1999) *Social Constructionist Psychology: A Critical Analysis of Theory and Practice.* Philadelphia, PA: Open University Press.

Pain, R. & Francis, P. (2003) 'Reflections on participatory research.' *Area,* 35, 46–54.

Petty, J., Guijt, I., Scoones, I. & Whompson, J. (1995) *Participatory Learning and Action: A Trainer's Guide*. London: International Institute for Economic Development.

Rancière, J. (2007) *The Emancipated Spectator*. London and Paris: Verso.

Seal, M. (2009) *Not About Us Without Us: Client Involvement In Social Housing*. Lyme Regis: Russell House Publishing.

Seal, M. (2007) *Working in the Homeless Sector: Worker Perspectives*. London: YMCA George Williams College Occasional Paper.

Seal, M. (2006) *Working With Homeless People: A Training Manual*. Lyme Regis: Russell House Publishing.

Seal, M. (2005) *Resettling Homeless People: Theory and Practice*. Lyme Regis: Russell House Publishing.

Smith, L. (1999) *Decolonising Methodologies: Research and Indigenous Peoples*. London: Zed Books.

Stoller, P. (1982) 'Relativity and the anthropologist's gaze.' *Anthropology and Humanism Quarterly*, 7: 2–10.

Terry, L. & Cardwell, V. (2016) *Refreshing Perspectives: Exploring the Application of Peer Research With Populations Facing Severe and Multiple Disadvantage*. London: Revolving Doors Agency.

Walker, M., Fredericks, B., Mills, K. & Anderson, D. (2014) '"Yarning" as a method for community-based health research with indigenous women: The Indigenous Women's Wellness Research Program.' *Health Care for Women International*, 35(10): 1216–1226.

9 Analysis and making recommendations

Grounding your data in community ways of knowing

The involvement of community members in analysis and the creation of themes is less covered in the literature than methods, ethics and principles of research (Byrne et al., 2009; Gillet-Swan & Sargeant, 2017; Holland et al., 2008; Nind, 2011). All too often it is at the point of analysis where research stops being participative, and certainly pedagogic, as Campbell explores within my own research in Chapter 13. Here we explore this dilemma and seek to find ways to keep participation meaningful. The method of analysing of PPIR also seeks to find a way between a pre-imposed thematic approach and a purely grounded approach that is in danger or orientalizing and de-contextualizing the researched. Methods of triangulation and grounding the data in the wider community are sought and explored.

Introduction

Why community members are missed out at the point of analysis is not clear. Some say that community members from particular communities are deemed as not being able to take part for reasons of age and implied limited capability (Byrne et al., 2009; Nind, 2011) through disability and cognitive functioning (Gillet-Swan & Sargeant, 2017), something most of the authors in the literature dispute. As Kellett et al. (2004) say, the barrier to empowering children as researchers is not their lack of adult status or supposed cognitive abilities, it is their lack of training in the area –'so why not teach them?' (Kellett et al., 2004, p. 332). Behind this is the idea that it is simply a matter of time, taking the time to train people properly.

Holland et al. (2008) did not train people in data analysis because they felt it would interfere with ways in which young people organically made sense of data. They found in the young people's culture a resistance to sustained and formalized engagement, of the kind they thought was necessary for thematic analysis. Instead they developed what they called 'analysis as process', whereby they had informal discussions with young people as to their views of themes the researchers saw emerging, and then 'analysis as a discrete activity', where they delved down into certain aspects of the data, and trained the young people in the data analysis techniques that were needed for that particular aspect.

Holland et al. (2008) recognized that as professional researchers in the research, they were filtering young people's perceptions. Later on in their article they recognize that, on reflection, some of this was about researchers not being able to let go of their expert status, and they continued to privilege their knowledge about data analysis. Petty et al. (1995) also list a number of exercises aimed at developing community members' analytical skills, from being able to code, to spotting patterns and distinguishing between rumour, fact and opinion, improving observational skills and discerning power relationships in the research process, including one's own bias and prejudices. While these activities are certainly participative in nature, I am not convinced that they unearth and build upon the organic ways the people make sense of data. Community members observe, draw out themes and discern bias and power relationships, we need these to be our starting points.

Thomas and O'Kane (1998), also working with young people, felt the key was to make data analysis physical, pictorial and 'fun', in keeping with the non-verbal approach of much participatory research (Chambers, 2010; Petty et al., 1995). I find the term 'fun' slightly patronizing, people want more than entertainment. Another way of looking at the concept behind the term 'fun', is that it has resonance with the community's natural ways of communicating, expressing themselves and making sense of the world. Alinsky put this as the rule that anything the 'drags on too long becomes a drag' (Alinsky, 1971, p. 85), and, as noted before, that, where possible, we should not go outside of the community's experience. Elsewhere (Seal & Frost, 2014) I have deconstructed the young people's expression of something being boring, which is not the desire for entertainment that adults often construct it as – it is that what is happening does not have resonance with them, and/or that the approach seems to be adultist. At the same time, we should not try and second-guess what the community's approach would be.

Again, an ethnographic approach can have macro, meso and a micro dimension. I worked with a group of rough sleeping homeless people to explore how they made sense of multiple sources of information, with the overall aim of understanding the dynamics of the rough sleeping community in an area new to them. They talked about having a chat (conducting informal interviews) with people to see who's who (working from the periphery to key informants) to conducting literature reviews (through accessing information through libraries). In terms of analysing the data they would look for themes, be that food access, shelter access, what agencies were useful or not, what the group dynamics were like on the street, etc.

At the same time, they recognized that the way themes manifested would be nuanced, and there may be other new things they needed to take account of. In analysing this they looked for patterns in what people were saying, and when people said the same things, but sometimes from different angles, displaying an organic grounded approach to theory making, as well as being able to thematically analyse. At the same time, they also had a finely honed sense of when someone was blagging or bullshitting, using organic discourse analysis to compare data to their own knowledge of context, speech patterns and use of language that signified authenticity. They could also examine people's syntax to see clichés or patterns that did not fit, anecdotes that did not ring true, empty categories, and took account of exaggeration and downplaying, again drawing on their knowledge of contexts.

Similar patterns emerged within the probation research with regards the criminal justice system, and learning about how the system works, and how to analyse knowledge gained to get the best out of the system. In other research detailed in this book, similar ways of analysing have emerged about the mental health system, the drugs world, both undergrounded and mediated through services, gangs and young people generally. On a meso and micro scale different team members were between them adept at detecting and analysing different data in different ways. In one of the probation teams Beth Coyne talks about in Chapter 12, one member was particularly good at being what we termed 'a bullshit detector', discerning statements that did not resonate, or come across as authentic. Another was very good at seeing pre-ordained themes within the data, picking up on ideas that we had agreed we were looking for. Another again was excellent at picking up new things in the data that we had not anticipated, and spotting patterns that were starting to emerge.

Between and outside of grounded, discourse and thematic data analysis

While there are many ways of conducting qualitative data analysis, one way of breaking it down is to distinguish three broad camps: thematic analysis, grounded theory and discourse analysis (Cohen et al., 2000). When I have discussed different traditional techniques of data analysis, and how they related to their organic ways of making sense of the world, community members often grasped the fundamentals of data analysis quite quickly, and even had many critiques of the approaches. I remember a community member neatly summing up these approaches as: you can have your ideas beforehand and look for things that fit them (thematic analysis), or you can build up from what people are saying (grounded), or you try and look behind what they are saying, and see where things aren't adding up (discourse analysis).

The same member was also very good at critiquing these approaches. On thematic analysis he said 'Isn't that just looking for things you want to find? Doesn't that mean you ignore what does not fit?' He critiqued a grounded approach for orientalizing what participants say: 'Why would you take what the person as saying as gospel, particularly when half the time they are just saying what they think in that moment.' He also questioned the groundedness of grounded theory – 'You still interpret, just later on' – referring to the axial coding stage where connections are made in the data. Discourse analysis he liked, but again asked 'Who are you (or is anyone), to interpret what some ain't saying – sometimes I pause 'cos the question doesn't make sense, and at other times it is not 'cos what I am saying doesn't add up, it's that I don't want to say what I really think to you.' This community member was extremely cynical about research and researchers, and he had encountered many. He was particularly disdainful towards those who thought they had gained access to his 'life world'. We noted in Chapter 8 Linda Smith's observation that many communities have a deeply ingrained cynicism towards research:

The term 'research' is inextricably linked to European imperialism and colonialism. The word itself, 'research', is probably one of the dirtiest words in the indigenous world's vocabulary. When mentioned in many indigenous contexts, it stirs up silence, it conjures up bad memories, it raises a smile that is knowing and distrustful.

(Smith, 1999, p. 1)

In the research in this book many community researchers gave accounts of 'playing' with the researchers they had previously encountered, sometimes giving accounts that were deliberately sensational, and/or played into what the researcher wanted to hear, and sometimes (and sometimes with the same researcher later) giving contradictory accounts, or deliberately mundane accounts and enjoying the frisson from seeing the researcher then getting disappointed or confused. When asked why they had done this, it was explicitly about power. They wanted to preserve the small amount of privacy they had, in a context when they were often heavily scrutinized. They did not want to give researchers, or anyone else, insight into what was really going on in their lives. Others wanted to gain power in the research process: denied power of *how* data was to be interpreted, they took the power back in *what* data was given away, and the portrayals that could then be drawn from these accounts.

Other community members described it as simply not being in their interests to let researchers know about their lives. I remember one of the Touch researchers was listening to a conference presentation denying the extent of gang and criminal activities going on in a certain city. The speaker cited speaking to one group of young people who said their activities were minor, and referred the research to another group who were involved in the real crime. When approached this group said their activities had similarly been exaggerated, and that it was another group who were really involved in criminal activity. This carried on through several groups, and the speak had concluded that there was no real activity going on. The peer researcher questioned this asking, 'And why would the young people want to tell you their business?'

One way phenomenologists have described to ameliorate this is by ascertaining what motivation people have for getting involved in research, citing community members' motivations as representation, political empowerment and informing change (Clarke, 2010), a desire to have their tales told, or their voices heard (Cohen et al., 2010). However, one community recognized that, for them, giving such a motivation to a researcher, whether asked or not, had been a way of them getting the researcher to believe their tale even more, and this was a ploy they had utilized on a number of occasions.

Equally poignantly, the peer researcher recognized the lack of accountability in more traditional research approaches, 'so who's interpreting those who do the interpreting?' When countered with descriptions of reflexivity he countered again saying that without client insight this was self-referential at best, and self-justification at worst. In recognizing the power dynamics of this, he explained that he had been in front of many judges and psychiatrists who had made judgements about what he was 'really' saying and thinking, assuming massive amounts about him, not knowing a whole lot of other things, and filtering it through their own understanding of the world – with no accountability and or come back.

Developing new paradigms?

I recognize that, so far, this is still seeing data analysis as filtered through traditional research paradigms. In many ways this is because community members' approaches often mirrored traditional approaches in their concerns, but were discernibly different in flavour in their approaches. While there is a danger of re-inscribing traditional approaches, there are also dangers in thinking we will find seeking to discover or uncover 'new' and 'exciting' paradigms. To seek the exotic can be to orientalize community members and their ways of knowing. However, while not necessarily 'new' or 'exciting', community members' organic ways of analysing data certainly gave us insight into certain aspects of data analysis, which did constitute an epistemological break. In all of the research described in the final section of the book, community members sought to find a more nuanced way through the data that displayed a different, more expansive collective interpretation of how data was to be made sense of.

Community members also recognized the limitations of seeing traditional data analysis approaches as separable and mutually exclusive, echoing feminist (Oakley, 1989) and post-positivist concerns (Archer, 2010, 2012). There was a desire not to impose professional researchers' or community members', preconceived ideas through a purely thematic approach, or to orientalize and over-privilege decontextualized individual interviewees' accounts through purely grounded analysis. Similarly, community members were keen that participatory research teams did not take a discourse analysis approach, interpreting the things people don't say and their inconsistencies, without interviewees' involvement, and again that any such analysis should be through the community members' cultural reference points. Community members see merit is all these approaches and thought that they could, and should, be combined in a more reflective model. What emerged was a model that sought to site data analysis beyond the research team, and even beyond being located solely in research interviewees' utterings.

One area of contribution that community members made to data analysis was around verifiability and triangulation. Community members elucidated an approach that foregrounded data analysis and the verification of its validity within wider community understandings. We called this approach 'grounding the data in the community'. The projects made a contribution through both the methods used, and interpretation afterwards. With the escape plan participants, as part of building up the picture of how individuals escaped entrenched rough sleeping, we spoke to two other individuals who might have insight into each person's life. This was in recognition that there would be multiple perspectives on that person's life. Where possible a worker's perspective and someone more personal, a worker, or perhaps a friend's perspective, was sought. These perspectives were then fed back to the individual, who reflected upon them. Sometimes there was a dialogue of interpretation of events, worker or friend giving insight into how the person presented, or things they had forgotten, and the interviewee feeding back other insights into their thinking at the time or other things that were going on for them.

After themes and analysis had been done, verification workshops were held with all parties, to see if the findings had resonance across the community. The intent of these were not to reject any themes, but to add nuance and perspectives that, again, the person may not have considered, and to give the individual chance to see their perspective in a new light and reflect further upon it. The intent here was not to achieve any kind of objectivity, such as taking an objective hermeneutic approach (Oevermann, 2002), but for the individual to achieve the 'best' subjective perspective possible. Verification took place in order to increase community members own, and others understanding, of the phenomenon, so that it would have resonance with the community's cultural context and ways of knowing. These verification processes were, at times, difficult, as people had to face their own contradictions and inconsistencies. I conducted a focus group within the escape plan that aimed at developing criteria for what constitutes having moved on from homelessness and rough sleeping. One community member realized that he had not, and was still hanging onto a number of issues – the group helped him to recognize this and start to move on from it.

In other pieces of participatory research, the group, when presenting themes, had to give an account of their reasoning and where the data had come from and their interpretations to a wider community and stakeholders, including other workers and homeless people who had not previously been involved. The verifications focus groups questioned them and offered different analyses, which at times, led to very different interpretations of data and events, and/or different recommendations. I will give an example of a changed interpretation. In a piece of research on client perspectives on mental health services, one participant said that she had been inconsistent in her interpretations and narratives of events, and this was a sign of her deteriorated mental state at the time. Through interaction with the focus group she changed her perspective on herself, seeing this as understandable behaviour in response to inconsistent service expectations, and that she was changing her behaviour to survive in the systems she was subject to. She recognized that she had internalized the narratives agencies had been giving her about her behaviour. She did this through hearing alternative agency accounts, and other client testimonies, within the verification focus groups.

To give an example of a changed recommendation (something we will come back to), a recommendation from a piece of research into client participation in a homeless service was for training service users in engaging with the management committee's processes as the service users did not feel fully equipped to do so. After the verification group the recommendation was changed. Instead it was recommended that the management committee should examine and change them, both to take in client perspectives and also because the processes of decision-making did not work for anyone on the committee (this perspective having come from a management committee member on the verification panel). The emphasis had shifted from an expectation to change within the client to one of change in the management processes.

I have found participants equally able to grasp the idea of building themes that have resonance across data and the usefulness of significant, illustrative, but isolated, cases. One community member in the probation research compared analysing data to aspects of the criminal justice system, where individual cases could create precedent and be illustrative of, and have relevance to, other cases. However, this was balanced against the weight of evidence in a particular direction, i.e. the more data that spoke to a particular theme the more that theme would hold sway. Within that same research community members elected to adopt particular interviewees as their 'mates', in that they would argue for the significant of particular things that interviewees said. At the same time, they agreed that they also had to find ideas and themes that went across the interviews. The tension and energy that emerged from the debates led to an enriching of the data.

From themes to recommendations

One of the tensions I have tried to be mindful of in much of the research I have been involved in is to ask ourselves whether we have got the right balance between remaining within the realms of the possible while simultaneously pushing those in power to make real changes. This tension is foregrounded when choosing which issues to investigate, but comes into even sharper focus when it comes to making recommendations. Indeed, current trends in research, particularly phenomenological research (Groenewald, 2004; Hycner, 1999), reject making recommendations, saying that their data is not generalizable. Other phenomenologists (Tucker, 2010) believe that researchers should present the data without offering either analysis or recommendation, saying that this is something the reader should do. However, for participatory research, the point of research is to change the world, not just to interpret it, and certainly not only to represent it.

For me, then, recommendations have to ride this tension, to enact and enable change, but always to push those in power and redress the balance slightly towards those with less power. In formulating recommendations, it is therefore important to consult widely about what the research is showing, and also about what is realistic in terms of what can be asked for. Using Alinskian terms, in identifying issues to investigate, you need to find common interest and make the issues winnable, immediate and concrete. The same principles apply to choosing recommendations. However, a little more depth is required in this process, and also with the criteria for the product – i.e. the actual recommendations.

Two of Alinsky's rules seem particularly pertinent here. The first is *Pick the target, freeze it, personalize it and polarize it.* This might sound ethically dubious, but a more neutral way of expressing it would be to make what you are asking for targeted at a person, or group of stakeholders, and that you ask them to do something concrete, and something within their power to do, although it might be a push for them. The recommendation should also be quite clear about what needs to change and who needs to change it, even if there is an expectation on both sides, the responsibility falls to a person. For example, in many of the micro levels of research I have been involved in there is often a desire for a generalized recommendation about 'improving communication'. This is the kind of recommendation is meaningful in that everyone can agree and it speaks to people's mutual self-interests, but is meaningless in that it does not put the responsibility onto anyone, and can conceal more difficult truths. In this case I have seen recommendations about communication concealing deeper feelings of isolation, disrespect or bullying that people are uncomfortable with because they are harder to deal with. If a recommendation buries rather than illuminates the true root of the issues under consideration, then the hidden need to be named.

In the probation research some of the workers seemed to be sabotaging the interview process. It had been agreed that referrals for the interviews would come via workers – i.e. the worker would ask the client at the end of a session whether they wanted to be interviewed by the research team. However, it became evident that this was not happening because referrals were not coming through. Some of the peer researchers also heard from other clients they knew that they had not been told about the project in their session with probation worker. While some may have just not taken notice, it was more endemic than that. Some of the researchers took direct action and started interviewing people in the waiting room, although the workers and receptionists then said that other clients had complained about this (though no evidence was forthcoming). We took this to the management group and a compromise was reached.

In the report we alluded back to these processes and said that this was beyond disrespect and showed a wider malaise in the culture of respect between clients, workers and management. We also polarized the possible consequence if this had been allowed to carry on. We named management as having a responsibility to develop training and support for staff (as stated before some of the sabotage came from staff resentment that they were not being listened to, or were being scapegoated), that as well as client, staff should be consulted on decisions, and that a contract should be developed between all three stakeholders about their working cultures, and that if this was breached, by any party, there should be disciplinary consequences. In other research we have asked named people to do things, such as asking the CEO to write a letter, or to convene a meeting about something. In another we said that to aid communication each management committee member should adopt a project and commit to getting to know it, to visiting it and talking to workers and clients a number of times a year – and commit to advocating for it in management meetings.

In doing this we also adhered to another Alinskian rule, that *the price of a constructive attack is in the providing of a viable alternative* (Alinsky, 1971, p. 56). While obvious in one sense, the principle also applies to a positive suggestion – i.e. that we need to name what we think will improve communication, and who has responsibility for it. Another principle, rather than a rule, about research recommendations is those who will be expected to take responsibility for them, have to know about them through the process of negotiating the recommendations – there should not be a surprise when published or launched. If possible if you can get policy makers and those with power to agree to them beforehand and make a commitment to them on the day of the launch, then all the better. Just before the launch I normally give the CEO a list of all the final recommendations, the thrust of which should already be known, and ask if there is one of them they can commit to on the day.

Another aspect of a successful recommendation is how it is sold to the decision makers. I have talked previously (Seal, 2006, 2009) about how the best arguments are economic (*this will save you money*), then political (*this may cost a little, but it will look really good*) and the worst arguments are moral (*this is the right thing to do*). Horribly cynical, I know, and I am not saying that policy makers are immoral, but their responsibilities are often primarily about making sure they stick within budgets, often being in control of the public purse. At the same time, they are expected to be moral, and this is a hard thing for anyone to manage. It goes back again to self-interest.

Recently I have been involved in some research locally about the living wage. One of the most powerful aspects of the living wage is that paying it to people tends to increase motivation, and therefore productivity or workers, and reduces absenteeism and turnover of staff – these things all cost. We made calculations about this, and found that paying the living wage saves money for the majority of businesses. We played to the self-interests of the businesses community. We may also have portrayed it in moral terms, and in a genuine sense, but behind the morality there was also a sound economic argument. Similarly, to make political gain and to look good is something we all want and need in public life. The reason I ask the aforementioned CEO to publically agree to one of the recommendations is because it looks good, it shows willing and is symbolic of their intentions – all of which is true; they know that to say 'I will take it back and think about it' does not sit well with people. Given the opportunity, people tend to do the right thing; as Ed Chambers says (Chambers, with Cowen, 2004, p. 21), it is in their self-interest.

I have been involved in several other examples. To promote the recommendation of the setting up of resettlement services for homeless people to support them once they had made a move out of a hostel into council accommodation, we calculated the cost of a flat being abandoned, and how often this happened with those not supported – and asked for less for the service. I have similarly argued for doctor registration schemes for homeless people and refugees on the basis that it costs four times as much to get the same service through Accident and Emergency, which is what clients used as a service of last resort. In a piece of work on homeless street drinking I argued for an arrest referral scheme to hostels. This was on the basis that it cost ten times as much to keep someone in the cells for the night, which was current practice, than to take them to a hostel. It was also a waste of police time.

Occasionally people need to be pushed a little to see this. Looking back to the voting campaign mentioned in Chapter 6, where a group of homeless people were being thrown out of B&B accommodation that they had lived in for years . . . when those in power did not respond we started a voting campaign and published the small majorities of local councillors – there were 2,000 people being effected. As said, this was an example of the application of another of Alinsky's rules, that the threat is usually more terrifying than the threat itself. In reality many homeless people would not vote, and may vote for those already in power; however, it served as a reminder that politicians are meant to represent all sections of the community. Interesting in this case the group went on to request that they held a 2-hour protest/ awareness raising event in the main square which the B&Bs where they were being decanted from overlooked. At the last minute the council withdrew permission because they said it would be embarrassing. The group of activists went ahead anyway, and stayed there until they were evicted four days later amidst far more publicity – sometimes the reality is greater than the threat.

Conclusion

Perhaps one of the most important things to ask for in the recommendations (Chambers with Cowan, 2004) is for an on-going relationship with those in power. I will come back to how to cultivate and develop these relationships in the next chapter. The importance of asking for it in recommendations is, first, to ensure that they are considered and acted upon accountably. Change may well be needed, but 'who decided this and how?' is the crucial question. Otherwise, often intentionally, the research can easily become another report that sits on a shelf. On a wider scale it is about establishing a new kind of relationship with community members (I would also include workers in this, as they are often the neglected stakeholder in terms of decision-making (Seal, 2009). The cultural change that PPIR privileges can be sparked by research, but it needs to be cultivated on an ongoing basis, and this often needs structures as well as will, or else that will can soon dissipate. A similar point can be made about dissemination, and this is what we will explore in the next chapter.

References

Alinsky, S. (1971) *Rules for Radicals: A Pragmatic Primer for Realistic Radicals*. New York: Vintage Books.

Archer, M. S. (2012) *The Reflexive Imperative in Late Modernity*. Cambridge: Cambridge University Press.

Archer, M. S. (2010) *Conversations About Reflexivity*. London and New York: Routledge.

Byrne, A., Canavan, J. & Millar, M. (2009) 'Participatory research and the voice-centred relational method of data analysis: is it worth it?' *International Journal of Social Research Methodology*, 12(1): 67–77.

Cohen, L., Manion, L. & Morrison, K. (2000) *Research Methods in Education*. London: Falmer-Routledge.

Chambers, E. with Cowan, M. (2004) *Roots for Radicals: Organizing for Power, Action and Justice*. New York: Continuum.

Chambers, R. (2010) *Provocations for Development*. Rugby: Practical Action Publishing.

Clarke, T. (2010) 'On "being researched": why do people engage with qualitative research?' *Qualitative Research*, 10(4): 399–419.

Gillett-Swan, J. K. & Sargeant, J. (2017) 'Unintentional power plays: interpersonal contextual impacts in child-centred participatory research.' *Educational Research*, 1: 1–16.

Groenewald, T. (2004) 'A phenomenological research design illustrated.' *International Journal of Qualitative Methods*. Available at: https://doi.org/10.1177/160940690400 300104 [accessed 15 February 2018].

Holland, S., Renold, E., Ross, N. & Hillman, A. (2008) *Rights, 'Right On' Or the Right Thing to Do? A Critical Exploration of Young People's Engagement in Participative Social Work Research*. NCRM Working Paper Series 07/08.

Hycner, R. H. (1999) 'Some guidelines for the phenomenological analysis of interview data.' In A. Bryman & R. G. Burgess (eds) *Qualitative Research* (vol. 3). London: Sage, pp. 143–164.

Kellett, M., Forrest, R., Dent, N. & Ward, S. (2004) 'Just teach us the skills please, we'll do the rest: empowering ten-year-olds as active researchers.' *Children and Society*, 18(5): 329–343.

Nind, M. (2011) 'Participatory data analysis: a step too far.' *Qualitative Research*, 11(4): 349–363.

Oakley, A. (1981) 'Interviewing women: a contradiction in terms.' In H. Roberts (ed.) *Doing Feminist Research*. London: Routledge and Kegan Paul, 1981, pp. 30–61.

Oakley, A. (1981) 'Interviewing women: a contradiction in terms.' In H. Roberts (ed.) *Doing Feminist Research*. London: Routledge, pp. 30–61.

Oevermann, U. (2002) Klinische Soziologie auf der Basis der Methodologie der objektiven Hermeneutik: *Manifest der objektiv hermeneutischen Sozialforschung*. Senckenberg: Universitätsbibliothek Johann Christian.

Petty, J., Guijt, I., Scoones, I. & Whompson, J. (1995) *Participatory Learning and Action: A Trainer's Guide*. London: International Institute for Economic Development.

Seal, M. (2009) *Not About Me Without Me: Client Involvement In Social Housing*. Lyme Regis: Russell House Publishing.

Seal, M. (2006) *Working With Homeless People: A Training Manual*. Lyme Regis: Russell House Publishing.

Seal, M. & Frost, S. (2014) *Philosophy in Youth and Community Work*. Lyme Regis: Russell House Publishing.

Smith, L. (1999) *Decolonising Methodologies: Research and Indigenous Peoples*. London: Zed Books.

Thomas, N. & O'Kane, C. (1998) 'The ethics of participatory research with Children.' *Children and Society*, 12: 336–348.

Tucker, S. (2010) 'Listening and believing: an examination of young people's perceptions of why they are not believed when they report abuse and neglect.' *Children and Society*, 25(6): 458–469.

10 Dissemination and impact
Accounting for and privileging process

As we have noted at several points in this book, a major criticism of participatory research is that its actual impact is minimal. Consequently, many authors have recently emphasized the importance of impact for participatory research (Cook et al., 2017, Pain et al., 2015; Reed, 2016), and explored means of achieving and recording it (Wallerstein et al., 2008; Cacari-Stone et al., 2014; Liamputtong, 2014; Ramaswamy & Ozcan, 2014; Greenhalgh et al., 2016). However, as Greenhalgh and Fahy (2015) point out, capturing the 'nonlinear chains and complex inter-dependencies of causation' (Ibid., p. 45) is not simple, and does not fit well into conventional models of capturing impact with predetermined measurement of particular outcomes. They go on to say that a meaningful participatory approach necessitates a focus on processes as well as outcomes.

Linked to impact is how research is disseminated, and who it is disseminated to (Cook, 2012). Chen et al. (2010) note that dissemination beyond an academic audience to community members and the general public is variable, and that myriad challenges to effective dissemination remain. In much of the research I have been involved in, impact has consistently been the aspect that we have given least attention to. Richard Campbell will recount in Chapter 13 how the Touch project ran out of steam and ideas when it came to dissemination and impact. I have vivid memories, towards the end of the project, of sitting in a European round table meeting discussing our findings with a disparate group that seemed more interested in networking with each other and eating the buffet provided.

Once we had ascertained their roles we found few were in a position to enact any of our recommendations, although all promised to try to get them to those who could, which they did not, and we never followed them up on it anyway. Our recommendations were quite long and rambling and either required very detailed knowledge of the processes we were talking about or called for wholesale paradigm shifts in policy agendas which were beyond the power even the highest policy makers – who, of course – were not there. We made promises to take things further, but no concrete plans were made and the mechanisms did not really exist for it, we had certainly run out of money, and our universities were expecting us to return to our day jobs. This demonstrated that the recommendation needed to be realistic and targeted at those who could actually enact change.

Within a piece of research for Groundswell, a certain city council had a memorable reaction to our recommendation not to have central hubs for homeless people. It was made clear that this was unwelcome. We found out subsequently that these were the central pillar of their new homelessness strategy, designed and commissioned before the research started which was not really in the participative spirit. They attacked our sampling, even though they brokered it. At another very expensive dissemination conference I remember having a cigarette outside with the few token homeless people present, who said they weren't going back in. They felt that the event was staged, boring, used language that was either over their heads or patronized them, and that the workshops weren't going anywhere – they felt it was a betrayal of the participatory spirit that the research had been conducted within. Interestingly a number of the commissioners and managers who were attendant at the conference joined us, as they had reached pretty much the same conclusion – all parties then started having what they later described as far more meaningful discussions about the research and what to do with it. Evidently the format for dissemination events needs to be thought of differently. At the end of the chapter I will explore how community organizing structures events to create maximum impact in terms of policy change. Simone Helleren, in Chapter 11, will explore the work of Harrison Owen (1997), who's open space approach is based on what happens in those informal sessions, such as the cigarette break I have just described.

Universities and the politics of Impact

I think we have to consider three dimensions of impact: the impact the research has on the stakeholders within it; the wider impact it has on the world; and the specific meaning 'impact' has within the academic sphere, which particularly in the UK, is very nuanced. As academia is still the place where much research is conducted, I will explore this first.

> Co-produced research may throw up impacts iteratively, on different time-frames, at different scales, and of a more or less tangible nature. The issue of demonstrating these impacts presents challenges. The quantitative measures and predictable pathways and mechanisms that are commonly used at present are unlikely to reveal more than a partial picture of impact. This is a key concern for a range of organisations who use co-production in research or in other activities – e.g. the creative sector, charities, service providers, community development and youth workers - as well as for Universities and their funders.
>
> (Pain et al., 2015, p. 3)

'Impact' looms large in the Research Excellence Framework (REF), the government mechanism for working out who gets governmental research funding in British universities. The REF is an interesting process in that it is supposedly one of peer assessment. Panels of academics and others consider the quality of research submissions from colleagues at other universities. Submissions are assessed as between one to four stars, with four stars being quality that is 'world-leading in originality, significance and rigour'; three star is world leading, but falls short of the highest standards of excellence, two star is research recognized internationally and one star nationally. Criticisms of the REF are numerous (Sayer, 2014). Critics say that it is biased towards, and consequently concentrates funding within, elite universities (Sayer, 2014).

Others (Watermeyer & Hedgecoe, 2016) say that the REF is methodologically conservative and biased against more innovative research such as participatory research, and that it judges quality narrowly in that, despite its protestations, it still sees research published in conventional academic journals as the gold standard. In addition, universities have their own internal processes for filtering out which research to submit. This adds another level of conservatism in that universities do not want to 'risk' their REF submission with research that might be controversial in findings or approach (Watermeyer & Hedgecoe, 2016). I have heard panel members within my own area talk about the importance of quality, rather than where the research is published, yet many university committee gatekeepers will only allow submissions through from certain academic journals (Kings, 2016; Watermeyer & Adam Hedgecoe, 2016).

Somewhat controversially, as least for the academic community who had previously not been required to have an impact on anything beyond itself, the 2014 REF included a criterion that the research should have 'an effect on, change or benefit to the economy, society, culture, public policy or services, health, the environment or quality of life, beyond academia' (HEFCE, 2012a). Impact accounted for 20% of the 2014 assessment score, the other 80% being the environment within which the research was conducted, and the quality and reach (nationally, internationally and worldwide) of the research itself. Impact in the 2021 REF is increased to 25%.

Cook et al. (2017) conducted a review of the impact case studies and dissemination of participatory research and found participatory research to be marginalized. Pain et al. (2015) similarly noted how traditional funding bodies, including HEFCE and RSUK, well as universities themselves, need to widen their conceptualization of impact to incorporate participatory research. Some of these issues that marginalize participatory research are structural, others methodological and others internalizations of these issues by participatory researchers themselves. Pain et al. (2015) note a central issue that the paradigms within which impact is viewed are not compatible with participatory research:

> [T]he attempt to measure 'impact' as a concrete, visible phenomenon that is fixed in time and space, that one party does to another party . . . whereas deep co-production is a process often involving a gradual, porous and diffuse series of changes undertaken collaboratively.
>
> (Pain et al., 2015, p. 4).

They go on to say that the '"donor-recipient" model of impact, where a single knowledge producer (University/academic) impacts on economy or society in a linear fashion, is not relevant to co-produced research' (Pain et al., 2015, p. 23).

Cook et al. (2017) concur saying that the model used for assessing impact is very much about the impact of the university directly, and the research findings as measured through publication in quality journals, rather than a reflection the impact of the research on all stakeholders, and incremental impact as it goes along. The definition of impact very much comes centrally from the university, and betrays the ethnopraxis approach of building from the definitions of impact held by the research participants. As Cook et al. note: 'The definition of impact by those with embodied knowledge is not given credence in frameworks for reporting (Cook et al., 2017, pp. 481–482).

A compounding factor within this is the REF process itself. Several authors (Chowdry et al., 2016; Kings, 2016; Watermeyer & Hedgecoe, 2016) note a process of cycle of conservatism, similar to that of research outputs, whereby universities are not confident in how they present impact case studies, and so rely upon conventional 'proven' approaches which privilege the robustness of the research output, rather than actual impact, and further rely on more causal, correlatable and positivist approaches to impact assessment. This in turn leads to a conservatism within the panels, sometimes caused by time constraints, whereby instead of engaging with alternative narratives of how impact could be reflected, they rely on what they know and what is obvious. At the same time Watermeyer & Hedgecoe (2016) note that the mechanisms designed to be a counter to this, such as the involvement of user groups as assessors, were tokenistic with unconfident members deferring to academics who often outnumbered them 1–12.

This bias extends to co-production in general, couched in REF terms as public engagement. Watermeyer & Hedgecoe (2016) noted a general antagonism towards 'public engagement', seeing it as too vague and therefore dismissible or curtailable. As they note 'the REF privileges a very specific type of engagement, which has less in common with the general public and more to do with the benefits accrued by predefined stakeholders' (p. 662). This tendency needs to be countered.

The NCCPE (National Co-ordinating Centre for Public Engagement) report in 2017 notes how those case studies that had public engagement fared no different than those that did not. They made several recommendations to the 2017 government review of REF. They recommended that, first, the guidance about public engagement and enhancing collaboration between HEIs and external organizations should be more extensively developed and, second, the definition of what constitutes 'underpinning research' in an impact case study be broadened beyond research measured by conventional research outputs. Third, they recommended that the assessment of the 'rigour' of the engagement undertaken be added to the assessment of the 'reach and significance' and that the definitions of 'underpinning research' and 'impact' should be developed. They also suggested that REF should encourage more engagement earlier in the research cycle and that the process of development of impact criteria be opened up to greater external input, through a more active approach to consultation and engagement. Finally, NCCPE (2017) suggest reviewing the process of recruitment of panel members. In a similar vein Pain et al. (2015) recommend that panels specifically take people on people who have knowledge of participatory approach and public engagement. Positively the Stern Review (2016) did just this, as well as calling for greater definition of public engagement, and emphasis on wider and more diverse recruitment, and for including public engagement to be incentivized within the REF.

Many participatory and co-production authors (Cook et al., 2016; NCCPE, 2017; Pain et al., 2015) call for other changes to the way that research impact is conceptualized. First is the issue of time, and this has several dimensions. Cook et al. (2017) note how, while the scale for REF is five years or more, impact measurement is often constrained by the funding regimes that work on much shorter time scales, and consequently measurement of impact 'often happen[s] beyond the dedicated lifetime of projects and were only captured serendipitously' (Cook et al., 2017, pp. 481–482) at best. Pain et al. (2015) talk about how time also needs to be front loaded, allowing for the developing of relationships, understanding and trust. The NCCPE (2017) also calls for parallel processes in the REF panels themselves, to ameliorate the tendency of academics to dominate and for their knowledge to be privileged. Additionally, time for developmental processes are needed if meaningful understanding of participatory research and public engagement, and criteria for them, are to be co-created within these panels. Pain et al. (2015) show how the separation of impact and research is an artificial construct and stems from a particular linear view. For them co-production and participatory research are

> centrally about impact. Impact is not a separate stage or endeavour, but a praxis that is built in to research processes; research and impact are so intertwined as to be indistinguishable. Impact is at the core of why and how co-produced research takes place. The purpose of the research is what brings people together, it drives them and drives the twists and turns of the process.
>
> (Pain et al., 2015, p. 6)

Secondly there are issues with the nature of the impact being an unpredictable process. As Cook et al. note:

> Changes in thinking are not observable and explicitly articulated. They tend to emerge cumulatively as part of the process of learning during the project. People may not, therefore, recognise their own learning (change) as it unfolds developmentally rather than as an unambiguous outcome.
>
> (Cook et al., 2017, pp. 481–482)

Pain et al. (2015) further note the tendency of impact measurement to privilege hard outputs, rather than soft outcomes. While true we should not underestimate that degree to which soft outcomes can lead to hard outputs. The most common reason for people leaving the team in the probation research (see Chapter 12) was that people gained employment and cited the project as a discernable factor in this. Also while the project did not last forever and relationships faded, people kept in touch and cited the project as being a definitive factor in this. While not a scientific correlation, it is certainly reported and felt by the participants as such and is not a soft outcome. I will come back to this issue presently when considering the impact of the project itself, as this is arguably one of the greatest impacts of participatory research.

Impact as a process

As Pain et al. sum it up, in participatory research 'impact happens all the way through co-production, not only *afterwards*' (Pain et al., 2015, p. 5). Some of these impacts are predictable, but many are not. One of the biggest claims of this book is that these changes happen, and are important. PPIR emphasizes the localized impact on the organization, the researchers and the researched. It is often the process of doing the research that has greatest pedagogic impact on how workers, community partners and the organization come to see each other, and themselves. Implementing the actions of the research is important, particularly in embedding this learning, but is not the only criteria of success. In all of the research described the participants reported that their participation had had an impact on them.

One of the reasons why the process impacts of participatory research is lost is that the importance of the impact on the local is also not recognized by the REF. Pain et al. (2015) detect and critique a trend to privilege traditional views of reach, favouring the international over the national, the regional over the local, the institutional over the personal and a wide reach over a deep one. Watermeyer & Hedgecoe (2016) also found this to be so when looking at impact case studies. Pain et al. call for 'an alternative approach, that focuses on the identification and development of a "suite of impacts" relevant to the immediate context and questions of each [individual] project to be considered' (2015, p. 12). I would agree, but concurrently we do not want to lose the major things we have to celebrate in terms of wider impact – we need to build in processes and infrastructures to ensure, and measure how, these wider impacts happen.

While the commissioner's words mentioned in the introduction were heartening at the time, the subsequent impact is important. A permanent client group was set up and other pieces of work were conducted. Some of the peer researchers went on to form a community interest company and were in turn commissioned to undertake training on the client experience for services in the area. The findings of the Commissioning Together project were presented at the National IOM Conference in 2016 to an audience of commissioners from across the country, many of whom went on work with Revolving Doors in changing their commissioning processes. On a more cultural level clients in the probation research, as well as seeing personal changes in themselves also saw changes in both their perceptions about the services and the services perceptions of them.

In the same project a worker remarked to me their biggest learning was being on the receiving end of an interview, and it made them realize just how intimidating a process it was. They said that it would change their practice in the future. Important in being able to account for these impacts is to find a way to maintain relationships with projects for some time afterwards. Preferably that is about building in, where possible, continuity projects although the structure of much research funding mitigates against this. University culture is also a factor. Pain et al. (2015) note that participatory research and co-production is rarely understood academically within universities, particularly the higher up the hierarchy one goes. Concurrently partnership working with community organizations and voluntary groups is still piecemeal and one sided (Pain et al., 2015). Universities need to encourage co-production and have infrastructures to develop and maintain relationships, and we need to make the case that this will create more and better research opportunities in the end.

Developmentally part of the emphasis on peer research within PPIR is that it leaves behind capacity within the organization. The aforementioned training and permanent client group in Wandsworth were a result of this capacity building, but were not facilitated by us. We heard about it through the personal and professional grapevine. However sometimes continuity projects can be built in. In the probation project we had a second strand to the project whereby we trained some champions within other probation services, a worker, a manger and a client, who set up their own peer research projects, a worker commenting later: 'The content is outstanding and I would like to thank you for the guidance provided and associated material that will prove of real value with our own service developments.' It was the ongoing relationship that enabled us to gather such comments. As part of the dissemination of the escape plan research we held workshops on the plan within agencies. One agency subsequently incorporated it as part of their core training, and as such produced data on its effectiveness and impact, this being a requirement of all casework within homeless services.

Similarly, the video made in the probation research was adopted by that service as a core element of their training programme, and so monitored through evaluations for years to come. With the Touch project, we maintained the relationship with the partners and had a number of events together, as well as an exchange scheme and a smaller research project. This meant we could have an event two years after the project finished to examine what impact we had had, and had some powerful testimonies as well as evidence of impact from case notes, newspaper reports and an account of changed local and national policy. While Pain et al. (2015) critique some events, as they are often to serve the interests of the academics rather than the community, they saw this as part of the mutuality of the relationship and valued the opportunity to genuinely gauge what impact the process had had on us all. Voluntary sector organizations are often more adept at recognizing the need, and dividend, of these longer-term relationships. Groundswell and Revolving Doors have worked with some organizations across a number of projects, processes and stages of development, for years, to the point where they would approach us as research partnership for projects they were developing.

Measuring less tangible impacts and questions of ownership

We, as participatory and co-producing researchers, also have some responsibility to look at how we are allowing the REF to influence us. Tellingly, Cook et al. (2017) in the review of how participatory project were reported and monitored in impact case studies noticed that the prevailing paradigm for reporting impact (the predominance of what is thought to be acceptable as impact, the observable and measurable) created a wariness of documenting less tangible impacts. While such impacts may be harder to measure, and less tangible in traditional terms, unless we collate them and argue for them both in papers and in our communities of practice, we will undoubtedly loose them. We have a duty to engage with the debates, set up centres, even if the institution does not properly support them and sit on the upcoming REF panels, otherwise our presence and perspective will not be present.

Both Pain et al. (2015) and Cook et al. (2017) have debates about ownership within participatory research. Pain et al. (2015) note that we should co-own research, and critique a doner/recipient model in favour of a transdisciplinary one, where it may well be the community that is having an impact on the academics. I think this mutuality may open the way for incorporating another neglected element of the REF – how research impacts upon teaching, something the Stern Review recommended (HMRC, 2017). In my own institution I have set up a critical pedagogy group, that also discusses participatory research that is beginning to be emphasized. The emphasis in the group is on both student and staff formation and we sits within the academic development unit. We are conducting research and foresee a case study coming out of it.

However, there is a potential down side to this mutuality. Cook et al. (2017) in their survey of participatory research through, and in the light of, the 2014 REF note that the question of ownership meant that many researchers were reluctant to take credit for impact, even if it is an expected outcome of such research. While they note the positive aspects of this they also note that it can have a consequence that 'academic researchers, the people who generally write the academic papers, tend to gloss over this aspect' (Cook et al., 2017, pp. 481–482). This would seem to place an emphasis, again on us, to engage, to write those papers and book, but not only engage in things that reap REF dividends, otherwise we re-inscribe these power relations. We also need to critique wherever possible, and not just in the few journals we have. I have always preferred writing books because of the relative freedom they afford and the undoubtedly further reach than a journal article. However, the co-written articles I have produced with community members have been largely fruitful, and they have been excited about producing something 'proper', although the process can be an education in what is, and is not, 'proper' about academic articles.

Dissemination: beyond the academic

For community partners, publication is seen as less important than 'acting and doing'. Publications that do occur are not necessarily in academic journals or even in traditional written form. This means opportunities for collating, learning and building on the impacts of participatory approaches to research through a meta-analysis of academic literature is not necessarily an effective way of locating impact.

(Cook et al., 2017, p. 486)

As Cook et al. (2017) note earlier, the REF debate is largely an academic concern, although there are knock-on effects in that other funds may not be forthcoming. However, the other side of the REF is that much research funded by research councils takes place within the elite universities. I have never been funded through such sources and have had to rely on a multitude of other avenues. In the UK participatory research network of over 40 researchers, only seven work at elite institutions; more come from the voluntary sector, and only eight are reader or above or senior management. I would agree with Cook et al. (2015) that a meta-analysis of academic research would not generally be appropriate, but that depends on what kind of meta-analysis it is, and also what academic papers participatory academics continue to produce. I think it is also worth making a distinction between the dissemination product, event and process. There is crossover between them, but we should not conflate them.

Dissemination products

As there are multiple ways to collect data and produce findings in participatory research, there are multiple ways to present and disseminate them. Most participatory research I have been involved in has produced a multitude of outputs or products. In the Touch project we produced:

- an hour long documentary that was shown at a number of documentary film festivals produced by the partners Chocolate films who filmed the research process; this was distributed via YouTube and on a DVD
- a number of films that were made by the young people on their experiences of violence, also on the DVD
- an album of raps from young people on their experiences of, and views on the solution to, street violence.
- a traditional research report and executive summary
- a series of PowerPoint presentations on different aspects of the research, including the findings for various audience and an account of the research process
- a set of guidelines for youth work practitioner on working with street violence, utilizing the films and music
- three articles in journals, one examining the relationship between worker and young person, one on participatory methodology and another on the general results
- a book for Policy Press
- a website that hosted all these materials and resources.

These all had different audiences in mind, and we held dissemination events that made use of one or more of these products depending on the audience. They were also produced at different times, the academic outputs following on later. In the probation research by far the most widely distributed outputs were the leaflets created by those on probation for other clients on how to get the most out of probation (which was distributed worldwide at the World Congress of Probation). The film was, as said earlier, used in ongoing training and was shown to the Secretary of State at the Ministry of Justice. The guidelines on how to undertake a peer research project have been distributed and used by probation services nationwide. The actual report has probably only been seen by those respective probation services and some of the clients. Table 10.1 gives a useful summary of the different products and their pros and cons produced by Tendulakar and Adjagnon (2016) for the Institute for Community Health.

While these schemas are useful, one of the criticisms of Chen et al. (2010) of participatory research is that the outputs and dissemination events rarely reach the community members themselves. What we need to do is find out, and build upon, community members' indigenous ways of disseminating information. In contrast Simone Helleren, in Chapter 11, goes into some detail about how we disseminated the escape plan. Homeless people tended to congregate in the communal spaces of hostels and day centres and relied on word of mouth, so this is how we got the information out. Unlike with the Touch project, we ascertained this from the outset, so to disseminate things this way was always built in.

Dissemination events and processes

I am sure we have all been to a lot of boring research launches where everyone gets up to have a say and to thank everyone else, and at some point a list of recommendations is read out. I am sure we have also been to events where everything seems to overrun and everyone says more or less the same thing. Perhaps consequently, as in the examples in the first few paragraphs of this chapter, the audience starts questioning what the event is achieving and whether the ensuing discussions are meaningful. Ed Chambers (2004) calls events, if they work, public dramas. Community organizing events and actions are indeed heavily scripted. Everyone knows what they are going to say beforehand, including those who are being asked to commit to changing things – why surprise them? And they will only say 'I'll have to think about that', as few public figures would be in a position to make commitments off the cuff.

The only tensions in their events are whether the power brokers stick to what they say, or instead become vague, in which case they will be pinned down, but again in a very scripted way. The events always finish on time and never take questions or contributions from the floor. They are not democratic, and are not meant. They are a power play whereby the strength or community members' presence in the room, turnout in organizing is heavily emphasized and the audience in always a majority of community members, dares the power that be not to agree with what are normally easily agreeable asks. The power brokers are always treated cordially and heckling is not allowed, it would give them a ready and easy excuse to walk away. The most important asks is for the person in power to commit to an ongoing relationship with the community members, probably in smaller numbers.

This is easy to agree to, but does commit that person to an ongoing dialogue, made in public, with the implicit threat that if the promise is broken they might

Table 10.1 Summary of the different products and their pros and cons produced by Tendulakar and Adjagnon (2016) for the Institute for Community Health

Types of product	Intended audience	Purpose	Pros	Cons
Comprehensive Evaluation Report with methods, all findings and recommendations (e.g. 10–15 pages)	Funders, individuals interested in replicating the program, advisory boards, programme staff, researchers	To provide audience with comprehensive understanding of evaluation methods and results	Comprehensive	Lengthy, not easily digestible, requires high literacy level and understanding of research
PowerPoint Presentation with methods, key findings and recommendations (e.g. 20–30 slides)	Community groups, programme participants, organizational senior management	To present an easily digestible birds-eye view of the key evaluation methods and findings	Visually engaging, easy to digest, highlights important points, can be used to lead audience in particular direction, slides can be customized to diverse audiences	Simplifies the findings, message quality is presenter dependent
Peer-reviewed manuscript with thorough discussion of evaluation methods, results, discussion of results and implications for the field. (e.g. about 4,000 words)	Academic Researchers	To disseminate research in a published academic journal, in order to share findings and lessons learned with the broader research community	Appealing to funders, helps connect you with others doing similar research for future research partnerships, advances the field	Limited audience, requires high research understanding and literacy level, inaccessible to majority

(continued)

Table 10.1 Summary of the different products and their pros and cons produced by Tendulakar and Adjagnon (2016) for the Institute for Community Health *(continued)*

Types of product	Intended audience	Purpose	Pros	Cons
Press release with brief methods and findings (e.g. 3–4 pages)	Media (e.g. radio stations, magazines, newsletters, newspapers)	To bring attention to a key health issue with a well defined community and talk about one strategy to address this key problem	Reaches wide audience, 'quick and dirty', brings more attention to your programme and health topic programme addresses, positions you as the 'expert'	Reaches only audience with media access
One pager with brief discussion of methods, and key findings (e.g. 1 page)	Everyone	To provide the audience with a 'quick and dirty' elevator speech overview of the evaluation findings	Widely accessible and easily digestible, transportable (can be passed around easily)	Lacks depth, often lacks full context
Video/documentary including interviews/ stories of participants, etc.	Online audience, national audience	To tell a story about how the programme has impacted the community	Limited audience, requires high research understanding and literacy level, inaccessible to majority	Reaches only audience with media access, expensive to produce, requires technology

(Adjagnon, 2016, pp. 2–3)

have to face the community in numbers again. Also important is that the organizers do not present; this is only done by community members. This is partly to grow leaders but also to show that the issues come from the community members, not the professionals. An interesting trick, particularly with politicians who may well naturally overrun, is that the timekeeping (people are normally given a matter of minutes to speak, with the bulk of speaking coming from community members) is normally held by a child, as the politicians would have to say no to a child who is asking them to finish. It would be a brave politician who would do that.

Conclusion

I am not saying that all dissemination events should be like this, but as a structure they could teach us some lessons. As I said in Chapter 9, I normally get the chief executive to agree to one of the recommendations at the event. The one I suggest is the one about having an ongoing relationship with them, and that a group is facilitated to enable this. It is this relationship that allows what can be a one-off event to become a process – a process of accountability. Simone will describe in Chapter 11 how this can be a highly developed process; the important thing is that there is one.

The importance of dissemination is that it has impact in that real changes happen in the lives of the researched because of the research. While the REF is flawed, participatory research is designed to have an impact in the spirit in which Impact was originally brought in in 2014. It is up to participatory researchers to engage with the REF and ensure that some of this original vision does not fade into academic convention. We also have to engage to argue that the concept of Impact has already been constricted, in that the interpretation of it marginalizes local impact and the impact that the process of research has on peers the researched and the academics.

We also have to ensure that our engagement with community members spreads to effect the universities' general culture of engagement with the community. Only then will we truly start seeing the longer-term impact of our research as mutual interest grows. It is also only then that we will see our research and reach spread beyond the local, as we network with other local initiatives until our reach becomes truly national, international and global, reflecting the diasporic reach many of our community members naturally have.

References

Cacari-Stone, L., Wallerstein L. N., Garcia, A. P. & Minkler, M. (2014) 'The promise of community-based participatory research for health equity: a conceptual model for bridging evidence with policy.' *American Journal of Public Health*, 104(9): 1615–1623.

Centre for Social Justice and Community Action (CSJCA) and National Co-ordinating Centre for Public Engagement (NCCPE) (2012) *Community-based Participatory Research: A Guide to Ethical Principles and Practice*. Durham: Durham University.

Chambers, E., with Cowan, M. (2004) *Roots for Radicals: Organizing for Power, Action and Justice*. New York: Continuum.

Chen, P. G., Diaz, N., Lucas, G. & Rosenthal, M. S. (2010) 'Dissemination of results in community-based participatory research.' *Medical Journal of Preventative Medicine*, 39: 372–378.

Chowdhury, G., Koya, K. & Philipson, P. (2016) 'Measuring the impact of research: lessons from the UK's Research Excellence Framework 2014.' *PLoS ONE* 11(6).

Chowdry, H., Crawford, C., Dearden, L., Goodman, A. & Vignoles, A. (2010) *Widening Participation in Higher Education: Analysis Using Linked Administrative Data*. London: IFS.

Cook, T. (2012) 'Where participatory approaches meet pragmatism in funded (health) research: the challenge of finding meaningful spaces.' *Forum Qualitative Sozialforschung/ Forum: Qualitative Social Research*, 13(1): Art. 18.

Cook, T., Boote, J., Buckley, N., Vougioukalou, S. & Wright, M. (2017) 'Accessing participatory research impact and legacy: developing the evidence base for participatory approaches in health research.' *Educational Action Research*, 25(4): 473–488.

Greenhalgh, T. & Fahy, N. (2015) 'Research impact in the community-based health sciences: an analysis of 162 case studies from the 2014 UK Research Excellence.' *Framework*, 13(232): 1–12.

Greenhalgh, T., Jackson, C., Shaw, S. & Janamian, T. (2016) 'Achieving research impact through co-creation in community-based health services: literature review and case study.' *The Milbank Quarterly*, 94(2): 392–429.

HEFCE, SFC, HEFCW, DELNI (2012a) Assessment framework and guidance on submissions (02.2011 updated version). Available at www.ref.ac.uk/media/ref/content/pub/ assessmentframeworkandguidanceonsubmissions/GOS%20including%20addendum.pdf.

HEFCE, SFC, HEFCW, DELNI (2012b) Main Panel A Criteria (01.2012). Available at: www.ref.ac.uk/2014/pubs/2011-02/.pdf.

Kings (2016) *The Nature, Scale and Beneficiaries of Research Impact: An Initial Analysis of Research Excellence Framework (REF) 2014 Impact Case Studies*. London: Kings College.

Liamputtong, P. (2014) 'Experiential Learning.' In D. Coughlan & M. Brydon-Miller (eds) *Sage Encyclopedia of Action Research*. London: Sage, p. 324.

National Co-ordinating Centre for Public Engagement NCCPE (2017) 'The role of public engagement in the REF.' Bristol: NCCPE. Available at www.publicengagement.ac.uk/ news/role-public-engagement-ref [accessed 27 February 2018].

Owen, H. (1997) *Open Space Technology: A User's Guide*. 2nd edition. San Francisco, CA: Berrett-Koehler Publishers, Inc.

Pain, R., Askins, K. S., Banks, S., Cook, T., Crawford, G., Crookes, L. & Darby, S. (2015) *Mapping Alternative Impact: Alternative Approaches to Impact from Co-produced Research*. Durham: Centre for Social Justice and Community Action, Durham University.

Ramaswamy, V. & Ozcan, K. (2014) *The Co-creation Paradigm*. Redwood City, CA: Stanford University Press.

Reed, M. (2016) *The Research Impact Handbook*. Aberdeenshire: Fast Track Impact.

Sayer, P. (2014) 'Five reasons why the REF is not fit for purpose.' *The Guardian*, 15 December 2014. Available at: www.theguardian.com/higher-education-network/ 2014/dec/15/research-excellence-framework-five-reasons-not-fit-for-purpose [accessed 1 November 2017].

Stern, N. (2016) *Building on Success and Learning from Experience An Independent Review of the Research Excellence Framework*. London: HMSO.

Tendulakar, S. & Adjagnon, O. (2016) *Dissemination Catalogue*. Cambridge: Institute for Community Health.

Wallerstein, N., Jetzel, J., Duran, B., Tafoya, G., Belone, L. & Ray, R. (2008) 'What predicts outcomes in CBPR?' In M. Minkler & N. Wallerstein. *Community Based Participatory/ Research for Health: Process to Outcomes*. 2nd edition. San Fancisco, CA: Jossey Bass, pp. 371–392.

Watermeyer, R. & Hedgecoe, A. (2016) 'Selling "impact": peer reviewer projections of what is needed and what counts in REF impact case studies. A retrospective analysis.' *Journal of Education Policy*, 31(5): 651–665.

Part 3

Notes from the field

Research in action

11   Reflections on peer and participatory research: Groundswell UK and The Escape Plan

Simone Helleren

Introduction

In this chapter, I explore three key issues commonly met when approaching peer and participatory research. To begin with is 'Peerness: the "who" of participation', unpicking the role of peer researcher and recognizing the complexity of peer research for the people involved. Second is 'Involvement in decision-making: how and how much?', highlighting some techniques and strategies for opening the space and getting out of the way to enable participation. Finally, 'Working with commissioners: how it helps and gets in the way' considers working within limitations and the benefits of partnering with experts. I am writing this chapter reflecting back on almost nine years of carrying out research with the charity Groundswell UK, with particular reference to a project called the Escape Plan. Prior to Groundswell I worked across the voluntary and statutory sectors with diverse groups focusing on 'involvement and participation'; as a facilitator I frequently used theatre methods.

I was a Groundswellian between 2007 and 2014. My reflections on it here are based on my personal perspective on the organization, beginning as a facilitator of a couple of workshops, then as trainer on Enterprising Solutions, Training Manager, Director of Training and Research and finally Director of Development. I started in an organization of three staff and two volunteers that grew to 17 staff and 20 volunteers and currently stands at 20 staff (14 with experience of homelessness) and 30 volunteers. It's a growing thing. In my various roles I facilitated training sessions and workshops; responded to calls for training and research proposals; wrote reports and a lot of minutes; messed up the petty cash doing expenses; lugged around a lot of flip charts. I didn't know much about homelessness or about research to begin with, which was good (mostly) because it kept me humble (mostly). Throughout I commonly refer to a 'we', referring to staff with permanent contracts, freelance peer researchers and group facilitators, volunteers and friends of Groundswell. This 'we' not only grew in numbers but also became more diverse, with more direct and different experience of homelessness.

Context

Groundswell UK is a charity which grew out of the radical, client and frontline worker oriented campaigning organization Campaign for the Homeless and

Rootless (CHAR) which became the National Homelessness Alliance, now Homeless Link. Groundswell, based in London, became an independent entity in 1996. From the start, the project was a product of the belief that 'people experiencing homelessness are not the problem but the solution to homelessness'. It has been, and continues to be, a project exploring ways of making space for people with experience of a phenomena in order to better describe it, to scrutinize and inform policy and practice, to get involved in improving it.

In the early days, working from the ground up, volunteers and a handful of paid staff organized Speakouts,[1] Forums[2] and funded 'self-help' projects.[3] From what I can gather, in the early days it was vital, unorthodox, part party, part project, angry and shouty. They had good cause: homelessness was about to reach its peak in 2003 (Homeless Link, 2015) Cardboard City[4] was two years from closing and the notion of listening to people actually experiencing homelessness was a novelty, at best. A tension perpetually explored by Groundswell, overtly or not, then and now, is power and how it is handled in distribution of help, especially related to homelessness, and in the legislation that shapes it. Key to this exploration are questions about the generation and perpetuation of knowledge about homelessness; knowledge which becomes the logic behind how we conceptualize homelessness, which in turn informs how we go about addressing it. Peer and participatory research grew naturally from the exploration of this tension.

About Groundswell's research

I joined Groundswell at particular point in homeless sector service development, at the beginning of 2006, towards the end of a Labour Government. The sector had been shaken up with new initiatives and guidance: the Social Exclusion Unit, the Homelessness Act 2002, and the introduction of Supporting People.[5] Involvement and participation formed a central strand of most New Labour flagship policies, and those pertaining to homelessness were no exception. Groundswell was well placed to provide guidance and support and service a new enthusiasm to 'consult' and 'involve'; we were recommended as a source of information on 'Speakouts and other means of consulting homeless people' in the government's Good Practice Guide to Developing Homelessness Strategies (ODPM: 2006, p. 17). Between 2006 and 2008 we cut our research teeth feeding local and regional strategies with the experiences and ideas of hundreds of people homeless in England at that time.

Over time, the research Groundswell produces has become more rigorous regarding the methodologies used, training provided for researchers, and research design. Despite our developments, obtaining recognition for the value and validity of the work has been a battle. Irrespective of rhetoric supporting participation and promotion of the 'user voice', policy makers, Local Authority managers and services providers – while curious – are sometimes sceptical of the methodological rigour and data quality of participatory research (Goodson & Phillimore, 2012, p. 11). This is not an unfamiliar state of affairs, motivating the cry from Claire Blencowe and colleagues below:

Participatory organizations should not be seen as the subjective 'other' to the objectivity of science, but rather as organizations acting as 'engines of alternative objectivity'.

(Blencowe et al., 2015, p. 408)

While Groundswell fought to be heard and have impact we were unusual in the impact we could have *through* the work of the project. The project itself is a vessel for dissemination and impact. For example, in the early days research findings fed into newsletters and informed topics for debate at local and national forums; later, findings informed training for homelessness sector staff and clients and the development of new Groundswell projects, notably Homeless Health Peer Advocacy (HHPA).[6] HHPA sits neatly at the nexus of findings from eight years of research,[7] and for the past eight years has been at the centre of the Groundswell programme of work.

Groundswell's research offer was limited by our areas of expertise, but we were happy to bring in experts or partner with another organization if commissioners had an interest new to us. We brought in filmmakers, artists, statistics experts. Bringing experts in gave our team of volunteers and staff the opportunity to experience different approaches to capturing and understanding the experiences and issues at hand. We would pretty much all take part in workshops, depending who had the time and inclination. There were always a few people looking bewildered and someone would nod off at some point. It was often lively; mostly in a circle with flip chart and sticky note. There were lots of breaks and biscuits; we ran out of milk and sugar all the time. Research planning meetings would be similar but we would, more frequently, sit around a table with an agenda and papers.

In our planning meetings I recall spending a lot of time on getting the 'group guidelines' section of the focus group introduction to everyone's satisfaction. We would rehash old debates and bring in new ideas from recent experience. Things took *time*. Practically, I would produce a draft design, topic guide, information sheet and consent forms; developed with assistance of various experts, responding to a commissioner's aspirations for the research. We would present on what we were trying to do, what we had come up with so far. Participants were invited to assist in improving the overall plan and details. We worked quickly; with surprise I note now we had a five weeks from inception to final report for a project involving four focus groups and 15 semi-structured interviews. We managed these hectic schedules but quickly learned how punishing they were on the staff team and the research. With over a year to complete, The Escape Plan was the most luxurious project we had worked on.

Meanwhile we were trying to build trust within our team, most importantly by listening and acting on what was said and ensuring people knew about the origins of decisions. Otherwise, we tried to be good administrators, clearly communicating, timely, on time. We tried to be flexible and supportive: addressing barriers to access to learning; planning and employment opportunities – paying travel; providing lunch; and providing personal and practical support. The potential of obtaining employment was a good incentive. Making work pay for peer researchers, financially, however, was unusual. We were always looking for ways to offer our team of Peer Researchers and facilitators the sort of employment that would help: long term, good rates, flexibility, and opportunities for progression. The Escape Plan, our first fully funded research project, enabled us to offer all of this to the two recruited Peer Researchers.

About The Escape Plan

The Escape Plan (Groundswell, 2009) was a qualitative exploration of the critical success factors that have enabled people to move on from homelessness. It aimed to use peer research methodologies to create an evidence base, then to use this evidence base to empower people currently experiencing homelessness, establish a good practice model for practitioners, and influence current and future policy development. The idea came about in 2007 while Groundswell was undertaking the peer research element of a study led by Mary Carter for Homeless Link and The Joseph Rowntree Foundation to explore the gaps in homelessness research. The study informed the themes of the Economic and Social Research Council's Multiple Exclusion Homelessness (MEH) Research Programme. One of the gaps identified was 'an evaluation of what works'.

The Groundswell team explored this question generally and in dedicated workshops with staff, volunteers, researchers and clients, who were at different stages of escaping homelessness themselves. Here we considered: the relevance of the question; who was in the ideal place to respond to it; and how we would capture their experience. Following success in the initial stages of funding bids, further workshops – with a group of peer researchers and one with people who had moved on from homelessness – fleshed out the methodology and began defining key terms which contributed to sampling decisions. Crucially, what constituted 'homelessness' and having 'moved on' from it?

Work on The Escape Plan began early in 2009.[8] Mike Seal, as lead researcher, was involved from the development stages, and the peer researchers were recruited and employed for ten months part time, several months before we began fieldwork. Together they finalized the methods employed, made final decisions on the definition of terms, sampling and recruitment of participants. The peer researchers, with assistance from the Groundswell team, went on to recruit and interview 25 people with experience of homelessness: 'Escapees'. Additionally, the Escapees were asked to identify two 'Significant Others' – people who had insight into their escape from homelessness. A total of 30 Significant Others were interviewed – a combination of friends, family and workers. Researchers used a variety of approaches to capture a life map starting at the beginning of homelessness to the point at which they identified as being 'moved on' from it. Interviews were audio recorded and transcribed, analysed by the lead researcher. The findings and recommendations were sharpened in three verification focus groups, one with Escapees, one with Significant Others and one with a mixture of the two.

The results were produced around September 2010 and included a report and a notebook to be used as a tool by people experiencing homelessness to plan their own Escape. The report elaborated on the seven areas the critical success factors sat within: Being involved in group activity; Changing your attitude towards yourself and others; Hitting rock bottom; Workers and services; Peer perspectives and client involvement; Social networks, family and relationships; and Coming to terms with the homeless experience. The notebook was nicely produced and pocket sized. It explained the research and described the participants, was divided in to the seven themes sharing the headline findings and posed questions with space to respond. Interest in the report came from as far afield as Canada and Australia; Escape Plan workshops continue to be facilitated by a homelessness sector user group.

Peerness: the 'who' of participation

As Mike highlights in Chapter 3, supporters of peer research suggest benefits including empowerment of the researcher, easier development of trust with participants resulting in more representative and reliable knowledge. This comes about because of what researchers share experientially, leading to deeper understanding. 'Peer research is justified in terms of efficiency in that it encourages closer intimacy and fuller discussion between researchers and researched, and fuller understanding of the data' (Alderson, 2001, p. 140 cited in Chapter 3).

This was the premise from which we sold the values of peer research. Researchers with experience of homelessness were more likely to develop trust with those experiencing homelessness and thereby to have the privilege of hearing a more full, perhaps more honest, accounts of what was going on. It seemed quite a claim and so we sought to back it up, conducting a questionnaire with 101 people who had participated in a Groundswell peer facilitated focus group; finding that 66 per cent felt they 'could be more open and honest when the group leaders are' people with experience of homelessness; 13 per cent when they were 'people [who] have not experienced homelessness'; and for 21 per cent it made no difference. Naturally, it is much more complex that this. How do the *differences* in our common experiences play out in the notion of 'peer'?

Goodson and Phillimore (2012, p. 4) in their book on Community Research point out the mess of terminology concerning those with 'insider knowledge' of phenomena. They conflate the terms 'peer', 'user' and 'citizen' into 'community researcher' and qualify it as someone who *could* be situated, geographically, in a community in which they undertake research, or could have 'shared interests or common experience' with a community not bound by 'spatial proximities or localized relationships'. I think this helps us better understand the complexity of the term, but it does not clarify it. Here, all I can do is point to some incidents where we came up against this complexity in the work.

The value of 'being peer' and declaring it was made apparent to peer researchers in training, and many if not all believed in and were motivated by the possibilities. However, how individuals handled their experiences in the field varied. Some spent an abundance of time sharing their experience and the interview could collapse into a series of brief statements that would trail off with 'you know what

I mean'. If the peer researchers had had a *particular* experience while homeless (for example, rough sleeping or success with Fellowship intervention), the interviewee might be reluctant to talk about their own experience of hostels or therapy in recovery for example. The familiarity could potentially do the exact opposite of what we had hoped.

Furthermore, our peer researchers experienced their homelessness differently: it might have been recent or many years ago; many were still in hostels or insecure accommodation; some endured long periods of rough sleeping, while others were squatters or had mostly sofa surfed. They were, unsurprisingly, more or less comfortable than they had imagined when it came to declaring their experience with strangers. Some felt either fraudulent (as their experience was long ago, short term, not as chaotic, for example), or reluctant to bring up and replay their past and regularly continuing experiences. People had engaged in the peer research training in the hope that they would find employment as researchers and trainers; we were appealing to their desire to nurture a new future but would require them to keep alive their experiences of homelessness in order to build trust with participants. Following fieldwork, in analysis sessions, we asked them to call on the experience of participants, holding their own to one side, while also reflecting on how their own experiences might affect what they saw in findings.

It was common in the sector to have service users contribute to presentations at AGMs and conferences, retelling their traumatic experience and how a service or project made the difference; many of us felt uncomfortable at this continual replaying, performing of homelessness and were concerned about the impact it was having on individuals. While Groundswell, in the main, avoided this, at times we wondered if we were keeping people in homelessness. The Groundswell team explored these tensions over time. I recall when our lead peer researcher at the time, Mark Flynn, said that he didn't mention his homelessness because when he did the interview would end up being all about him, highlighting a procedural rather than personal issue. From this point on, Groundswell researchers informed participants that 'I have experience of homelessness but I'm here to find out about you and your experiences.'

I was pretty pleased with the new introduction but I noted when reading transcriptions of focus groups and interviews that individuals would maintain an approach that suited them irrespective of what we may have agreed. Effectively addressing part of this complex issue (i.e. people felt free to reveal as much or little of their own experience as they chose), we left aside *how* what they brought opened and/or closed the personal account of interviewees. By the time we started on The Escape Plan there were many more people in the Groundswell office than before with permanent contracts and who had experience of homelessness. All of them handled how they spoke about their experience differently. The experiences they had were differently useful. But there was always the danger of reifying past experiences; how ethical was it to keep experiences that frequently looked like trauma so present through the work?

Media opportunities frequently brought this issue to the surface. Journalists were keen to hear just how bad it had been for peer researchers and facilitators, before it came good. The Escape Plan proposal included the production of a film to aid the dissemination of findings. Unfortunately, the media company's time could not flex around our own, and the film was produced in the middle of fieldwork. As a result it focused on the two peer researchers, Mike (Spike) Hudson and Andrew Campbell, as men who, having been homeless, were able to change their circumstances, find homes and jobs, and create balance in their lives. Despite the initial positive spin, some of the very worst moments of the researchers' time being homeless were pawed over in the film. There was an abundance of distant shots of them looking alone on a park bench, looking thoughtful from a bridge down at the traffic, uncomfortably holding signs with some early findings written on pieces of cardboard, statements such as 'never give up'. We managed to influence some of the editing but there was tension in the team over the results that were screened on a community television station. It remains a warning for how collaborators and funders can push a fairly good research project into the realms of what Mike makes reference to in Chapter 2 as 'voyeurism at best and pornography at worst'. 'It is pornography in the sense that it will reveal lives and voices, but not take responsibility for changing them, and in purely presenting them allow others to be voyeuristic, to sensationalize and to orientalize' (Chapter 2 in this volume, p. 37).

The notion of peer could be seen to interpellate a 'Them and Us,' combative and unequal relationship between people using services and those working in them and making decisions about them; the very relationship that we were trying to agitate. While still using the 'peer' terminology, and focusing on people with direct experience of homelessness, Groundswell's attention shifted towards all the different people involved in homelessness; frontline staff, administrators, policy makers, etc. We recognized that the more multifaceted our experiences, the better picture we could get of what was going on and where to begin to make change. It was marked by a literal shift in how the organization described itself, from enabling 'people with experience of homelessness to create solutions' to 'inclusive solutions to homelessness'. Handling the complexities of 'who' is involved and how they can use their experience remains a question of standpoint or positionality that is best worked through, reflexively, within a team of researchers. *How* to manage this reflexive process is addressed by Mike effectively in Chapter 4.

Involvement in decision-making: how and how much?

Who made the decisions though? This question makes my head spin. I can say for certain that decisions taken at Groundswell within and outside its research were, in the main, the subject of a lot of discussion and that, while I was there, a multitude of perspectives contributed to the smallest and most significant ones. We flirted briefly with 'consensus decision-making' but time was mostly too tight to allow for it, and not just our time; the team (mostly volunteers, freelance peer researchers and facilitators) were neither time- nor cash-rich. We had more and less successful workshops and meetings. Some would say they felt heard and that their experience was valued, others that they definitely did not – possibly both would change their minds. It is very difficult to tell when people feel free to say what they want, whether we have all been completely understood and if perspectives are success-fully incorporated. I would naturally ask people and get others to ask people 'Do you see yourself in this? Is this what you meant? Will this work better?' If they said 'no', we would seek to understand and try again – but even if they said 'yes', it is very difficult to tell if people feel free to say what they want . . . However, the more trust we built, as a project, with all the collaborators we worked with over the years, the more willing people were to say 'no', 'no, you haven't understood'. This resistance and working with it is something of a sign of progress.

Taking a participatory approach requires us to become sensitive to where the power is and where and when it flips or subtly drifts from one person to another throughout the research process. It requires a commitment to locating power in our thoughts, actions, use of language and space. It is about painfully unravelling the strands of power that run through our relationships and adjusting, minutely and drastically. It is a process of perpetually learning, adjusting, checking, learning and adjusting again. While it is fairly easy to see where it goes wrong I think it is not so easy to see when it goes right. For me it is a practically wordless thing running beneath a group conversation that is passionate and littered with 'yes, what they said and . . .', 'but, what about when . . .', when people have new thoughts, epiphanies and disagree and are alright about it. A delicate and precious thing. I would say that passion is always involved, caring about a subject more than how we are all looking to one another. As Blencowe says, 'It is about holding things open rather than prescribing possible pathways of understanding or action' (Blencowe et al. 2015, p. 405).

Holding things open is quite a thing, like stopping in the middle of a sneeze. It's much cleaner, easier, more satisfying even, to close a debate down with a solution we can all live with. In 2006 I discovered Open Space Technology (Owen, 1997), and borrowed heavily from it in how we facilitated workshops. It is, in short, a method to bring diverse groups of people together around a specific question or theme, to debate and plan action. It runs on the passion people bring regarding the question or theme and the responsibility they are prepared to take in addressing it. It is 'open' in that there is no agenda. Furthermore, there are a series of principles and one law that guide the progress of the session.

The principles, question or theme, line the wall of the space. The group begins in a circle to establish an agenda and for the remaining session attends smaller group discussions around items suggested by participants. The law, which we made good use of, is the Law of Two Feet: if you are not learning something or contributing something, use your feet (or whatever you possess to get you about) to take you somewhere you can. This included outside with the smokers, by your self-reflecting, or buzzing from group to group. Whether people used the Law to its full effect is debatable – but the promise of freedom was there, the rec-ognition that individuals will have surprising areas of interest and expertise, and that some individuals will try to drown out or dominate all others – but in this case you needn't stay for it. The four principles, likewise, help to create the sort of space that nourishes difference of opinion and frees participants from domination and control.

Getting out of the way

I advocate, if you can't hold things open, get out of the way. If there is the opportunity to almost completely remove oneself, you should get out of the way. A
small step towards this is handing over the flip chart marker. In my mind a good
example of this is Escapees in The Escape Plan selecting their Significant Others;
effectively making sampling decisions; reminiscent of 'snowball sampling', and
yet distinguishable in that it wasn't just people they knew but those who they felt
had significant insight into their own experience. *To know me better, what happened
to me better, look through these eyes.* The benefits of getting out of the way are also
apparent in the dissemination of the findings. I made some attempt to follow up the
current use of The Escape Plan findings and found that the notebooks continue to
be used in St Mungos, the homeless charities, Recovery Colleges in London and
Bristol. I would put this success down to the resources we developed which provide
an accessible framework – based on research findings – that enabled us to get out
of the way and leave groups of people using homelessness services use them for
themselves.

Working with commissioners: how it helps and gets in the way

Getting out of the way and holding things open to enable participation depends,
to a degree, on the freedom and the flexibility one has. Prior to The Escape Plan,
Groundswell research had been largely determined by commissioners. We bid
for contracts to deliver evaluations for service providers and consultations to
feed into Homelessness Strategies. While commissioned research occasionally
forged partnerships that enriched the expertise, breadth and rigor of Groundswell's
research work; limitations imposed by budgets and conservative thinking around
the possibilities of participatory research more frequently got in the way.
Participatory research done well requires time and is not a cheap alternative; there
is still a need to make this case.

Methodologically, the Local Authority work involved peers (people with experience of homelessness) in developing and facilitating questionnaires and focus
groups and contributing to verification events. I distinguish Peer from Participatory
here in that they were people who didn't have experience of homelessness in those
specific geographic areas. The central questions and sampling decisions were made
entirely by commissioners. The design of the research began with semi-structured
interviews, which informed a Likert Scale questionnaire, the findings from which
would be fleshed out in Focus Groups. On rare occasions we managed to convince
commissioners to agree to include Verification and Recommendation building
events. Here clients and front line staff were encouraged to attend and participate in
a day of small group discussion. We used techniques from Open Space Technology,
Citizens Jury and a lot of voting with sticky dots, to establish a vibrant, fun and as
equal as possible environment to encourage open and honest discussion, agreement, and commitment to taking new ideas forward. These events would help to
shift the project from 'peer' to 'participatory', albeit at the final stages. They were

the most resource-intensive element of any research project and commissioners were frequently unable to see how the investment in this more participatory approach could dramatically increase the benefits of the research project.

When commissioned by service providers, Groundswell had more opportunity to propose more participatory approaches that engaged with clients and staff as decision makers in the entire process. The methodology would be negotiated with the service and, in most cases, a steering or advisory group including clients and staff was established to see the project through to dissemination and beyond. They were asked to apply their experience to decisions about: key questions, sampling, methods, topic guides and questionnaires, recruitment of participants, and timing. This process was both a learning experience and encouraged ownership of the research, to help embed the process of participatory work. This worked. Sometimes, to great effect: in one case, a user group established in a research project continues some 13 years after working with Groundswell; another service provider has continued a programme of annual participatory evaluation; another is well into the recommendations from an evaluation of member involvement undertaken five years ago. Despite the obvious benefits, commissioners would frequently select a lighter option because of budgetary and time limitations. As mentioned previously, The Escape Plan was the least limited research project we had. I believe that this fact is linked inextricably to the continuing impact of the project.

Conclusion

I firmly believe that participatory approaches to research can create new knowledge and provide us with the insight required to address pernicious issues. When talking about impact we should be talking about legacy beyond changes to policy embedding an awareness of participation and involvement of people usually shut out of knowledge production, as 'engines of alternative objectivity' (Blencowe et al., 2015, p. 408). That 'embedding' requires the quality of commitment and passion which can only be wrought in the crucible of experience. Manifesting this 'crucible of experience' of participation requires flexibility and resources. These things are worth fighting for.

Finally, participatory research requires deep thinking about ourselves, our subjectivity. When we ask people to call on *their* subjectivity we need to account for the complexities of self and how the telling of it affect us. Especially when the experience we are drawing on is traumatic, we need to apply sensitivity and humility, make use of theory and experience to work with people. Thankfully Mike's Chapter 3 draws out the strands of this complex task and how we might practically manage the reflexivity required to understand *how* our experiences both open up and close down how we see ourselves and the world that we seek to better understand.

Notes

1   Groundswell facilitated hundreds of Speakouts around the UK including National Super Speakouts. They were typically events that brought together people experiencing homelessness, sector staff, local councillors, MPs and civil servants. They made use of interactive techniques for people to communicate their experiences and debate local

issues affecting people experiencing homelessness. Speakouts were listed in the guidance for the 2002 Housing Act as one of the recommended techniques for consulting with homeless people.

2   Self Help Forums brought together people from all around the UK who were all using their experiences of homelessness to make positive social change.

3   GAS, The Grant Award Scheme, was open to people experiencing homelessness to set up projects. It awarded over £250,000 to more than 500 homeless-led self-help groups. This gave people the resources and support to "do it yourself" and create their own solutions to homelessness.

4   Cardboard City is the name given to a massive settlement of people experiencing homelessness near Waterloo station where the Imax Cinema is currently. It was populated between 1983 and 1998.

5   Supporting People and the Quality Assessment Framework (QAF) 2003 established standards expected in the delivery of housing-related services and was used as a contract management tool for 'ensuring continuous improvements' (Sitra, 2010, p. 3).

6   http://groundswell.org.uk/what-we-do/health/homeless-health-peer-advocacy/

7   Groundswell's body of research has demonstrated that for people experiencing homelessness health issues are pernicious, devastating and expensive. They cause and are caused by homelessness and prevent people moving on from it. Poor use of health services and barriers in health services for people experiencing homelessness are consistent across the country, as is the efficacy of peer support.

8   The project was funded by City Parochial and The Ashden Trust, and supported by a partnership that included Newman University College, Thames Reach, a London-based homeless sector service provider Homeless Link, the national membership organization for frontline homelessness agencies, and Geoffrey Randall, independent researcher.

References

Blencowe, C., Brigstocke, J. & Noorani, T. (2015) 'Theorising participatory practice and alienation in health research: a materialist approach. *Social Theory & Health*, 13(3/4): 397–417.

Goodson, L. & Phillimore, J. (2012) *Community Research for Participation.* Bristol: Policy Press.

Groundswell (2009) *The Escape Plan: A Participatory Research Study Creating an Evidence Base of the Critical Success Factors That Have Enabled People to Successfully Move on From Homelessness.* Available from: http://groundswell.org.uk/what-we-do/peer-research/the-escape-plan/ [accessed 7 January 2018].

Homeless Link (2015) *Let's Make the Difference: A Manifesto to End Homelessness. Homeless Link.* Available at: www.homeless.org.uk/our-work/campaigns/policy-and-lobbying-priorities/manifesto-to-end-homelessness [accessed 8 February 2018].

The Office of the Deputy Prime Minister (ODPM) (2006) *Homelessness Strategies: A Good Practice Handbook.* Available at: http://webarchive.nationalarchives.gov.uk/20120920035214/http://www.communities.gov.uk/documents/housing/pdf/156720.pdf] [accessed 7 January 2018].

Owen, H. (1997) *Open Space Technology: A User's Guide.* 2nd edition. San Francisco, CA: Berrett-Koehler Publishers, Inc.

Sitra (2010) *Using the Quality Assessment Framework.* Available at: www.sitra.org/policy-good-practice/quality/ [accessed 12 May 2017].

12 Courage of our convictions

Participatory research in the criminal justice system

Beth Coyne

Introduction

This chapter will present a brief précis of the methodology and findings of two service user involvement projects in probation settings, and one in a prison. It will also set out a number of key findings that are of interest to the discussion here about participatory pedagogy, its use, its value and its limitations. We will begin with some context of the time and the Transforming agenda and how we undertook the projects before going on to examine the impact of involvement Rehabilitation on service users themselves including the effect of pro-social modelling between peers, the identity theory of desistance and use of language.

Background

Revolving Doors Agency (RDA) is a charity based in London working across England and Wales. Its focus is on policy and practice concerned with adults with multiple and complex needs who are in repeat contact with the criminal justice system (the revolving door of prison, release and reoffending) that is often driven by associated needs and issues such as poor mental health, substance use and homelessness. In 2013 Revolving Doors Agency was commissioned by the National Offender Management Service to develop materials to support service user involvement in the criminal justice system. The project led on from a recent Clinks production of a toolkit of service user involvement in criminal justice (Hayes, 2011) and the purpose of the RDA work was to test and review putting service user involvement into practice in a range of settings. The project included two probation trusts and three prison settings. This chapter will focus on the two probation projects and one prison. We aimed to conduct meaningful service user involvement projects in each of the settings we selected, and to record the challenges and successes of each in order to help other trusts and establishments learn from and replicate the processes.

About the services – probation at the time

Prior to 2011 Probation services in (England and Wales) were arranged via 35 Probation Trusts, all centrally accountable to the Ministry of Justice. The whole system was delivered by public sector employees, with some voluntary and charitable sector provision working alongside or commissioned by the public sector. Probation services were on the cusp of a major transformation. Under the Secretary of State for Justice at the time, Chris Grayling – a programme called Transforming Rehabilitation was set to completely transform the landscape of probation provision in the UK.

> I want to bring in the best of the public, private and voluntary sectors to help us achieve this and we will design a competition process which allows a range of organisations, including mutuals, to bid to deliver services.
>
> (Ministry of Justice, 2013, p. 3)

Another key element of the proposals was:

> new payment incentives for market providers to focus relentlessly on reforming offenders, giving providers flexibility to do what works and freedom from bureaucracy, but only paying them in full for real reductions in reoffending.
>
> (Ministry of Justice, 2013, p. 6)

Opening up probation services to private providers, and establishing Payment by Results contracts was a sea-change in the delivery landscape. The House of Commons Justice Committee (cited by Richard Garside in the Centre for Crime and Justice Studies) said:

> In place of a single probation service, operating locally, there will therefore be: 'two probation services (the new National Probation Service and the contracted provider) in every locality delivering similar services side by side and sometimes via one another. Each will have to form working relationships with other local organizations, bodies and services for the delivery of the joint or complementary services which characterise effective local work with offenders.' 'Ministers should recognise,' the Committee continues, 'that there is a potential risk that this will lead to inefficient use of resources, and confuse accountability at local level.' Introducing a more complicated structure, with a higher risk of inefficiency and the greater potential for confused accountability, does not sound like a very good basis for effective reform.
>
> (Justice Committee, 2014, p. 45)

Our projects were affected by the understandable suspicion and reticence from hard-working staff who were anxious about this impending change. Early sessions had moments of hostility - In several sessions with probation staff we were asked if Revolving Doors Agency was part of G4S or Serco (major supply chain companies bidding for contracts in the new Community Rehabilitation Contracts) and despite assurances, we felt that this suspicion continued, that we might sell our findings to the highest bidders to give them an advantage. It felt at times that staff used this suspicion as a reason not to engage with what we were trying to do. For example: when we asked staff to tell their clients that we were conducting research and to ask them to come and speak to us on the way out, we found that very few people were doing this.

Practitioner training: pro-social modelling

The Offender Engagement Programme was a three-year change programme for Probation Trusts focusing on the one-to-one relationship between the offender and 'the engaging practitioner'. Part of the Offender Engagement Programme was the development, national dissemination and promotion of an approach called SEEDS. The SEEDs model is Skills for Effective Engagement, Development and Supervision. A key element of this approach included pro-social modelling – for the probation officer (or offender manager) to model or demonstrate positive behaviours that they would expect to see in return, for example, politeness, being on time, having a positive attitude.

In particular, as Trotter (2009) has found, there is some evidence to suggest that pro-social modelling by peers can be effective, and this is a key principle of for example, peer research. Seeing your peers in a position of trust and responsibility, seeking your views and opinions, undertaking to act on them and then feedback to you, and then doing so, can be transformational for someone who sees themselves and people like them as lacking agency or opportunity.

> Modelling pro-social values by workers appears to influence the re-offence rates of their clients. There is also some evidence that modelling by other offenders also influences re-offence rates. I found in an Australian study . . . that clients placed on community work sites with other offenders had higher re-offence rates than clients placed on community worksites with community volunteers or by themselves. This was particularly so with young offenders (aged 17 to 21) and was evident after risk levels had been taken into account. This is certainly consistent with theories of differential association and a range of research studies pointing to the influence of peer group association.
>
> (Trotter, 2009, p. 150)

I would argue that the next stage in this would be for people to spend time with offender peers doing non-offending and non-punishment activities – to see another side to their peers and what they are capable of and like in a different social setting. To some extent our projects provided this space, and we discuss the positive relations that were formed amongst the groups in more detail further on in this chapter.

How we delivered the projects – getting started

The project began with seeking partners – RDA wrote letters to the Chief Executives of probation trusts and prisons across England, setting out the parameters of the project and inviting interested trusts and prisons to get in touch. The response rate was low. We first met with senior staff in the probation trusts – Chief Officer, communications officer, Senior Probation managers. RDA presented the rationale and benefits of service user involvement and following discussion a peer research project was chosen to be supported in both sites.

Recruitment

Posters were made up by the communications officer and an outline of the project circulated to offender managers. In one trust, 17 names were put forward in the first three weeks and in the other, only eight after two months and a great deal of chasing and prompting. Names were vetted by senior staff for risk and appropriateness. Some were screened out, because they were deemed to be too vulnerable at the present time, or had very recently commenced probation and there was a lot of coordinating of services to support them going on. We held information days which were drop-ins at the probation office, where the two coordinators were available to run through the project, answer questions and to take each interested participant through a brief questionnaire – asking why they want to do the research, what they hope to get out of it, any issues with mobility/childcare/reading/writing, and what dates/times they could attend trainings.

Venue

We had imagined it would be very important for training to take place away from the probation offices and that clients would welcome a neutral or more positive venue (such as a library, community centre or office space). This was something we asked about on the initial information day. To our surprise, everyone was happy for the training and meetings to take place at the probation offices. Perhaps the choice of Probation was in fact about reclaiming the space (reference) and challenging/remembering what it is for – a place of change for the people who use it. Initially, we had to ask for the key each time we wanted to use the toilet in one office. After a short while however, we were trusted to keep hold of the key for the duration of the time we were on the premises. It was interesting to see the shift in how people carried themselves within the probation office as they got used to the increased access in the space. Mike Seal describes in Chapter 4 the importance of liminal rather than safe spaces and in this way the probation office felt very much like a transitional space, the beginning of a change process. This change was the way in which people viewed themselves and the interaction with probation shifting from a largely negative experience, in which they lacked agency and experienced shame, to one in which they had agency, could affect change and see themselves as something more positive.

Activities and training

We held several days' training in research techniques and methods, and batted around a number of options for the content and direction of the research to take.[1]

In terms of a peer research typology, we positioned ourselves in the second approach as per Beresford's (2013) description:

> Three broad approaches to involvement in research projects are also identified. First is user involvement research, where input from service users is added to existing arrangements; second, collaborative or partnership research, where service users and/or their organisations and researchers and/or their organisations jointly develop and undertake projects and third is the user-controlled research where service users and their organisations initiate and control the research.
>
> (Beresford, 2013)

Observations on group forming and dynamics

One group was smaller and coalesced quickly – they were a young group and this probably helped build early rapport. The other was more diverse, with a greater age range and people from different socio-economic backgrounds. Both groups started out with more people but lost a few over time, with people not attending sessions. It was interesting how disappointed and let down by this behaviour other members of the group were. Possibly participants felt this as a transgression of acceptable behaviour within a group and this perhaps links back to the efficacy of peer pro-social modelling.

As in any group of people, there was considerable support offered around, with some individuals taking others under their wing, and strong relationships were formed. One of the transformative elements of the work was what I saw as shaking off the shame associated with being on probation that a number of participants felt. In particular, this was often people from more middle class and privileged positions who were surprised and embarrassed to find themselves 'in this situation' i.e. attending probation. Forming meaningful friendships with other people also on probation seemed to lessen the extent to which they saw involvement in the criminal justice system as a shameful thing, and allowed them to make some kind of peace with it – along the lines of 'it happens to all sorts of people'. I revisit this later as part of the analysis of identity and its impact on desistance.

Service user involvement in a prison setting

The prison work was much more challenging. It took a long time to get started, and felt mired in process. We had several meetings with the management team, often with several key people absent, at which we agreed terms of reference, and limits of the scope of the work. The management were keen to tell us about initiatives they already had, like the Listeners service, or wing representatives, with the suggestion under the surface that they already do this and don't need to do more. There was a lot of passing over of responsibility – it was often the person who was missing from the meeting who needed to take the next step, and then the next meeting would be spent catching that person up on what they had missed, only to be told that they didn't have time or capacity to help for a few months. When we got into the detail of the work, there was a definite lack of buy-in to the process. We sent round a document asking what changes had been made as a result of the previous service user involvement that people were so keen to insist had been happening. We asked:

Changes made in your area as a result of prisoner feedback/input: *'You Said We Did': Please list all changes you can think of and where the suggestion came from. Please also give names of anyone else you think we should speak to or who might have ideas about changes that have happened.*

The response we got to this detailed question was **"work is ongoing ready for HMIP in August"**.

We were not encouraged or able to form a group of prisoners to give training to or to engage in t a longer-term project. Rather we were offered the opportunity to do ad hoc events and a highlight of the project was the World Café activity.[2]

World Café is a methodology[3] for inviting comments and opinions on a particular theme, that is done by rotating participants around tables where they build iteratively on the comments of the previous users of the table. Setting up such an activity in a traditional Victorian prison was a challenge and an eye-opener. I arrived at the prison with bags of kit – paper cups and plates, biscuits, fruit as well as decorations – metres and metres of brightly coloured bunting, traditional red and white checked tablecloths and bunches of gerbera to put out in plastic cups for vases. I set up an old fashioned training room (like a large cell) with bars for walls and bars on the window, peeling paint, lino floor . . . in a couple of hours it was transformed into a warm and cheerful looking venue.

When the prisoners were brought in I remember having a moment of doubt – was this going to work? Would they think I was ridiculous for decorating the room like a children's tea party? The session was productive and the buzz was palpable. My favourite moment came as one of the biggest and hardest-looking blokes there motioned to the flowers on the table and said, 'Nice gerbera, Miss'.

At the end he asked if he could take a flower back to his cell. Naively I said of course, and there formed an orderly queue of prisoners to collect a gerbera in a plastic cup each. I'm pretty sure they wouldn't have got past the screw on their floor with their prizes but I didn't know that at the time.

Later we did negotiate (after forming a positive relationship with the Governor) to be able to hold a Joint Working Group with experienced and new representatives and we held a few of these in succession. However, there was a considerable churn in prisoners and a number of meetings were cancelled when lockdowns happened. Unlike the probation projects then, the prison project was beset by false starts, stalling from staff, a sense that existing programmes were 'enough'. I never got to work with a consistent group of people, to form the dynamics of a group, to participate in training or undertake research.

I believe the challenge is that much greater within a prison environment because prison is situated that much further towards the punishment end of the punishment – rehabilitation spectrum of services, the sense of 'them' and 'us' is (understandably) greater than in probation and staff are not ready there to embrace techniques and mindsets that stress the contribution service users can make to services. Service user involvement requires giving up of a modicum at least of power and control, and a prison environment is one in which the power and control exercised by staff over service users is a defining characteristic.

Highlights of the projects

In the Probation projects, a key success of the work was the positive involvement and influencing of Her Majesty's Inspectorate of Probation (HMIP). HMIP is an independent inspectorate, funded by the Ministry of Justice and reporting to the Secretary of State, who undertake regular inspection of Probation services in England and Wales, and their findings are published publically. The findings and recommendations of HMIP are taken seriously by Probation Trusts as regular reviews of performance and quality.

In 2011 we held a session at Revolving Doors Agency to which senior members of HMIP and people who had been in contact with the criminal justice system were invited for the latter to describe their experiences, both of probation and of service user involvement. The group described many aspects of their treatment and experience in probation that had had negative impacts on their lives and mental health, and also described the positive learnings and impact they'd experienced through being part of service user involvement programmes at Revolving Doors Agency and elsewhere. This session resulted in a commitment from HMIP to look at Service User involvement in their inspections – its existence, accessibility, quality and impact.

In one of the probation projects the outputs achieved were a report and recommendations which were presented to the staff team at an event at the local college. This again, was a liminal space – a place of learning and self-development. A particular highlight of the project was a short film the research team produced, led by one of the group with skills and experience in film production and editing. A highlight for the research team was being invited to show the film to the then Secretary of State at the National Offender Management Service (NOMS) offices in London.

The report and recommendations included sections that we were given assurances would go on to be incorporated into staff training – 'What makes a good probation officer' and 'Involving service users in sentence planning'. These sections presented several findings: the importance of being listened to, the ways in which a probation officer could demonstrate empathy and being non-judgemental, and the finding that many people on probation were unaware of their 'sentence plan' or their ability to influence and have input into it. As Glover (2012) has it, 'Choice and autonomy are given lip service, as "personal support plans" remain locked in office cabinets and designed and managed by professionals' (quote from Terry & Cardwell, 2016, referencing Glover, 2012).

The group were keen to share their experience and knowledge of how probation works with people coming into the service for the first time. This is a common theme in service user involvement projects and speaks to the desire amongst most people regardless of their circumstance, to help others. This is a powerful driver for people and a huge potential benefit for the services and for other service users. In one of the probation projects the team produced a leaflet about what to expect and how to make the most of your time on probation. It seemed the group found producing this quite cathartic/therapeutic – a realization that even if they didn't set out with the best attitude towards the probation offer, they did (through the project and their own growth and development) come to be positive and constructive in their dealings with probation. This was particularly true for one participant, who acknowledged when he started on probation he was angry and aggressive, and made a point of not engaging. It was powerful to hear him speak of the benefits of 'giving it a go, listening to what they say', and his wish to encourage others to do the same from the outset.

The Joint Working Group in prison did a similar thing – producing a new 'First Night' booklet where they shared their experiences and set out what you can expect on your first night and first few days in prison. There was a real recognition of the stress and fear experienced in these early stages and again, a sense that people had come through difficult times and were stronger now as a result of them. The clients were actively seeking to help others through the same experience – and as McNeill (2006) has it in his description of identity based desistance,

> Typically later in the process of change, involvement in 'generative activities' (which usually make a contribution to the well-being of others) plays a part in testifying to the desister that an alternative 'agentic' identity is being or has been forged.

We will see again later the impact of this kind of 'evidence' of a changed self, this is an important contribution that service user involvement activities can have in the desistance journey.

The Probation Game – video

In one of the probation projects the group made a short film:

> a comedic fiction poking fun at the thoughts and feelings of both staff and service users. For an added joke, the probation officer and the service user are played by people in the opposite positions. This film is based on real research undertaken by real probation service users to help improve the service for everyone.

> (Video/film credits from Revolving Doors, 2014)

The film's central premise is an enactment of initial appointment between service user and offender manager – repeated three times. In the first, the service user is unwilling to engage – she's taken drugs before coming, she gives one word answers and her body language is distinctly 'off'. In the second, the probation officer is cynical, bored of his job and suspects the worst of the person in front of him. The film makes use of though bubbles to convey what's going on in each of their heads. In the third, both parties are as bad as each other and the conversation pretty much grinds to a halt. The film makes use of direct quotes from the research . . . 'you just don't care', 'sentence plan . . . what?' and the single message is that both parties need to be engaged, open, trusting and willing to **engage positively in the process**.

Integrating the identity of 'offender' and moving forward

What struck me watching the film again was that the young man who produced it (working long hours and roping in friends to help get it finished on time) had had a previous experience as a film maker (student and commercially employed). I get the impression he was able to bring some of his former self into this experience of his present self (on probation) and that this helped him to reconcile and make sense of his current situation (someone on probation). Shortly after making the film, he was back working in film production.

Another example came from the other probation project. One of the participants had described her own shock at finding herself in trouble with the law – she was a middle class mother, and struggled with the sense that being on probation wasn't the sort of thing that someone like her should experience. She felt a great sense of shame. She was an extremely talented cake maker and made a themed cake for the launch of the findings event – it was stunning, and had a garden theme to represent growth and development. Again it felt that she had used her skills and interests and in bringing them to the project, integrated an aspect of her current self (being on probation) that she felt so awkward about, into an element of herself that she felt more positive about (being a talented cake baker).

Impact on self-perception – identity and desistance

In this chapter I argue that participation in the research projects positively impacted on participants' sense of self, enabling a shift to a more positive self-perception, perhaps enabling them to reconcile and move on with their lives. This is not new, as Mike Seal describes in Chapter 3. I am conscious of falling into the trap of re-inscribing the professional/community power divide 'emphasising the dignity and respect to be sought between user and provider, without any attempt to change the balance of power within it' (Braye, 2000). It is not surprising that it is often the most palatable for workers and it can also be the least challenging to their practices and structures (Seal, 2009). Having said that, these warnings are aimed at the practitioners, and I participated in this project as a facilitator, not a probation officer.

Throughout the project and in writing toolkits for staff I have been persuaded that service user involvement in criminal justice is particularly powerful and impactful because desistance is encouraged by an improved sense of self and one's own capabilities – a confidence to change and live differently. Effective desistance from crime requires a belief in your own capacity to live differently. Bushway and Paternoster (2013) describe it as

> a rational choice-based identity theory of desistance. Part of this process is that the offender begins to think that his current, working identity of a criminal offender is no longer desired and begins to think of a future self that is free from crime. This future self consists of both a feared self that the offender does not want to become and a possible self that they now aspire to and are motivated to become.

Service user involvement and particularly peer research can facilitate this shift in self-perception, from recipient of services/being talked to and having plans made about you to being in charge of something, driving it forward, telling others what you've found, how you've analysed it and what you recommend for the future. As such the participant gains a concrete example of their ability to do things differently. As Cahn (2004, p. 21) describes it: 'Co-production is a capacity based approach to involvement rather than a deficit approach, where the community moves from being seen as passive recipients of services and burdens on the system into are equal partners in designing and delivering services.'

In both the probation projects, a number of participants went into paid employment during the project. We can speculate on the link between participating and being able to secure work, but one participant's example made this link explicit. She was attending an interview for a sales assistant position in a supermarket. During the interview she talked about the peer research project she was involved in, how it involved speaking to and presenting to senior members of staff in the organization and how much she enjoyed helping others in the team. She was offered a supervisory position and told us she felt it was a direct result of her experience and skills gained through the project.

A service user involvement project also changes the relationship and dynamic between the individuals and the professionals – what Beresford (2013) calls 'othering' – and we saw on a couple of occasions the shift in these relationships. In particular, when the Chief Officer came to do a session with the group. We'd been together for a few sessions by then, and a group dynamic had formed, we felt comfortable together. It was interesting to see her nervousness when she came in to the room, a sense of the tables being somewhat turned. One of the group in particular was passionate and articulate and asked follow up questions, giving the Chief Officer something of a grilling. You could feel the sense of confidence that grew in him during the session, and it was interesting how many times he came back to things she said over the weeks, it had obviously been an important exchange for him.

Another occasion where we really saw a change in the dynamic was in the interviews with probation officers. Again there was a nervousness – on both sides – with the probation officers feeling wary and anticipating being 'caught out' somehow or made to say something they might regret, and the researchers feeling that this was an opportunity to show themselves in a different light, and perhaps conscious of being able to 'turn the tables'. Although perfectly cordial, there wasn't a particularly friendly atmosphere. One question from the researchers changed all this. 'Why did you get into this work?' The workers paused, seemed visibly to relax – as if 'this is an easy question'. The answers – invariably 'because I wanted to help people and to make a difference' – seemed to break down a barrier between researchers and officers and there was a moment of warmth and mutual understanding. When officers said things like 'I'd tried a couple of other jobs, hadn't liked them' or 'I didn't get on very well at school' or 'my aunt was a probation officer and I really respected her' the researchers saw a different, human, fallible side.

Use of language and speech acts

The research asked probation officers and clients to list the most important attributes of a probation officer. We then ranked the responses, as below.

Top ten – client

1. Makes a difference/helpful
2. Understands (empathetic)
3. Cares
4. Listens
5. Trustworthy
6. Non-judgemental (especially on crime)
7. Friendly/human
8. Positive about things (and clients)
9. Challenges me (doesn't collude)/truthful
10. Respectful/encourages and enables

Top ten – worker

1. Listens
2. Follows through and does what says they will
3. Respectful
4. Challenges me (doesn't collude)
5. Friendly/human
6. Consistent
7. Encourages and enables
8. Understands (empathetic)
9. Explains things/is clear
10. Positive about things (and clients)

It is interesting how important 'cares', 'trustworthy', 'makes a difference' and being 'non-judgemental (especially on crime)' scored highly for clients, but didn't register for workers. While their responses show these characteristics in different ways – e.g. 'follows through and does what says they will' is a way of demonstrating 'trustworthiness' and being 'friendly/human' and 'empathetic' could be synonymous with caring – there was a sense of the need for clients to have these attributes named – 'I care about you' or 'I'm not here to judge you'. As Wittgenstein might have had it – the use rather than the meaning of what offender managers/probation officers say might need to be made more explicit in order to register for clients. McNeill (2006) citing Rex (1999) describes how 'probationers interpreted advice about their behaviours and underlying problems as evidence of concern for them as people, and 'were motivated by what they saw as a display of interest in their wellbeing'.

There was a discussion during a meeting between an offender manager and the peer researchers about the point when an offender became an ex-offender. The worker felt that the important turning point was where the client started calling themselves an ex-offender. McNeill (2006) cites Maruna and Farrall (2004) who suggest that it is helpful to distinguish primary desistance (the achievement of an offence-free period) from secondary desistance (an underlying change in self-identity wherein the ex-offender labels him or herself as such. The Peer researcher said that they found the point where the worker started calling them an ex-offender equally important, as it gave them some independent affirmation. This is referenced by Terry and Cardwell: 'People must be able to imagine themselves beyond the identities of addict, offender, or mental health patient. This new identity must also be reaffirmed by others' (quote from Terry & Cardwell (2016), citing Farrall, 2005, p. 23). As Austin (1962) has it 'can saying make it so?' Clover (2011) describes identities as being 'both self and socially defined or confined'. McNeill (2006) goes on to say 'offender managers' role might be constructed as prompting, supporting and sustaining secondary desistance wherever this is possible (McNeil, 2006).

Both of these examples, where the client seems to require the explicit naming of the thing – that the offender manager cares, or sees them as an ex-offender, bring to mind Austin's (1962) work on language. I would argue that these are illocutionary or indirect speech acts that have a greater communicative power than the words alone – that they are greater than the sum of their parts. In other words, these are transformative acts of speech that can change the world around us – making the other person see that we care and are interested in them as a person by the things that we say, and changing a person's self-perception and perhaps even their behaviour – by describing them using a particular label (ex-offender) rather than another (offender). As per the point earlier about pro-social modelling I wonder whether the act of participating in the research helped consolidate people's own ideas that they were moving towards being ex-offenders themselves.

Conclusion

In this chapter we have seen some of the issues that arose from a selection of service user involvement projects in different settings. We have examined the potential benefits of involvement, particularly in a research project to service users themselves and how in some settings (difficult macro-level change such as new national policy or more micro-level such as a prison setting) meaningful service user involvement can be at risk of sabotage or never getting off the ground. We have argued that involvement can help individuals reconnect with their own sense of agency, and a positive self that can help them move forwards in their journey.

Notes

1   Details are available in M. Seal (2016) *Running a Peer Research Project With Offenders in the Community: A handbook for Staff.* London: Revolving Doors Agency.
2   More information in Revolving Doors Agency (2016) *Improving Your Prisoner Involvement Systems: A Toolkit for Staff.* London: Revolving Doors.
3   www.theworldcafe.com

References

Austin, J. L. (1962) *How to Do Things With Words.* Cambridge, MA: Harvard University Press.

Beresford, P. (2013) 'From "other" to involved: user involvement in research: an emerging paradigm.' *Nordic Social Work Research,* 3(2): 139–148.

Braye, S. (2000) 'Participation and involvement in social care.' In H. Kemshall & R. Littlechild (eds), *User Involvement and Participation in Social Care: Research Informing Practice.* London: Jessica Kingsley Publishers, pp. 9–28.

Bushway, S. D. & Paternoster, R. (2013) *Identity and Desistance from Crime.* First online: 30 September 2013. Available at: https://link.springer.com/chapter/10.1007/978-1-4614-8930-6_4 [accessed 2 January 2018].

Cahn, E. (2004) *No More Throwaway People: The Co-production Imperative.* New York: Essential Books.

Clover, D. (2011) 'Successes and challenges of feminist arts-based participatory methodologies with homeless/street-involved women in Victoria.' *Action Research,* 9(1): 12–26.

Farrall, S. (2005) 'On the existential aspects of desistance from crime.' *Symbolic Interaction,* 28(3): 367–386.

Garside, R. (2014) *The Coming Probation Privatisation Disaster.* Centre for Crime and Justice Studies. Available at: www.crimeandjustice.org.uk/resources/coming-probation-privatisation-disaster [accessed 7 February 2017].

Glover, H. (2012) 'Recovery, life long learning, social inclusion and empowerment: is a new paradigm emerging?' Referenced in L. Terry & V. Cardwell (2016), *Understanding the Whole Person.* Available at: www.revolving-doors.org.uk/file/1845/download?token=3jprn2sc [accessed 7 February 2018]. (Glover (2012) originally from P. Ryan, S. Ramon & T. Greacen (eds), Empowerment, Lifelong Learning and Recovery in Mental Health: Towards a New Paradigm. New York: MacMillan, pp. 15–35.)

Hayes, C. (2011) *A REVIEW of Service User Involvement in Prisons and Probation Trusts* Clinks, London. Available at: www.clinks.org/sites/default/files/Service%20User%20Findings%20Sept%2011.pdf [accessed 7 February 2018].

Justice Committee (2014) *Twelfth Report: Crime Reduction Policies: A Co-ordinated Approach? Interim Report on the Government's Transforming Rehabilitation Programme.* Available at: https://publications.parliament.uk/pa/cm201314/cmselect/cmjust/1004/100402.htm [accessed 7 February 2018].

Maruna, S. & Farrall, S. (2004) 'Desistance from crime: a theoretical reformulation.' *Kölner Zeitschrift für Soziologie und Sozialpsychologie*, 43: 171–194.

McNeill F. (2006) 'A desistance paradigm for offender management.' *Criminology & Criminal Justice*, 6(1): 39–62.

Ministry of Justice (2013) *Transforming Rehabilitation: A Strategy for Reform*. London: HMSO.

Revolving Doors Agency (2016) *Improving Your Prisoner Involvement Systems: A Toolkit for Staff*. London: Revolving Doors.

Revolving Doors (2014) *The Probation Game*. Luton: Courage of our Convictions productions, video/film.

Seal, M. (2016) *Running a Peer Research Project With Offenders in the Community: A handbook for Staff*. London: Revolving Doors Agency.

Shadd, M. & Farrall, S. (2004) 'Desistance from crime: a theoretical reformulation.' *Kolner Zeitschrift für Soziologie und Sozialpsychologie*, 43: 171–194.

Trotter, C. (2009) 'Pro-social modelling.' *European Journal of Probation*, 1(2): 142–152.

13 The absent lens of the peer researcher

Reflections on and beyond a research project into youth violence

Richard Campbell

Introduction

My name is Richard Campbell, and I was a peer researcher for the Touch EU project investigating how youth workers can work with young people who are both perpetrators and victims of street violence, including the nature of that violence. The research with young people was broadly participatory research (Kemmis, et al., 1998; Petty, et al., 1995. The aspiration of the project was that the voices of young people would substantively inform the research process and that my knowledge and experience of the topic, as well my experience of being a youth worker, would inform the project and help assess 'what worked?' in order to improve practice. An integral aspect of the project's approach was the use of two peer researchers from the UK who had personal experience of the issue and understood the local context. I was one of these peer researchers. As Mike Seal explores in Chapter 3, there is a large body of literature on peer research. However, there is also criticism about the tokenism of some of this participation, particularly with young people. This includes accusations of manipulation, unequal power-relations and the adult focus of such research. It is often adults who frame research questions, choose the methods and control the analysis; for the most part and children are unequal partners (France, 2000).

This chapter investigates the concept of a peer researcher from the perspective of someone who has undertaken the role. I aim to look at what makes for good and bad practices in engaging peer researchers in research. It also explores my transition from being a community support worker to becoming a peer researcher, assessing the degree to which I had reach and impact on those young people's lives. My audience is academics, universities, community members, and, in particular, other peer researchers who may wish to reflect on how they have, or may, experience involvement in research. I wish to share thoughts on how to improve the community research base on using community practitioners as peer researchers.

My role will be clarified, evaluated and explored through reflections on my two year experience as a peer researcher. Throughout the process I kept a critical reflective journal for my studies which is the basis of my reflections. I will explore how my identity as a researcher developed, and reflect on the skills I think are necessary to underpin this role. In particular I will focus on the need to learn complex academic language, the importance of creativity and building on existing skills, personal development, and clarification of what is powerful about the role of a peer researcher. I will assess the adaptive, dynamic impact I had and the methodologies I learnt (and needed to have learnt). I argue that peer researchers are able to directly access certain perspectives that academic and professional researcher cannot. We can have a unique impact, but there is good and bad practice in enabling this to happen.

The journey to using academic language

My first steering group meeting was also my first encounter and involvement with academics. The steering meeting was a high profile academic round table. We did not attend all of the steering groups and, reflecting back, to have done so would have been valuable to the research. This is where peer researchers have the potential to demonstrate their importance to the research. To have had at least one peer researcher in every steering group meeting would have been useful. It would have enabled us as peer researchers to develop our critical thinking, confidence in our expertise, and would have given academics perspectives from practitioners and community points of view. A more meaningful engagement would have allowed us, as peer researchers, to increase our self confidence, belief in the validity of our knowledge, develop our self-esteem, and given us confirmation that our views mattered and could effect change. It would also have given us broader personal development opportunities, extending our social and networking skills through working with both academics and participants. Steering groups need to consult with peer researchers to understand and move forward with the problems that the research may encounter. Peer input would give members of the committee insight into the skills peers have acquired that may help with implementing solutions – practitioners and peers have expertise and a history of working in this sector that is often untapped as a resource. Similarly workers should have attended. Early negotiations with workers revealed that they had similar suspicions about academics (Seal & Harris, 2016).

The language used in the meetings we did attend was often very academic and served to intimidate. Over the last three years, I have increased my academic language through working with Dr Martin Glynn from Birmingham City University who I met in 2012 during my role as a peer researcher. Dr Glynn took the time to examine my work and identified that I needed more training and support, particularly on research methods and academic frameworks for research – the training on the project had not properly equipped me. I needed support in helping me develop my academic skills, which he has done. It is so important to support peer researchers to identify such needs. At times, particularly when I started, I felt very alone, low on confidence and on reflection did not receive enough training. My involvement in the planning and execution of the research was therefore not as meaningful as it could have been. In fact, I was put to the side a number of times doing the research, as I do not believe they had trust or faith in me to deliver some academic tasks for the research.

There are dangers in doing this with peer researchers. Rather than building their confidence, it can decrease it. After completing my MA in youth and community work I became a guest lecturer and student mentor at Newman University, which aided my transition from being a peer researcher to being a researcher in general. I gained a much better understanding of academic language and how to use it when presenting my ideas. Reflecting back, I strongly believe that doing my Master's, either in the process, or after completion of the project, would have enabled me to develop into a much better peer researcher. It would have given me knowledge and understanding I needed to prepare me for my role as a peer researcher. The amount of reading and writing I had to do throughout my masters showed me how much I missed out on. I was not given or allowed the training and time to become a disciplined peer researcher, and certainly not an academic, or achieve some balance between these roles.

As this was my first time in the world of academics it would have been ideal to have had a mentor to support and enable me to find that balance and manage my transition from community member to academic. Academics must be very careful that peer researchers do not become simply facilitators and mediators between young people and academic researchers, or just data gathers, but valid researchers in their own right. Positively this experience made me determined to understand the world of academia and academics, and this is the path career I now want to pursue.

Becoming a peer researcher, and then going on to study for my Master's degree, created a change in the way I present my work. Being in an academic environment for a few years helped shape and transform my academic thinking and writing. The experience of becoming a peer researcher and doing field work and academic assignments strengthened this. For example, I was very good at being descriptive when I first started, but struggled to apply my knowledge and write academically. Undertaking study and field work concurrently meant I had to apply more academic concepts, and this started to transform my academic writing. It also improved my research abilities. By gathering a variety of information from different perspectives and authors, I started to increase my reading, writing and knowledge of academic frameworks. It also impacted on methodologically as I started using more than one method to collect data on the same topic. This assured the validity of research through the use of a variety of methods. I captured different dimensions of the same phenomenon and deepened as an academic and peer researcher.

I also deepened my organic knowledge of techniques such observations, interviews, program documentation, recordings, photographs, books and using quotations that represent program participants in their own terms. Capturing participants' views of their own experiences, in their own words, became paramount for me. I started to harness the learning and skills I already had from the multiplicity of roles I managed daily; as a peer researcher, guest lecturer, student mentor and practitioner into my new role as a research and academic. This wealth of experiences in multiple settings, combined with a new academic analytical perspective, meant I became a grounded researcher and an ethnographer. I saw the purpose of the fieldwork I did and used it in my everyday practice. This in turn enabled me to conduct better research and developed my academic writing. This transformed my work in that when I presented my work, I had a critical attitude. Having embraced critical analysis means that now writing academically appeals to me. I reflect critically on my work all the time, often keeping a record and journal of those experiences and conceptualizations.

I have found myself penetrating deeply into subjects much more profoundly, exploring ideas that require greater knowledge and understanding. This has been to an ever greater depth than when I engaged in higher education and the peer research project and means I now want to pursue study at doctoral level. My view on my career has also been transformed through peer research and academic engagement. Since being a peer researcher I have concentrated on creative literacy work, assisting in institutions such as schools, university, educational centres and community organizations. This has given me a tremendous sympathy for oppressed people in society and an intellectual desire to understand the dynamics of that oppression. I have contributed via speaking at conferences, facilitating student learning, holding workshops and advice sessions, special events, further research, international visits, guest lecturing and student mentoring with a goal of building community, skills and knowledge in education, youth and community work and community organizing settings. This has culminated in my developing the Bless centre.

What difference did it make being a peer researcher?

As a peer researcher, trust was a real key. Trust was also important to the groups of young participants and practitioners that took part in the research project. It was essential in making data collection and interviews with young people meaningful. As Mike Seal mentions in Chapter 3, many authors consider trust to be vital to youth work and the helping professions (Goetschius & Tash, 1967; Perlman, 1979). Participants in the research also valued trust. A trusting relationship with a street-based worker acted as a counter to some of the other dehumanizing experiences and symbolic violence (Bourdieu, 1990a and b) young people had been subject to in their relationships with adults. As some of the young people said, they have been in front of a lot of workers and been subject to care, justice and social systems all their lives. They had to find a way to discern how and why any new worker would be different. One of their criteria was to *know* the real motives of the worker, and be convinced that the worker cared about them as individuals. Only then could a trustworthy relationship begin.

Trust was needed in research, and not just for methodological purposes, or just between participants and peers, it was essential for all parties involved in the research project. Peer researchers were the link between all parties involved, from academics practitioners, young people, communities, and other sectors. One of the distinctive features of this project was the use of peer researchers in this way. We identified that young people and those involved in violence may mistrust perceived authority figures (Decker & Van Winkle, 1996) and members of the educational establishment, including university researchers.

By involving peers, researchers broke down barriers between researchers and the researched. As part of this we had to tap into the illogical side of trust, especially when working with people whose sense of trust had either never been present, or had been shattered (Seal & Harris, 2016). Sometimes we trusted in participants knowing that they may well betray that trust. This was done in the belief that giving such trust will eventually elicit more trustworthy behaviour and develop therapeutic trust.

However, this was no simple task. Referring back to my journal, I talked to Dr Mike Seal about the complexities of this, and how expectations for peer research needed to be managed. During my time as a peer researcher part of my job was to engage with young people and get them to open up. However, it was not sufficiently taken into consideration that I could not just walk in to the home and say 'right tell me about your life' or 'I need to ask you a few personal questions'. Although I was a peer researcher with experience of the topic being investigated, both peer researcher and participants, would automatically put up our defensive barriers, leaving peer researchers feeling very anxious to challenge or be criticized for not doing 'their role'.

It was vital for me as a peer researcher, and someone working in this sector, when speaking to young people to establish what it was that made them trust their workers. As noted already, two themes they mentioned were firstly, authenticity and secondly, that they believed the worker cared about them. In my experience, when on the road, it can seem that you are alone and can never get out of situations and go through the necessary transitions in your life. Having someone listen, and being listened to, that can understand the nuances of this, can relate it to their own life and share it back with the participant, is what brings trust. I remember young people saying to me 'yeah we heard it all before'. As young people they were used to being treated as consumers or objects and their previous experience of research was no different. Peer researchers with knowledge of this and an ability to share similar experiences were needed.

It felt like being a mediator between academics and young people, as some young people never really trusted the academics in the research as they did not have this experience to give. There were times when the academics in the research team would approach young people, but would be shut down in their conversations. I remember young people asking me 'Are they police or private investigators?' They had some kind of sixth sense and could see right through academics and people in higher authority. They could not see themselves in them. Having a 'road' background, and knowing some of the unwritten rules of how respect and trust are mediated in marginalized communities where violence prevails meant that I could work with their sixth sense, and see what it would take to establish credibility.

Trust was something that I had to demonstrate explicitly. As a peer researcher I adapted how to demonstrate trust to my audience and participants involved in this research. I had to show that we were not just using them for the purposes of the research, but were going to give something back. I worked hard to create that trust, to have impact on their lives, and to deliver the passion that conveyed authenticity.

I needed to show I cared about them and that the research was a reflection of this. They needed to know that we were investing in them personally as a peer, this made all the difference. They had to be convinced that I was genuine in wanting to make sure their voices were heard. At times I challenged the research managers to make sure we delivered that, and they were aware of this. Interestingly it was when I started to make these challenges with my research team that I felt a growing level of respect for me, not as a youth or support worker, but as a researcher with some important ethical views to take into consideration, and ideas that must be listened to.

Time and commitment were also vital factors in trust. Within the Touch project spending time with young people over several days and weeks and months was so important in building trust. There was a point when I was based in Islington in North London where the academic gave up on collecting data from young participants, they had got all they felt they could, and needed. I thought that there was both more to get, and that the young people needed support which we were ethically bound to give. As a youth and support worker with a street background, this experience enabled me to complete the task of gathering data through continued interactions with these young participants around street violence, and to support them in their processes when they opened up, and the things going on in their lives. It was my commitment to the responsibilities of what a trusting relationship means, and my resilience in going back to London time and time again, that proved to be a tipping point. This led in time to a breakthrough where I was allowed into their 'circle of trust'. Any research using peer researchers needs to adopt a process to research that recognizes and enables this commitment to be developed. It needs an approach to ethics that entails following through on supporting people, and part of that is that we give back. Some of these young people I still keep in contact with today. We need to reflect on the trust-building process and the depth it requires.

Street, creativity, and validity

Recent research has found that people who have been involved in street violence prefer to speak to someone who is perceived as credible (Decker & Van Winkle, 1996), and participants' perception of the validity of the peer researchers' personal experience is key. However, it goes further than this – participants in the Touch project needed to identify with, or at least see aspects of themselves, in the peer researcher, giving me a massive advantage in this. Through my experiences from the 'road', and having a practitioner background of youth work and working with BME groups, I had developed a variety of transferable skills (for example, research-ing information, presentation, project management, negotiation and decision-making). As importantly as having these skills was that I could articulate them. As the young people related to aspects of my experience, it meant that they could see some of those skills in themselves. I was a mirror of them, and this helped them start to see that they also possessed many transferable skills.

An added factor was that I had something to give – as a music producer, which was one of the creative methodological approaches I used, conducting music workshops with the Islington detached youth team on their buses. When undertaking my Master's degree, I studied ethnography, which was something that really interested me as a creative person with an interest in sociology. Ethnography is the study of social interactions, behaviours and perceptions that occur within groups, teams, organizations and communities. As we were researching young people and street-based violence, I felt this creative element was overlooked and under-emphasized in the Touch research. The use of creative approaches should have been expanded upon as it can be methodologically within ethnographic research. Most importantly, it was a feature of both the young people's, and my, interests. A positive example is where I took group of young participants from Germany and London and spent time creating the Touch audio musical LP called 'Young voices of the streets'. This had a strong emphasis on exploring the nature of the social phenomenon of violence. Its unstructured free narratives were still able to be coded, and were far more effective than seeing the data through the lens of a closed set of analytical categories.

My credibility and being allowed into the circle of trust also meant that I could challenge their constructions of violence. At first some of the rhymes they created were clichéd and focused on postcodes, violence and sexist statements. I encouraged them to challenge their own self-perceptions, and explore how they really experienced violence and what it meant to them in their lives, introducing ideas like symbolic and structural violence that they may not have encountered before – I had earned the right to do this, both through the demonstration of my commitment and through my experience as a music producer, and it changed radically the lyrics that they created. This is something that I am very proud of as a peer researcher in terms of my contribution to the research. It captured so much key data and highlighted and gave depth to several themes. It also allowed me, and the young people, to be creative with a sense of purpose, rather than feeling like the people who collected data. Capturing these ethnographic perspectives was paramount.

I was also in a unique position to make judgements about the validity of the data, and to interrogate it with both the young people and academics. That I had been allowed into their circle of trust, and been given permission to develop an understanding of young people's lives, was a determining factor in the assessment of the data. That I had had to get close and become a reliable trustworthy person to the young participants in order to gather qualitative information and research data in turn made the data more trustworthy. This was where we came into our own as peer researchers. We helped to keep explanations made based on partial evidence in check. People's utterances became a starting point for further investigation, rather than an end point. As peer researchers we helped to keep the research grounded. As we were accepted in the circle of trust with young people, we could meaningfully check out what people really thought, and then go back and check it again, sometimes challenging it. Only through this iterative and developmental process did the research begin to unfold young people's multi-layered perspectives and truths. Only through this process did we truly start to co-examine with young people their encounters with street violence and what it meant to them. We enabled the research project to explore with the young people what they really wanted to say. This enhanced the quality of data and kept things in line with the stated aims to the research to give young participants a better understanding of their local realities, to give them the tools to analyse their situation themselves, to truly involve them in learning and in decision-making, and to move forward on the issues.

Evaluations of data were solution-oriented – we did not dwell primarily on problems, but rather focused on learning lessons from both successes and failures (Florin, Chavis, Wandersman & Rich, 1992). The level of control given to young people in a research project shapes the research, the tools and methods to be used, and the extent to which young people felt motivated to take part and continue with the project. The more control and decision-making power young people are given during the research, the higher the level of ownership will be, and the richer the data.

I guess that was why my journal ended up at 25,000 words after finishing the Touch project, and much of the learning from this has yet to be mined. Developing 'Young voices of the streets' taught me a lot as a peer researcher about the interpretation of cultural behaviours. Rather than studying members of a cultural group as an outsider, we need to understand their worldview as they define it. Reflecting back now, if I had had more space and time to develop these creative spaces it would have had a positive impact on the research, as well as developing my academic skills as peer researcher. Nevertheless, the interviews, videos and music recording enabled us to study people's lives, or should I say the academics in the research team were able to analyse and examine participants' ways of life, customs, meaning of behaviours, meaning of language, and culture over a period of time.

New learnings (data verbalization)

After being a peer researcher for the Touch project, and completing my Masters in youth and community work in 2015, I continued my academic development with Dr Martin Glynn from Birmingham City University, one of the world's leading criminologists and specialist academic and educational writers. I read his book *Black Men and Invisibility* and wanted to learn more. I remember going to Dr Glynn's house where he had over 3,000 books and had read them all. Reflecting back on my time as a peer researcher and academic with Newman University and sharing this with Dr Glynn, I realized that I had so much more to learn, that what I had been taught had been partial and patchy at best, and that what I had learned was only a start. I had only really been taught enough to undertake the aspects of the research that the academics wanted me to undertake – I had not been taught enough to truly engage with the process, to reach my own potential, and in turn, for the research to reach its potential. In particular my analysis of the data had been minimal, and this made me realize that a new way of enabling peer researcher in data analysis and presentation needed to be developed.

Dr Glynn became my academic mentor. I would go to his house after finishing work to improve my reading and writing and understanding of research. This was the start of things to come during the year of 2015. As a peer researcher back in 2011 I was left wanting to create new ways to present research. I wanted to conduct and present research in a way that embraced not just privileged academics, but the community, organizations and corporate sectors, bringing academia to the streets and to communities. Dr Glynn and I decided to develop an approach. We took a music studio setting to present different forms of lectures, to create impact in our communities and enable learning to take place.

So, as a music producer in 2016, I convinced Dr Glynn to record a version of his doctoral dissertation – that took him two to three years to write. He distilled his thesis down to a 12-minute single called 'Silence', produced by myself. My journey had meant that we have developed a new way of presenting data called 'Data Verbalization'. This is an approach that communicates and disseminates research data using performance approaches and techniques 'Data Verbalization Lab' examines, explores and interrogates the interdependent relationship between method (*Data Verbalization*), theory (*critical inquiry*) and practice (*performance*). 'Data Verbalization Lab' is about researchers, academics, & practitioners experimenting, devising, and engaging creatively with research data, designed to generate wider environmental, social, and cultural impact. We hope that the forthcoming book *Speaking Data and Telling Stories: Data Verbalization for Researchers* will be an invaluable resource for researchers, scholars and related practitioners who want to strengthen their ability to communicate and disseminate research data using live performance (*spoken word*) approaches and techniques. *Speaking Data and Telling Stories* will be a vital text that provides guidance for anyone wanting to generate wider environmental, social, and cultural impact using research data creatively.

Further learning about methodology as a peer researcher

What follows are some observations on other aspects of the research process. I do not necessarily have answer to the questions they raise, but wanted to highlight them as issues of concern, some of which Mike Seal has examined throughout the book.

Qualitative research

Since being a peer researcher I have developed a more comprehensive understanding of qualitative research as a means of investigating the *why* and *how* of processes in order to develop concepts. Qualitative research is sometimes defined as interpretive research, and interpretations can be incorrect or biased, and the findings may be controversial. In this regard my approach to research has become a lot more rigorous and disciplined because if people do not like the results, the first thing they will do is criticize the rigour of your methods. Given that the peer researcher is considered to be a vital aspect of the research instrument, qualitative research cannot depend upon traditional approaches to address concerns such as bias and credibility. Qualitative research can also work with, not against, quantitative research, playing a key role in 'validating' it or providing a different viewpoint on the same social phenomena.

Ethics and the researcher–participant relationship

The relationship and intimacy that is needed between the researchers and participants in participatory studies can raise a range of different ethical concerns. Participatory researchers face dilemmas such as respect for privacy, at the same time as seeing the need to establish honest and open interactions, and avoiding misrepresentations. Ethically challenging situations may emerge if researchers have to deal with such contradictory issues, and they will need to choose between different strategies in conflict if they arise. In such cases, disagreements between conflicting demands of participants, researchers, ethical guidelines, the funding body and society may be inevitable.

The method to be utilized needs to explain, clarify and elaborate the meanings of different aspects of participants' human life experience. Researchers have to interpret people's experiences because they are involved in human activities. The principle of 'no harm' to participants ought to be considered by researchers, who should be aware of the potential harms that might be inflicted upon study subjects. Obviously, sometimes a conflict between the right to know (defended on the basis of benefits to the society) and the right of privacy (advocated based on the rights of the individual) will need to be ameliorated. Development of personal relationships with participants are inevitable and desirable when collecting data. Therefore, researchers should seriously consider the potential impact they may have on the participants and vice versa, and details of such interactions should be clearly mentioned in research proposals and detailed in researchers' reflective logs. Overall, the role of the researcher as a stranger, visitor, initiator, insider-expert or other should be well defined and explained.

Data gathering and data analysis: peer research and youth and community workers as ethnographers

In qualitative research, data is collected from a multitude of sources, and explores multi-layered narratives, in order to produce an interpretation of the meaning of participants' experiences. An interview comment sheet could assist the researcher to note the feelings of informants, as well as interpretations and comments that occurred during the interview. Data collection needs to be as overt as possible, and findings should be recorded. When a researcher aims to study the culture of certain people, living their lives alongside them may be inevitable. This is also something that a youth and community worker does as part of their job – they are in this sense 'natural' ethnographers. However, this method of collecting data is a subject of debate from an ethical point of view. The presence of the researcher amongst people of a particular culture necessitates their informed consent, but the nature of this consent becomes problematic the longer their presence goes on. Yet, ironically, it is this length of time that makes the perspective of the youth and community worker unique and their research meaningful. In order to gain meaningful data, youth and community workers as ethnographers need to know the ethnographic process. There are eleven steps defined in ethnography that are meant to assist researchers (Geertz, 1973; Gluckman, 1961). These steps include participant observation, ethnographic record, descriptive observation, taxonomic analysis, selected observation, componential analysis, discovering the cultural theme, cultural inventory and, finally, writing ethnography.

My learning from the content of the research: symbolic and structural violence

This notion of symbolic and structural violence was probably the concept that had the most resonance with me. It played to my self-interest and aided my develop-ment as a peer researcher, practitioner and academic. As was noted in the Touch project (Seal & Harris, 2016) when we talk about violence we tend to just consider physical violence. The notion of 'symbolic violence' comes from the work of Pierre Bourdieu. It represents an extension of the term 'violence' to include various modes of social/cultural domination. Symbolic violence is the unnoticed (subconscious) domination that everyday societal habits and conformities maintain over the conscious individual. Symbolic violence should not be confused with 'media vio-lence'. It is not related to the acts of murder and mayhem portrayed on television. Actually, symbolic violence is not normally even 'recognized' as violence. For example, gender domination, and gender itself (say, in the construction of sexual-ity) represents one prominent arena of symbolic violence. Through institutional-ized modes of 'discipline and punishment, as Foucault noted (in his work *Discipline and Punish,* 1979), violence has acquired a positive social value, without much thought going into the violence involved in these practices. Indeed, Bourdieu tells us that such 'soft' violence has been mostly overlooked in social theories, and is subject to 'misrecognition' in everyday life.

Bourdieu's theory of habitus allows us to see people's attachment to things like cultural practices as learned and habituated. Violence becomes a part of the vocab-ulary and lived lives of communities, such that they do not even notice it. However, a community's habitus should be seen as the product of social conditionings, and it can be endlessly transformed. It is open to modification and reconstruction through developing the reflexive agency of the community through educational practices (Bourdieu, 1990a). For generations the school has been seen as the site of these social conditionings. In this sense education is used as the 'field' to habituate a cultural identity. My fieldwork research concentrated on this subject. If we are to understand why street violence occurs, and is an ever-present element in young people's lives, we need to understand how all forms of violence are embedded in their realities and routines of daily life, and how one form of violence can nurture another). Symbolic violence also refers to the imposition of a system of symbolic meanings upon groups 'in such a way that they are experienced as legitimate (Jenkins, 2002, p. 104). It is 'violence which is exercised upon a social agent with his or her complicity' (Bourdieu & Wacquant, 1992, p. 167). This legitimacy obscures existing power relations, often making them unrecognizable to, and mis-recognized by, agents (Kim, 2004). This includes demonization and structural/symbolic violence towards young people (France, 2000; see Symbolic Violence and Public Space (Ghannam, 2002) and coverage of youth work and symbolic violence (Cooper, 2012).

Conclusion

My journey and experience as a peer researcher is now over. I would like to conclude with some thoughts and recommendations for research teams considering using peer researchers, people considering becoming peer researchers, and even students doing their field research on something they have experienced themselves.

- In contemplating undertaking participatory research and qualitative research with peer researchers the research team should prioritize recruiting the right type of peer researchers for the topic being investigated. Peer researchers should be interviewed to see if they have the required ability, skills, and potential, to develop the academic knowledge required. Peer researchers should have passion, interest, basic knowledge of the research that they will be undertaking and be willing and ready to undertake lots of reading and writing.
- Peer researchers should always be aware of the precise nature of and reason for their involvement in a study. This is in order to minimize the impact of undesirable personal issues coming up. The probability of interviews unearthing vicarious trauma for the peer needs to be evaluated and appropriate support put in place. Research teams should have schedules that provide peer researcher with sufficient recovery time and reduce the risk of emotional exhaustion. The project should allow ample time for analysis of the data and ameliorating other emotional aspects of the research. It is also necessary for the researcher managers to be familiar with signs of extreme fatigue and be prepared to take necessary measures before too much harm is done.
- Research teams should make sure that there are clear protocols for dealing with peer researchers' distress so that both parties involved in research can use them if necessary. As it is not easy to predict what encounters are likely to lead to distress, peer researchers should therefore receive sufficient training in predicting situations. Adequate professional supervision and supervision sessions directed at learning, developing insight and skill development are essential for peer researchers. This fosters their ability to carry out research professionally while building confidence.
- Research teams should provide peer researchers with opportunities for self-development and self-care, and facilitate the process of self-reflection and self-monitoring. It is necessary for peer researchers to continuously update their investigative skills and methodological knowledge.
- Peer researchers should strive to find novel techniques to better carry out studies in the field in natural organic settings. This requires peer researchers

to work in close collaboration with other members of the team and under direct supervision, and they need to feel able to discuss and resolve issues as they arise.

- Peer researchers can benefit and develop by conducting research in different settings and at all levels. There should be clear guidance, frameworks and training for peer researchers conducting research, so they can shape their creativity. This should include explicit ethical protocols, guidelines and codes.
- Peer research can be very beneficial to academic students, youth and community workers, practitioners and other sectors helping bridge the gap between academia and community, thus enriching academic research. Peer research should be more collaborative while not losing sight of the goal to improve peer researchers' learning and developments and help them through their transitions and changes.

References

Bourdieu, P. (1990a) *In Other Words: Essays Towards a Reflexive Sociology*. Cambridge: Polity Press.

Bourdieu, P. (1990b) *The Logic of Practice*. Cambridge: Polity Press.

Bourdieu, P. & Wacquant, L. (1992) *An Invitation to Reflexive Sociology*. Cambridge, UK: Polity Press.

Cooper, C. (2012) 'Imagining "radical" youth work possibilities – challenging the "symbolic violence" within the mainstream tradition in contemporary state-led youth work practice in England'. *Journal of Youth Studies*, 15(1): 53–71.

Cushion, C. & Jones, R. L. (2006) 'Power, discourse, and symbolic violence in professional youth soccer: the case of Albion Football Club.' *Sociology of Sport Journal*, 23: 142–161.

Decker, S. & Van Winkle, B. (1996) *Life in the Gang: Family, Friends and Violence*. Cambridge: Cambridge University Press.

Florin, P., Chavis, D. M., Wandersman, A. & Rich, R. (1992) 'The Block Booster Project: a systems approach to understanding and enhancing grassroots organizations.' In R. Levine & H. Fitzgerald (eds) *Analysis of Dynamic Psychological Systems*. New York: Plenum.

France, A. (2000) *Youth Researching Youth: The Triumph and Success Peer-research Project*. Leicester: Youth Work Press.

Geertz, C. (1973) *The Interpretation of Cultures*. New York: Basic Books.

Ghannam, F. (2002) *Remaking the Modern: Space, Relocation, and the Politics of Identity in a Global Cairo*. London and Berkeley, CA: University of California Press.

Gluckman, M. (1961) 'Ethnographic data in British social anthropology.' *The Sociological Review*, 9(1): 5–17.

Goetschius, G. & Tash, M. J. (1967) *Working with Unattached Youth: Problem, Approach, Methods*. London: Routledge and Kegan Paul.

Kemmis, S. & McTaggart, R. (eds) (1998) *The Action Research Reader*. 3rd edition. Geelong, Victoria, Australia: Deakin University Press.

Kim, K.-M. (2004) 'Can Bourdieu's critical theory liberate us from the symbolic violence?' *Cultural Studies-Critical Methodologies*, 4: 362–376.

Perlman, H. H. (1979) *Relationship. The Heart of Helping People*. Chicago, IL: University of Chicago Press.

Petty, J., Guijt, I., Scoones, I. & Whompson, J. (1995) *Participatory Learning and Action: A Trainer's Guide*. London: International Institute for Economic Development.

Seal, M. & Harris, P. (2016) *Responding to Youth Violence Through Youth Work*. Bristol: Policy Press.

14 From relationships to impact in community–university partnerships

Randy Stoecker, Karen Reece
and Taylor Konkle

The centrality of relationships in community–higher ed partnerships

From the early days of service learning to today, many academics have put relationships at the center of community-higher education partnerships (Beran & Lubin, 2012; Lillo, 2016). This is partly because trust is a central issue in such partnerships (Kaye, 1990; NCAI Policy Research Center and MSU Center for Native Health Partnerships, 2012), especially given the history of many communities' interactions with academics that have practiced an extractive or colonizing model of research (Smith, 2012). This also means that academics must learn about and practice respect for community members' beliefs, and cultural practices (Rink, Montgomery-Andersen, Koch, Mulvad & Gesink, 2013). Writers emphasize communication (Blouin & Perry, 2009; Sandy & Holland, 2006; Stoecker, 2009; Strand et al., 2003), mutual understanding (Sandy & Holland, 2006), and mutual commitment (Stoecker & Tryon, 2009) as core characteristics of these relationships. Effective communication is particularly important to clarify goals, roles, responsibilities, and expectations (Blouin & Perry, 2009).

Some analysts even propose typologies of relationships between academics and communities. Stoecker (1999) distinguished initiator, consultant, and collaborator relationships, preferring the collaborator model as the most participatory academic-community relationship. Clayton et al. (2010) differentiated exploitative, transactional, and transformative relationships, preferring the transformative model. Similarly, Hicks et al. (2015) emphasized relationships that maximize democratization between faculty, students, and community. In general, the focus is on relationships of mutual benefit or reciprocity (Shappell, 2015; Porter & Monard, 2001).

Although the relationship is important, the emphasis on relationships can make it seem as if the goal of community–higher ed partnerships is simply to have a relationship. This perspective neglects the question of whether that relationship has impact. The most understudied topic in all of community–higher ed partnerships is impact (Clarke, 2003; Sandy & Holland, 2006; Blouin & Perry, 2009; Stoecker et al., 2010; Stoecker & Beckman, 2014). Are any of those relationships creating social change and advancing social justice? In this chapter we will present a case of relationships that also had a strategy and helped to produce real change. We will begin by discussing how our relationships developed from the first-person standpoint of the community.

Karen Reece—the community leader

In 2015, I worked with Randy Stoecker on a project with Justified Anger, an initiative seeking to reduce racial disparities in Madison Wisconsin—which has some of the most extreme Black:white racial disparities in the United States (Race to Equity report, 2013)

As the Director of Research and Program Evaluation for Justified Anger, I was excited to work with a team of students that effectively increased my own very limited capacity and the capacity of the organization. Randy's approach to this project was to have the community state the specific needs and then guide his capstone class to develop a way to meet those needs. This approach ensured that our organizational needs were truly met as opposed to an approach where the students develop a project and then ask community to participate.

As this project wrapped up, I started the thinking about other ways to engage university research for social justice work around Hip-Hop. Even though Hip-Hop—a culture born by African American youth in 1970s New York City to provide entertainment and speak out against oppression—is the most popular music genre, surpassing rock and pop music (Harris, 2017), it remains stigmatized and marginalized.

In Madison, and many other places, Hip-Hop has become code for African American people and allows discrimination against events that draw large crowds of people of color without labeling it as such. Rap artists, 80% of whom are African American, have struggled over the past three decades to gain a foothold in Madison's nightlife. After many failed efforts to organize over the years, the Urban Community Arts Network (UCAN) formed in 2010 to unite Hip-Hop artists and fans and to begin to chip away at the stigma Hip-Hop faced. When Madison nightlife stages were inaccessible, UCAN created performance opportunities in outdoor spaces and community centers. To gain access to stages in nightclubs, UCAN began calling meetings with local elected officials and the police department to address these issues. The dominant narrative was that Hip-Hop shows drew crowds that were violent and disruptive and that it was too much of a risk for venue owners to host this genre. This narrative persisted even though there was no empirical data backing up the claim.

I became president of UCAN in 2011, and long wished we could gather the data assessing the actual risk that Hip-Hop posed. I pitched to Randy the concept of developing a data set that could answer the question of whether Hip-Hop really was more violent than other music genres. Randy found this concept interesting and we continued our partnership, planning this new research for the next fall's capstone course.

An outcomes model for partnerships

How do we go beyond just having good community–academy relationships to actually accomplishing things together? Karen saw the potential for research to confront the fears of music venue owners about Hip-Hop and potentially open up those venues to more Hip-Hop shows. Randy Stoecker had been working on a model for how community–academy partnerships could produce real change through research. That model inverted the traditional service learning model that puts student learning first, some token charity service second, support for community third, and social change last. The new model starts instead with specifying a social change goal and then building a sense of community around that goal. The "service" is an organized knowledge project supporting the social change goal. That knowledge project is used to educate everyone—community, researcher, students, and the broader public—to achieve the social change (Stoecker, 2016).

What are knowledge projects in this model? This is where another model, called *project-based research*, comes in. It is similar to what physicians do when they treat medical conditions. The process begins with diagnostic research to determine the cause and characteristics of a social problem or issue. Next, with that diagnostic information, we can gather knowledge on how to solve it—creating a "prescription." Then we implement the strategy and evaluate how well it works (Stoecker, 2013). In this chapter we will show how we put into practice both of these models, starting with a first person account from the professor.

Randy Stoecker—the professor

I entered the relationship with Karen Reece motivated to fight racial injustice. I am the parent of a multi-racial daughter, a teacher of increasingly diverse students, and a resident of a city whose progressive reputation is challenged by increasingly visible racism in nearly every facet of the community. I had a long history of doing community-based research (CBR) and community organizing technical support with a variety of community groups that I could offer.

I had been working on a model of using capstone courses to do CBR projects. With a group of skilled and advanced students, I could do CBR projects that were bigger and could have more impact than if I did them alone. And because capstone courses are not restricted in content and instead are supposed to integrate a broad swath of what students have learned, CBR projects seemed the perfect focus. Each capstone can be devoted to a single CBR project designed with a community group to focus on the specific issue they are addressing. The project with Justified Anger together was not as impactful as I'd hoped (though Karen has helped me see how Justified Anger has picked up on some of the work), but I found with Karen a very comfortable working relationship. She loved being in the class with the students and the students loved having her in the class. Our standpoints felt very compatible and complementary in a way that allowed students to get two perspectives that combined rather than clashed.

Toward the end of that project Karen introduced me to UCAN, and educated me on discrimination against Hip-Hop in Madison. UCAN had a ready set of research ideas and a clear vision of why they wanted research and what they would do with it. My only concern was that, aside from a basic mainstream knowledge of Hip-Hop, I was pretty ignorant. But the project called out to me. In the previous year I had watched on TV as my daughter's boyfriend—a student in UW-Madison's innovative First Wave scholarship program supporting students to do Hip-Hop—performed spoken word at the Kennedy Center. I had attended a First Wave performance event featuring one of the students in my community organizing class—a student who had begun the class with skepticism, and at the end performed for the class. In both cases I was awe-struck at the depth of meaning and emotion I witnessed. So this opportunity felt deeply right even while I felt embarrassingly ignorant. When I revealed my own self-consciousness about my ignorance, Karen urged me to reflect on how community group members feel when they are confronted with the exclusionary language of academia and how disempowering that can feel.

What about the students?

Randy and UCAN met over the summer to develop the project and a syllabus for the capstone course. The project we settled on was a study of calls for service to the Madison Police Department from 2008–2016 for all bars with entertainment licenses, to which the students would then add data on whether there was a performance at the time of each call and what the genre of the performance was. UCAN provided the readings on Hip-Hop for the syllabus, along with contributing to its overall structure.

Much of our discussion was about what the students needed to know for accomplishing the project. That is different from the dominant model that emphasizes what students should learn *from* the experience rather than what they should learn *for* it. Existing literature on community–campus partnerships has been overwhelmingly concerned with student outcomes—how much students learned or how much their attitudes changed, with community outcomes being almost ignored (Warren, 2012; Reeb & Folger, 2013; Schmidt & Robby, 2002; Stoecker & Tryon, 2009). That prioritization risks further exploitation of marginalized people, and it may not be warranted on pedagogical grounds. When we look closely at the research, the extra intellectual benefits service learning might provide are small at best (Warren, 2012; Reinke, 2003; Parker-Gwin & Mabry, 1998) and sometimes the practice can even reinforce problematic attitudes and perceptions (Medina, 2011; Mitchell, 2010; Billig & Eyler, 2003, p. 15).

If we use the new inverted model described earlier, which makes change the priority, we can establish the knowledge tasks required of all partners, and can consider what students must learn to fulfill those knowledge tasks. There is certainly substantive learning—students need to learn about the issue on which the project is focused. But in this new model they also need to learn professional skills such as project planning and management, teamwork, facilitation, group-centered leadership, and research methods and judgment. We typically don't tell students about any of this strategy. They either enter the experience thinking it will be just another class or, as some of our students did, worrying that it will follow the traditional service learning model. A first-person capstone student account illustrates this concern.

Taylor Konkle—the student

My first experience working with a university service project was in my junior year when I went to Peru with an on-campus organization whose mission was to "build a worldwide movement empowering the poor in their fight for equal access to healthcare, education, and a safe home." I signed up thinking this might be a great field experience with the potential to "make some kind of a difference." But leading up to the trip there were no cultural competency trainings, no informational sessions—just a packing list sent out three weeks before we left. I felt like I was going into the trip not knowing what to expect, but I was still excited for the "adventure".

When we got to Peru, we were informed that we would be working in rotating clinics alongside Peruvian doctors for four of the five days. The last day was to be focused on a development project building a concrete staircase in a low-income community that was built on dry and sandy slopes.

On the first day of clinical week, our roles as assistants were vaguely defined. We were supposed to assist in whatever ways they asked—in Spanish, and understanding Spanish wasn't a prerequisite for this trip. The second day I was paired with a dentist and another student from a different college. Almost immediately, I was assisting the dentist in filling cavities. We could only work on the worst problem per patient and the decision to pull that tooth or fill that cavity was made quite abruptly. I thought, "my training is in the social world, not dentistry. I am not training to be a medical professional." The trip for me was plagued with uncomfortable situations, introspective moments, but most of all a sense of undeserved power.

I knew, after that trip, I wouldn't commit to that type of service-learning again, but it also didn't close the door to working with other diverse communities. My academic career focused on problems in the world around food systems, development abroad, sustainability, and poverty. It's not the type of course material that elicits non-action. Conversely, it inspires thinking, action, and change. Otherwise, quite frankly, it could be overwhelming focusing on all the bad.

In my major, Community and Environmental Sociology, we were required to take a capstone course. There were two types of capstones to choose from: One was a literature study with a decent amount of career preparation and the other was a community-based research project. I chose the community-based research project with Randy Stoecker because I wanted to work with another community in a more controlled setting where we could discuss background information on the community and learn about its culture.

The process of our partnership

Beginning

Our capstone class had nine enrolled students and a paid Service Learning Fellow from the University of Wisconsin Madison's Morgridge Center for Public Service to assist with student reflection and project logistics. We began with UCAN leaders presenting Hip-Hop history and culture to ensure the students understood the genre was more than just music and entertainment, and that an underlying racial context was driving the narratives (UCAN leaders attended most classes to help direct the research project). We then did reading and training in the essential skills needed for the project: teamwork, project management, facilitation, group-centered leadership, and specific research skills. There was some tension between the critical perspective the students had learned through most of their coursework, and the research methods perspective that the results "will be what they will be" and may not support that critical perspective. We did not know, for example, whether the data might show that Hip-Hop was associated with more violence.

There was also some anxiety early on. The project was to study police calls for service to all Madison bars with entertainment licenses. Randy had a network relationship with the Madison Police Department (MPD) and was tasked with getting the initial data. He had past experience with such data in another city, but didn't know if MPD might be different. The students anxiously wondered when they would receive the data and what it would consist of. With a project lasting only a semester, students felt there was no time to waste. It felt strange to plan how to use the data without knowing what it was. The Service Learning Fellow was trained in helping students identify and reflect on such anxieties, providing a valuable service. Thankfully, Randy quickly secured the calls for service data. MPD also volunteered a second database of charges filed from the calls for service, and provided ready assistance on understanding and interpreting the codes used to describe the calls and charges.

The challenge was that the data contained over 10,000 calls for service. In thinking about the "scope" of a community–campus partnership project, one important consideration is whether it is doable in one semester. It was very clear that we needed to make the data set fit our capacity. After discussion, Randy, Karen, and the students first eliminated all calls between 4am and 7pm, since those would not be connected to a music event. Second, we eliminated calls that were irrelevant to our research question or would not be tied to behavior at an event, like liquor license checks, 911 pocket dials, traffic accidents, etc. That brought the data set down to a bit over 4,000 calls. Randy was still concerned, but believed completing the project within one semester was possible, and was prepared to complete it himself if it took longer. We also decided to turn the research question into a hypothesis, using standard hypothesis language, to test what we saw as the dominant cultural stereotype. The hypothesis we were testing was that Hip-Hop attracted more violence. Then our null hypothesis was that there is no difference between Hip-Hop and other music genres in attracting violence.

As we began to understand the project's scope and complexities, we also started to see the different tasks and skills needed to complete it. We listed the tasks and skills on movable whiteboards and the students then listed themselves where they perceived their own skills. The skills included communication skills, data analysis skills, technological skills, writing skills and much more. Thus we could fit students into roles that suited their skills and determine needs for further training.

The main data task was that the MPD data did not have any information on who may have been performing during the time of a call and what their genre was. We then needed a plan for collecting and coding that performance data. UCAN leaders and the students jointly created a list of every possible source of performance announcements, including the city alternative weekly, a local specialty music magazine, online sources, and sundry other possible sources. We divided up the calls by venue, with each student having a roughly equal number of calls to gather performance data for. We had students maintain their own spreadsheet, and charged one student with checking each person's data before importing it. A subgroup worked on how to code performances for genres. They created their initial list, gave it to UCAN to review and revise, determined the easiest ways to code all the artists, constructed the spreadsheet, and trained the class in its use.

Collecting the data and moving toward analysis

Matching performances to police call data wasn't as easy as students hoped. There were many police calls where the students could not readily find performance data. This led us to reach out to music venues to see if they could provide old event listings that included the artist and the date. The students were much more optimistic than Randy that, if they just asked venue owners, they would get the data. Some venues responded and others didn't respond even after several follow-ups. Several times they were receptive until someone said, "we are trying to find out if there is a difference between types of music genres and violence . . .". Sometimes the venue manager, owner, or booking agent was initially responsive, but never followed-up.

This was frustrating for the students and we spent time debriefing both the logistics and emotions of this data collection experience. The students found it difficult to think about analyzing data that seemed "incomplete" even though both Karen and Randy tried to reassure them that this is the reality of research. From the student perspective this was really difficult to accept. Students are taught throughout their college experience that the most complete papers and most complete assignments receive the best grades. It was hard to imagine proceeding with a somewhat "incomplete" data set along with being unsure whether venue owners would come through with more information. We were trying to get the most complete data set possible, and some students lost sight of the possibility that an incomplete data set could still provide a valid analysis.

The students also had varying levels of engagement with the project. Some were committed almost to the point of risking their other schoolwork. Some were barely interested. Some were sick at inopportune times. But, in contrast to the traditional service learning model, where students are sent out to fend for themselves, Randy played the role of project leader and kept close tabs on everyone's progress. When a student was falling behind to the point of impeding the group progress, he stepped in to rearrange the work and do some of it himself to keep the project on track. This showed students that the professor was not above doing the actual work, and reinforced the importance of the project.

Continuing the commitment

In the traditional service learning model, where student learning is the priority, when the semester is done the project is done, whether it is any good or not. In the model we used, the project wasn't done until it was done well. As the fall semester ended we did a few initial analyses with the data that we had collected, but we realized that we had only scratched the surface of what the data could tell us. So we had to decide what to do. Randy had become used to such projects growing— this was his third capstone project that expanded beyond the initial course into the next semester. Karen was happy to have a more complete analysis even if it meant waiting until the spring. Five of the original capstone students signed up for credit to continue the project in the spring, and the Service Learning Fellow also continued. So we continued on, digging even deeper for performance and genre data, combining the two data sets, and designing a variety of analyses using a triangulation strategy to compensate for the gaps in our data.

And while we found more data, the data set remained incomplete. As the spring semester continued, we realized that we needed to do the analysis before time ran out. The students felt much trepidation over having a data set with holes in it, and often got sidetracked by small details in the data. Randy intervened by urging the students to "stay out of the weeds"—making quick decisions on problematic details rather than getting paralyzed by the imperfection. Randy proposed that students fill in missing data by looking for patterns in existing data and using existing knowledge of music venues. For example, when students knew that a bar had regular performances on certain nights, and booked a consistent genre, they could fill in the missing data with those patterns. Karen agreed with this strategy and gradually convinced the students to move onto data analysis with a good rather than perfect dataset.

Another motivator for students to move to analysis was the opportunity to present a poster for the university's annual undergraduate research symposium that spring. The symposium provided the first opportunity for students to present initial findings to other people in the community. So the students switched into analysis and now had a deadline to meet. The poster included a map of the downtown Madison establishments showing the places with more calls for service, and graphs that analyzed calls by genre from different standpoints. Having the deadline to finish the poster presentation for the symposium forced the students to stay "out of the weeds" and wrap things up. The students came together as a group and made difficult decisions about what the final analyses would be and how to present the results and conclusions.

Impact

The study had an impact even before it was completed. While we were doing the research, the study was covered in a lengthy feature article for one of the student newspapers (Solotaroff-Webber, 2016), so the word was out. Additionally, an incident occurred at a Hip-Hop concert where an argument between two women resulted in an intervening staff member getting hit in the head with a bottle, requiring stitches. The venue hosting this concert immediately announced a one-year ban on Hip-Hop there. The resulting outrage from the Hip-Hop community prompted the venue to host a community conversation about their future booking practices. UCAN also increased its advocacy for a city-sponsored task force on music and entertainment that would investigate why Hip-Hop was underrepresented on city stages and make recommendations for changing this. This idea was supported by various city agencies, but had stalled in the process of determining specific language and staffing needs. The incident with the venue, public knowledge of the research we were undertaking, and the public outcry put pressure on the City of Madison to accelerate the formation of the task force.

On the evening of the student research symposium, UCAN hosted a community conversation about the upcoming City of Madison task force on equity in music and entertainment. Karen was excited to bring the poster to the meeting, spread it out across the table, and explain the approach and results to community members. The reaction ranged from confusion over the project's complexity to excitement over having such a detailed analysis, but everyone was thrilled to see the conclusion showing that Hip-Hop was not associated with more violence than other genres. UCAN now had data to support an argument the community could only make anecdotally for the past 15–20 years.

The students spent the next few weeks completing analyses and writing up the final report. UCAN networked with local news media and prepared a press release to ensure the study would be covered and released to the public. The final report was covered in two local newspapers and a music and entertainment website, and then picked up on the websites of the TV news stations. The coverage varied in tone, but all respected the work that had been done and recognized that the study could not support the dominant narrative about Hip-Hop attracting more violence than other genres in the city. Since then, the study has been cited by reporters and community members in news articles and public discussions. It was used as foundational information for the new city music and entertainment equity task force—established three months after the public release of the report—for the police department, and it has been published in a peer-reviewed journal (Fearing-Kabler et al., 2018). This was the end of an academic project for the students, but fueled the fire in UCAN's fight for equity.

Discussion

Randy:

This project has reinforced in me the importance of going beyond the relationship emphasis in the community–university partnership literature to look at how to move those relationships to impact. By using the new model that starts with change, then community, then service, and then learning, we could give community impact the importance it deserves. We started with UCAN's social change goal—to end racialized discrimination against Hip-Hop in Madison.

We were able to build a sense of community among students, the professor, and UCAN leaders. The students who continued had a cohort experience that is exceedingly rare in higher education. A number of them came out to UCAN meetings that were some distance from campus, and attended the annual Hip-Hop awards. I also attended my first Hip-Hop awards show, and have been at three UCAN events since then. Our sense of community was not the alienated and euphemized "mutual benefit" exchange of student volunteer hours for student education but the mutual goal of fighting racial injustice.

The "service" we performed far outpaced the typical "hours" model where students provide untrained labor for a limited time. We did high-end, high-stakes research. This was also a massive project—the kind of thing many researchers wouldn't touch without a big grant. But I had 10 students, counting the Service Learning Fellow, and I knew from previous projects that we could do something big. This model of partnering one class with one group for one research project has so much more impact than the individual student placement model of most service learning practices. It also shows the value of the diagnose-prescribe-implement-evaluate cycle in the project-based research model. This research project was an amalgam of evaluation and diagnosis. By asking how much violence is associated with Hip-Hop compared to other genres, we were "evaluating" the effects of an input—Hip-Hop—on an outcome—violence. We were also diagnosing how much of a "problem" Hip-Hop was in relation to violence. UCAN is now taking that research into the policy arena with the city's task force on equity in music and entertainment. They will hopefully produce prescriptions that can be implemented and then evaluated.

The learning part of the equation was placed where it belongs—at the end of the list rather than the beginning. Once we had the change goal, and Karen and I had enough of a relationship to do the basic outline of the project, we could figure out what students needed to learn—not for themselves but for successfully carrying out the project. Of course they learned much more than that, but the important learning was that which prepared the students to do the project successfully. The project management and teamwork skills they learned, I believe, played a large role in that experience. By carefully tracking the project every week, and having team assignments that were broken up into individual assignments, we were able to keep things on track, hold each person accountable, and troubleshoot before little issues turned into big ones.

So yes, relationships of trust and respect are important, but they are not important as an end in themselves. Without respect for the community's expertise, those of us on the university side could have easily gone down a research path that would have been uninformed and uninforming. UCAN's expertise on Hip-Hop, music genres in general, and the Madison music scene were crucial in shaping the research to be valid and reliable. Showing trust and respect encourages people on the community side to contribute their expertise rather than withhold it out of worry their ideas will be dismissed or discounted. But all of that trust and respect is enacted within a context of seeking to achieve a mutual goal and develop a strategy for achieving it. Without the goal and the strategy, the trust and respect is wasted.

Karen:

I'm not sure the students or Randy realized exactly how groundbreaking this research could be, although it was difficult to hide my excitement. I had been trying for at least five years to find a way to do this project. I never had any doubts that the students and Randy would be able to produce something useful for us.

As a small community organization and one focused on Hip-Hop, we were used to dealing with stigma and not being taken seriously by other more established organizations. Even though we knew Randy and the students were taking this seriously and showing respect to the problem at hand, we didn't really know what to expect as a final outcome. As we approached the end of the first semester, it was clear that we would not be quite finished with the work. The coding step was an enormous undertaking and there are only so many hours in the day. I knew Randy would continue long enough to give us some kind of final report, but I did not anticipate that six students would continue on and dedicate significant time and energy to seeing this project through. This commitment, by itself, showed UCAN that other community members really did care about seeing equity in this area. This commitment validated UCAN's participation as an equal partner with the University of Wisconsin.

Community academic partnerships CAN be beneficial to both the academic and *the community sides of the partnership. A critical piece of this project was that Randy and the students listened to and heard the community need before developing the research project or even the research question. This helped to ensure that we were asking a question appropriate to the context and could then design appropriate methods. With my academic roots and research training, I was surprised at how much I expected a power imbalance. I looked at Randy and the class as being much more knowledgeable than we were and was hesitant to "get in the way." A critical factor in establishing UCAN members as equals came when even the methods were designed with us at the table. Even though some UCAN members did not understand the process of research design, they were able to speak their expertise as the methods were developed. When UCAN expressed concern about an approach or interpretation, the researchers listened and treated us as equals. We also realized that the success of the project required our expertise in the process of data analysis. We were the true experts in the room and in the city that could appropriately characterize music genres and the categories certain events or venues would fit.*

It was essential to turn the traditional service learning model on its head to take this project from a transactional experience to a transformational experience for all involved. The entire process began with UCAN stating and defining a social change goal. Because of our collaborative process, we developed meaningful relationships with the students that deepened when six students continued on for a second semester. Through our discussions, research, and data analysis, we developed true allies in the students who were committed to finding the truth about the inequities in Madison's entertainment scene. A challenging piece of this project, as with any research project, was the potential impact of bias. UCAN had a pretty clear idea of what we thought the conclusions would be, although I remained confident that the data would be useful whether or not the conclusions confirmed our expectations. Having a group of independent researchers provided a level of objectivity that maintained the project's integrity. That said, the students respected our input in the interpretation of the data and framing of the conclusions. This approach allowed UCAN to control the public narrative, but gave us a method to strategically deliver results to the broader community so they would be recognized as coming from a respected University and not just the assumedly biased, and often disregarded, opinion of a community organization. The final report allowed us to rule out violence as a diagnosis for the inequities we observe. UCAN could then use this report as a foundation to move the task force on equity in music and entertainment past the usual discussion of public safety and directly to root cause analysis informing a prescription to treat this issue. We are hopeful that the process of building allies in the research process will also prove useful as we look for funding and support to implement the recommendations "prescribed" by the task force. For the first time, thanks to this project, we are seeing the conversation progress.

Taylor:

I have learned that community-based research projects can amount to something more than just a completed task, a job well-done, or a good grade. Upon signing up for the capstone course with Randy, I knew I would be receiving a grade, which undoubtedly was an extrinsic motivator. But once the process began, I had an intrinsic desire to provide an outcome for this community that was actually useful. In fact, it was as if all six of us remaining students shared this common goal when proceeding with the project into the next semester. This alone created a close relationship with each other and a close relationship with UCAN. With the focus more about the community and less about the specific learning of us students, our common goal was achieved and learning was inherent in the process.

While most of our meetings were in a classroom, the skills and learning we acquired during this research project transcended the average classroom experience. The skills we gained included how to listen and effectively communicate with different groups of people, how to work with others, and how to navigate and use resources outside of the classroom to create a successful outcome. Personally, I was able to fine-tune my data analysis and data management skills, experience community and passion in the research process, and discover more about myself as an academic and as a member of society. Further, this research project has opened my eyes to the injustices that exist in the Madison Hip-Hop and entertainment community and I now have a greater awareness of these issues.

References

Beran, J. & Lubin, A. (2012) 'Shifting service-learning from transactional to relational.' *Journal of Jewish Communal Service*, 87(1/2): 88–92.

Billig, J. & Eyler, S. H. (2003) 'Enhancing theory-based research in service learning.' In J. Billig & S. H. Eyler (eds), *Deconstructing Service-learning: Research Exploring Context, Participation and Impacts*. Greenwich, CT: Information Age Publishing, pp. 3–24.

Blouin, D. D. & Perry, E. M. (2009) 'Whom does service-learning really serve? Community-based organizations' perspectives on service-learning.' *Teaching Sociology*, 37: 120–135.

Clarke, M. (2003) 'Finding the community in service-learning research: The 3-"I" model.' In J. Billig & S. H. Eyler (eds) *Deconstructing Service-learning: Research Exploring Context, Participation and Impacts*. Greenwich, CT: Information Age Publishing, pp. 125–146.

Clayton, P. H., Bringle, R. G., Senor, B., Huq, J. & Morrison, M. (2010) 'Differentiating and assessing relationships in service-learning and civic engagement: Exploitative, transactional, or transformational.' *Michigan Journal of Community Service Learning*, 16: 5–22.

Fearing-Kabler, A., Konkle, T., Laitsch, J., Pierce, H., Rater, C., Reece, K., Stoecker, R. & Varelis, T. (2018) 'Is Hip-Hop violent? Analyzing the relationship between live music performances and violence.' *Journal of Black Studies*, 49(3): 235–255.

Harris, V. (2017) Hip hop dethrones rock as most consumed music genre in the U.S., Nielsen Music stats reveal. *New York Daily News* July 18, 2017. Accessed January 4, 2018 at www.nydailynews.com/life-style/hip-hop-dethrones-rock-most-consumed-music-genre-u-s-article-1.3336085.

Hicks, T., Seymour, L. & Puppo, A. (2015) 'Democratic relationships in service-learning: Moving beyond traditional faculty, student, and community partner roles.' *Michigan Journal of Community Service Learning*, 22(1): 105–108.

Kaye, G. (1990) 'A community organizer's perspective on citizen participation research and the researcher–practitioner partnership.' *American Journal of Community Psychology*, 18(1): 151–157.

Lillo, S. (2016) 'Rapport at the core: Relationships in service-learning program development.' *InterActions: UCLA Journal of Education and Information Studies*, 12(2): 1–22.

Medina, E. (2011) 'Innovation in education: The influence of service on stereotypes.' *Michigan Journal of Social Work and Social Welfare*, 2(2): 132–151.

Mitchell, T. D. (2010) 'Challenges and possibilities: Linking social justice and service-learning.' *Michigan Journal of Community Service Learning*, 17(1): 94–97.

NCAI Policy Research Center and MSU Center for Native Health Partnerships (2012). *'Walk Softly and Listen Carefully': Building Research Relationships with Trial Communities*. Washington, DC, and Bozeman, MT: Authors. Accessed January 4, 2018 at www.ncai.org/attachments/PolicyPaper_SpMCHTcjxRRjMEjDnPmesENPzjHTwh OlOWxlWOIWdSrykJuQggG_NCAI-WalkSoftly.pdf.

Parker-Gwin, R. & Mabry, J. B. (1998) 'Service learning as pedagogy and civic education: Comparing outcomes for three models.' *Teaching Sociology*, 26(4): 276–291.

Porter, M. & Monard, K. (2001) 'Ayni in the global village: Building relationships of reciprocity through international service-learning.' *Michigan Journal of Community Service Learning*, 8: 5–17.

Reeb, R. N. & Folger, S. F. (2013) 'Community outcomes in service learning: Research and practice from a systems theory perspective.' In P. H. Clayton, R. G. Bringle &

J. A. Hatcher (eds) *Research on Service Learning: Conceptual Frameworks and Assessment: Communities, Institutions, and Partnerships.* Sterling, VA: Stylus, pp. 389–418.

Reinke, S. J. (2003) 'Making a difference: Does service-learning promote civic engagement in MPA students?' *Journal of Public Affairs Education*, 9: 129–157.

Rink, E., Montgomery-Andersen, R., Koch, A., Mulvad, G. & Gesink, D. (2013) 'Ethical challenges and lessons learned from *Inuulluataarneq* – "Having the Good Life" study: A community-based participatory research project in Greenland.' *Journal of Empirical Research on Human Research Ethics: An International Journal*, 8(2): 110–118.

Sandy, M. & Holland, B. A. (2006) 'Different worlds and common ground: Community partner perspectives on campus-community partnerships.' *Michigan Journal of Community Service Learning*, 13(1): 30–43.

Schmidt, A. & Robby, M. (2002) 'What's the value of service-learning to the community?' *Michigan Journal of Community Service Learning*, 9(1): 27–33.

Shappell, A. S. (2015) *Cultivating Mutual Relationships in Service-learning.* Summer Service Collaborative Conference, Xavier University, Cincinnati, OH.

Smith, L. T. (2012) *Decolonizing Methodologies: Research and Indigenous Peoples.* 2nd edition. London: Zed Books.

Solotaroff-Webber, H. (2016) Hip-hop a threat? Local organization, professor hope to uncover truth once and for all. *The Badger Herald*, November 29. Accessed December 12, 2017 at https://badgerherald.com/artsetc/2016/11/29/hip-hop-a-threat-local-organization-professor-hope-to-uncover-truth-once-and-for-all/.

Stoecker, R. (1999) 'Are academics irrelevant? Roles for scholars in participatory research.' *American Behavioral Scientist*, 42: 840–854.

Stoecker, R. (2009) 'Are we talking the walk of community-based research?' *Action Research*, 7: 385–404.

Stoecker, R. (2013) *Research Methods for Community Change: A Project-Based Approach.* 2nd edition. Thousand Oaks, CA: Sage Publications.

Stoecker, R. (2016) *Liberating Service Learning, and the Rest of Higher Education Civic Engagement.* Philadelphia, PA: Temple University Press.

Stoecker, R. & Beckman, M. (2014) 'Making higher education civic engagement matter in the community.' In J. A. Laker, K. Mrnjaus, and C. Naval (eds) *Citizenship, Democracy, and the University: Theory and Practice in Europe and North America.* New York: Springer.

Stoecker, R. & Tryon, E. (eds) (2009) *The Unheard Voices: Community Organizations and Service Learning.* Philadelphia, PA: Temple University Press.

Stoecker, R., Loving, K., Reddy, M. & Bollig, N. (2010) 'Can community-based research guide service-learning?' *Journal of Community Practice*, 18: 280–296.

Strand, K., Marullo, S., Cutforth, N., Stoecker, R. & Donohue, P. (2003) *Community-Based Research and Higher Education: Principles and Practices.* San Francisco, CA: Jossey-Bass.

Warren, J. L. (2012) 'Does service-learning increase student learning? A meta-analysis.' *Michigan Journal of Community Service Learning*, 18(2): 56–61.

Wisconsin Council on Children and Families (2013) *Race to Equity: A Baseline Report on the State of Racial Disparities in Dane County.* Wisconsin Council on Children and Families.

15 Using Volunteer-Employed Photography

Seeing St David's Peninsula through the eyes of locals and tourists

Nika Balomenou and Brian Garrod

Introduction

Volunteer-Employed Photography (VEP) has been described as a powerful but underused and undervalued research tool (Garrod, 2008; Balomenou and Garrod, 2016). Indeed, there is a growing body of scientific evidence to suggest that participatory photographic techniques such as VEP allow complex meanings to be conveyed and permit study subjects to express their views more efficiently and effectively. It is argued that this is because the medium of photography is more sensitive to the multidimensional nature of experiences than is written text or the spoken word. On this basis, it is argued that VEP proves itself useful in investigating tensions between locals and tourists in tourism destinations. The area of St David's Peninsula in the Pembrokeshire Coast National Park (PCNP) in West Wales was therefore chosen for the case study. The growth of tourism in the area has led to there being a ratio of 143 tourists to every resident in the late 2010s, which has resulted in tensions between the locals and tourists. Local people were asked to photograph aspects of the PCNP that give them a sense of attachment to place. They were also asked to attempt to capture aspects of the area that they did not particularly appreciate. Tourists, meanwhile, were asked to take photographs to illustrate why they chose to visit PCNP. They were also asked to take photographs of aspects they did not particularly appreciate if they happened to come across them. Participants were asked to keep photo-diaries and to describe what aspects of the PCNP they would change if they were given the opportunity, as well as to explain why. This chapter focuses mainly on the methodological issues that arise from the use of VEP. A critique of the methodology with the view of it being used in different contexts is presented in this chapter.

Background

Volunteer-Employed Photography (VEP) is one of a range of participatory research techniques which focus particularly on the visual dimension of a person's experience, be it of the place where they live or somewhere they are visiting, of a special event or of their daily routine. VEP has close similarities with another technique, known as photo elicitation, with which it is often confused.

Photo elicitation is widely considered to be a dynamic and useful tool for social research and it seems to have appealed to many researchers over the years. In photo-elicitation interviews, the researcher typically presents the interviewee with photographs of the interviewee's own world and uses them as prompts to discuss issues of interest to the researcher (Danford and Willems, 1975, Jenkins, 1999). It allows insights and understanding to be gained that could well be missed or may not even be discernible using other methods (Banks, 2001).

Emmison and Smith (2000) note that photography has been employed as a technique of psychological research. One such approach they term 'autophotography'. The difference between autophotography and photo elicitation is that with autophotography, the person taking the photographs is not the researcher but the research subject, who thereby participates directly in the study. The subject is also charged with the task of interpreting the photos to the researcher (Emmison and Smith, 2000). Zillier and Rorer (1985) used an autophotographic approach to investigate shyness, where it was found that shy people are less likely to include other people in their photographic representations of themselves.

Clancy and Dollinger (1993), meanwhile, used autophotography to examine sex-role differences. Some of the outcomes of this study were that men were more likely to take photographs of themselves whereas women tended to take family-orientated photographs, photographs of groups of people and activities (see Emmison and Smith, 2000). Autophotography has also sometimes been employed in ethnographic research. For example Prosser (1998) cites the work of Worth and Adair (1972), who taught Navajo Indians how to operate a video camera and asked them to record some of their traditions and rituals in order to represent them accurately. Crang (1997) also mentions an example in which the British Broadcasting Corporation (BBC) gave video cameras to individuals to make their own video logs under the umbrella of the *Picture Post/New Society* reportage tradition (Keighron, 1993).

In view of the central importance of photography in tourism, and the close links that are recognized to exist between the two, it seems only reasonable for researchers to apply photographic techniques of this kind in a tourism context. According to Crang (1997) "the possibilities of using film (be it still or video) to help understand the processes by which the people engage with and make sense of the world, in tourism in particular, seem significant".

While the term 'autophotography' has often been used in psychological and ethnographic research, this term is not widely understood outside of these disciplines. Tourism researchers, therefore, have often adopted a similar technique but called it by a different name. Among the most common terms used are 'visitor-employed photography', 'resident-employed photography', 'reflexive photography' and 'self-directed photography'. In order to avoid confusion, therefore, the term 'Volunteer-Employed Photography' (VEP) will be used throughout this chapter as a catch-all for such techniques.

This terminology makes more sense: in all cases the approach involves the use of photography by people volunteering to take part in the study. Moreover, the term is generic and thereby transcends disciplinary barriers. It would be clumsy to use a technique called 'visitor-employed photography' in psychology, where the participants may not be visitors at all but perhaps hospital patients or prisoners. At the same time, the term 'autophotography' seems to imply that the photos are of or about oneself. This may well be the case in psychological or ethnographic applications of the technique. However, arguably the term would seem much less applicable in a tourism application where participants are being asked to photograph external features such as pleasing landscapes or interesting museum exhibits.

What is Volunteer-Employed Photography?

VEP is an experience-recording technique, where the participants of the study are each given a camera and are asked to take photographs according to a particular task that has been set for them by the researcher (Balomenou and Garrod, 2014). The participants are requested either to explain why they have taken each photograph to the researcher in an in-depth interview after the event, or take explanatory notes when taking the photographs, putting them into a photo-diary or photo-log.

Haywood (1990: 25) considers the VEP technique to be highly appropriate to the tourism context, believing that photographs "reveal something about us – how we see and interpret the world and the people and places in it, and all the meaning and associations we conjure up". A number of other researchers have also indicated a considerable potential for the VEP technique in tourism research. Yet there have been very few practical research projects adopting the VEP approach. It is apposite, therefore, to consider what the principal advantages and disadvantages VEP has as a research tool.

Positive aspects in the use of VEP

One of the problems identified in social research that may be a source of bias, and is also blamed for making the participants wanting to 'please' the researcher, is the so-called 'power relationship' between the researcher and the participant (Prosser, 1998, p 102). However, it can be argued that in the case of VEP, the asymmetry in power between the researcher and the participant that is usually an issue in other research techniques may actually be greatly reduced (Loeffler, 2004). The participant is empowered in the VEP study, as he or she is the one who defines the issues that will be captured in the photographs and will be analysed in the interviews or the diaries. This means that the participants are able to address precisely the issues that interest them, instead of being expected to reflect on those issues chosen by the researcher.

Additionally, when talking about perceptions of places and experiences, it is more revealing to ask the research participants to identify issues that are most important to them, rather than the researcher having to guess, make assumptions or even use secondary data to identify them. Loeffler (2004, p 539) highlights the fact that the respondents are the ones to determine what precisely will be photographed. Participants are telling their own story and have greater control over the research process, as they are the ones who decide what to photograph (Markwell, 2000, Balomenou and Garrod, 2014). Similarly, Taylor et al. (1995) note that VEP is a way of "capturing without reshaping" the natural environment. VEP clearly has important conceptual strengths in terms of the way in which participants are empowered to steer the research process and to enable their expertise, experiences and knowledge to be drawn out.

Some commentators argue that one of the major weaknesses of photographic methods is the potential for subjectivity to enter the research process and this is one of the reasons why some researchers in the social sciences hesitate to trust, let alone use, photographical methods (Prosser, 1998, Linfield, 2011). VEP enables participants to express their particular points of view, experiences and biases, which the researcher then interprets and draws conclusions (Loeffler, 2004). Such data must surely be biased. Yet arguably this feature is one of the strengths of VEP rather than one of its weaknesses. VEP seeks to capture participants' perceptions, understanding and feelings about an area, activity or experience, and these can only be different for each participant.

Another topic touched upon by many visual researchers is that photography is less restrictive than most other media of communication. Indeed, participants in VEP studies often indicate that words were not sufficient to explain their opinions or experiences (Loeffler, 2004). Carlson (2001, cited in Loeffler, 2004) mentions that photographs have the advantage of reflecting emotions better than spoken or written words. VEP is thus sensitive to the multidimensionality of people's opinions and experiences (Jurkowski, 2008, Swanson, 2015).

Additionally, VEP asks people to do something they may have never done before, which requires a commitment from them and probably a considerable investment of time. Those who agree to take part in the study thus tend to feel involved in the research process. That way, participants feel that they are able to make their own personal contribution to the objectives of the study, for example in deciding how a wilderness area should be managed (Haywood, 1990, Taylor et al., 1995). It has been argued that novel, quirky and intriguing research methods can more easily engage the "increasingly sceptical participants" (Haywood, 1990, MacKay and Couldwell, 2004, Schänzel and Smith, 2011). This also argues in favour of the use of VEP. Even though participating in a VEP project can take up a significant amount of the volunteer's time, a number of researchers have commented that participants generally enjoy the experience (Cherem and Traweek, 1977, Haywood, 1990, MacKay and Couldwell, 2004, Deale, 2014).

Even though the first groups of researchers who used VEP considered it to be a useful technique, with potential for extensive future use, they were sceptical about the logistics involved. Where regular 35 mm cameras were used, there was always a risk of not getting the cameras back. Early disposable cameras were also quite expensive to buy, while the photographs were generally only in black and white and generally of poor quality. More recently, however, the cost of disposable cameras has fallen considerably and people can also use their mobile phones, making it possible to use a large enough sample of participants to render the technique replicable (Cherem and Driver, 1983, Ross, 2011).

Weaknesses of the VEP method

Researchers who have used VEP have identified some weaknesses of the technique. In this section, the proposed weaknesses of VEP are separated in two categories: conceptual and practical. The practical issues depend largely on the way each research team decides to apply the technique, whereas the conceptual issues have more to do with the VEP approach as a whole, highlighting a number of proposed theoretical weak points in the technique.

Conceptual issues

The first and probably most widely discussed issue with VEP is the level of commitment required from its participants. As Markwell (2000) highlights, this kind of study requires a certain degree of commitment on the participants' side. Chenoweth (1984) notes that the method can be obtrusive as it requires people to undertake a task which involves quite a lot of time and effort while they are on holiday (Chenoweth, 1984, MacKay and Couldwell, 2004). People might start off with the best intentions but neglect their task after a while.

It can be argued, nevertheless, that the high level of commitment required by the participants might not be the only reason why those who are initially very keen to get involved might not actually complete the task they have been given. It is impossible for the researcher to have complete control of the project, no matter how clear the instructions he or she gives. For example, it is difficult to avoid influences from other members of the party (Haywood, 1990, MacKay and Couldwell, 2002) or social media users (Lo and McKercher, 2015). People that are asked to participate and are members of a group often find themselves to be receptors of advice from other members of the group, advising on what to photograph and what to leave out, advice which is sometimes difficult to ignore. In some cases, people understand the importance of VEP studies but they are not keen camera users. Much as they might want to participate, they might feel intimidated by the process of taking photographs. They might not want to draw attention to themselves and therefore do not use the camera as often as they would like to (Haywood, 1990) or they might want to enjoy the moment more than spending time engaging with technology (Tribe and Mkono, 2017).

Another issue that is often raised is that the researcher might create a kind of bias by asking participants to take 'meaningful' photographs. Because of this, the participant might be in pursuit of 'significant' photos (Loeffler, 2004). Participants might feel obliged to see the world around them in a way they would not do were they not participating in the study (Chenoweth, 1984). One way around this problem could be for the research team specifically to address the issue and ask the participants to behave as they would if they were not participating in the research. However, this is much more easily said than done.

Last but not least, researchers have touched on the potential problem of participants either actively or sub-consciously replicating of the images that made them decide to visit the area in the first place, for example scenes and panoramas they have seen in brochures and on postcards (Loeffler, 2004). Whether participants are influenced by the pre-constructed images they have of a place is an open question. However, a number of researchers have worked on this particular aspect of tourism photography and some argue that people use photography to prove that they have visited a destination (Markwell, 2000; Urry, 2002). Preconceived images may therefore play some kind of role in determining the photographs participants take for the VEP study.

Practical issues

Some concerns are expressed that some scenes or subjects might not be photographed as they may be inaccessible (Taylor et al., 1995) or might involve vulnerable social groups or people (Germain, 2004). Events might not be captured because of the challenging environment, the limitations of the equipment or the nature of the activity (Haywood, 1990, Loeffler, 2004). Climbers can be considered as a good example for this point; it is difficult to climb, admire the view and juggle with a camera at the same time. Some areas that might be important for the tourist experience such as some museums and art exhibitions limit or even ban the use of cameras (Haywood, 1990).

There are also some disadvantages associated with VEP which may be related to the way in which the research team has chosen to apply the technique. For example, Haywood (1990) notes that because the participants in his study could only keep the camera for a single day, it was likely that they only visited one site and their photographs only illustrated one particular theme. Similarly, in Sugimoto (2013) there were restrictions in the time the participants had to participle in the study. In the case of Cherem (Cherem and Driver, 1983), limitations were felt to occur because of the nature of the activity the participants were engaging in; the participants were canoeists, who may be travelling fast in one direction and there was always the danger of a ducking for either the participant or the photographic equipment (Cherem and Traweek, 1977, Traweek, 1977, Cherem and Driver, 1983).

The list of weaknesses of VEP seems long. However there are some points that need to be made in order to ensure that the method is considered objectively. The first is that all the researchers who used the technique concluded that this method is underutilized and they recommend further investigation of its potential. The second is that a significant period of time has elapsed since some researchers have used the technique (Cherem and Traweek, 1977, Traweek, 1977). Subsequently, there have been technological advances that have reduced the cost of cameras and photographic development, making the use of the technique much more cost effective.

St David's Peninsula: an introduction to the area

According to the National Park Management Plan 2003–2007 (2003), Pembrokeshire Coast National Park (PCNP) is the only coastal national park in Britain. The park has a coastline of 186 miles (299 km) and has been designated primarily for its coastal scenery. It includes seven Special Areas of Conservation, three Special Protection Areas, one Marine Nature Reserve, six National Nature Reserves, 75 Sites of Special Scientific Interest and 80% of its coastline is designated as SSSIs. It also includes 257 Scheduled Ancient Monuments, 1,019 listed buildings and fourteen Conservation Areas. More than 1.2 million visits were made to the area in 2004. Pembrokeshire Coast National Park attracts many walkers, as the Coastal Path is designated as one of fifteen National Trails in England and Wales.

At the same time, the park suffers from a number of socio-economic weaknesses. As described in the National Park Management Plan 2003–2007, 21% of the population in Pembrokeshire receive a key social security benefit, whereas the UK median is 12%. Additionally, the employment rate is 61.4% comparing to 73.5% for the UK. Average gross weekly earnings are 70% of the national figure.

Narrowing the focus down, St David's Peninsula received more than 500,000 visitors in 2006 (personal communication with Tourism Information Centre staff), while no more than 3,500 people live in the peninsula. This means that there are 143 tourists to every resident. Local income is largely dependent on the tourism industry. Informal interviews with residents suggest that more than 54% of the houses in St David's are holiday homes. This creates problems such as inflated house prices which lead to local people being unable to buy properties in the area. In addition, a tools factory closure in the area in December 2006 affected more than 50 families as more than 50 jobs were lost.

It is clear from this data that tourism is a very important source of income for the local economy. It is also evident that there is plenty of potential for conflicts to arise between locals and tourists, and between local people and the planning authorities.

Case study of St David's Peninsula: method

This is the first research study to use VEP in a tourism planning context, with both user groups – locals and tourists – asked for their input. The study is unique in that it has been designed with the specific objective of feeding into the planning process.

Three pilot surveys were undertaken before the man study. Each involved a random sample of ten tourists. Every fifth person passing in front of the researcher outside the Tourist Information Centre in St David's was asked to participate. If the fifth person was member of a group, the member of the group whose birthday was next was asked to participate. Depending on the person's answer, the researcher either noted their approximate age and other obvious details such as if the person was a member of a group, if they were on holidays with friends or family if the person refused to participate, or explained what the study was about and proceeded to a short semi-structured interview. Some of the data gathered through this interview were demographic and some related to people's perceptions on planning issues as this study is mainly concerned with the planning issues that arise from the research.

After the interview, the researcher provided the participants with a research pack that comprised a bag, a folder, a coded camera, a coded photo-diary, an explanatory letter and a pen. There were also planning-related questions in the photo-diary. For example, having recorded that they had taken a photograph, participants were asked to identify the main feature of the photo and whether the photo conveyed a positive or generally negative connotation for them. If on the other hand the meaning was considered to be positive, participants were invited to suggest what would spoil it for them. If the photograph was considered to convey a negative meaning, the participants were invited to suggest what would improve the situation.

The purpose of the first pilot study was to see if the material put together was user-friendly and if it worked well in the field. The researcher asked the participants to return the camera and photo diary to the Tourist Information Centre staff. Eight out of ten participants returned their camera and photo-diary.

The photo-diary, questionnaire and information letter to participants were adapted after observations made by the researcher and the participants were taken into account, and this modified questionnaire was then used in the second pilot study. The participants were asked again to return the camera and photo-diary to the Tourist Information Centre staff. Eight out of ten participants returned their camera and diary.

The changes to the questionnaires, diaries and letters of the first pilot study were considered successful, so the only change to the third pilot survey was the return method: a stamped and addressed envelope was included in the participants' research packs. Five out of ten participants returned their cameras and diaries within two weeks of the day the pack was given to them and two more participants replied within six weeks. It was therefore decided for the main study that the researchers would be asked to return the cameras and diaries in drop-in boxes; if they found that difficult to do they would have to send their cameras and diaries back at their own expense.

After two weeks of intensive sampling for each category, 145 cameras were distributed to tourists and 54 cameras to locals. The response rate was 78% for the tourists and 45% for the locals. The time spent interviewing each tourist was approximately 24 minutes. Presently, efforts are being made to recruit more locals in order to obtain a similar size sample. Data were coded and stored in NVIVO, a software package that allows flexible interrogation and analysis without losing sight of the individual.

Significant indications

The primary result from this study is that the quality of the responses is very rich. The photos, in conjunction with the interviews and the photo-diaries, provided a high-quality dataset which will be able to demonstrate the utility of VEP in informing about planning issues and disputes.

Most of the participants who returned their cameras seemed to be happy with the number of photos they were asked to take. A number of participants actually used the whole film to take photographs for the project. However, a large number of the sample did not take twelve photographs. There were comments made by participants that maybe ten photographs would have been easier to take and make comments on.

It also seems that the digital photography option is the way forward. The participants in the case study were given 27-shot disposable cameras with a built-in flash. This means that upon their return, the cameras had to be sent away to be developed. It was observed that not all the photographs were usable. In some cases, especially in night shots, the participants were not always using the flash in order for the camera to capture what they see. In other cases, it seemed that the participants thought that they had actually taken a photo, and noted it in the diary, when they had not.

The general feeling of enjoyment and commitment to this kind of study has been identified in the literature by a number of researchers (Durrant et al., 2011). This proved to be very strong motivation in recruiting volunteers to this study, as a large number of participants commented on the enjoyment this project offered and wished the research team luck for the results of the study.

It is also evident from the data that there are some very important planning issues, and these are raised by both groups. These include issues such as commercialization, the factory closure in St David's, scenic beauty and its importance for tourists and locals, wishes for the area to remain unspoilt without too many tourists and the desire of local young people aged between 16 and 29 to move to a bigger city with more job opportunities are difficult to ignore.

The most evident planning issue that arose, however, was the problem of the second/ holiday homes. This issue was mentioned by local participants many times with close to 70% making comments on second homes. Moreover, this was the major reason why it proved extremely difficult to recruit local participants. During the design process, it was decided that from a list of the residents, three hundred would be randomly chosen and approached in order to be asked to participate. It was also decided that if one person on this list was not at home, the next door would be knocked. However, this decision resulted in a fortnight of door knocking without impressive results. This did not surprise the locals when they were asked for their advice on this issue, as they were convinced that this is due to the large number of second homes in the area.

Conclusion

The data strongly suggests that VEP has considerable potential as a tool for examining planning issues. According to the literature, as well as the experience of the researcher, there are indeed some evident drawbacks in using VEP. However, VEP also has clear strengths. In particular, the technique has the potential to empower people to demonstrate how they feel about important planning issues. It enables tourists to show why they have chosen to visit a certain area and to explain why they would not repeat their visit. It also enables the local community to demonstrate what gives them a sense of place and what they actually do not like about it and would like to see changed. Clearly there are grounds to suggest that VEP should be considered an effective planning tool in areas where conflicts between user groups arise and need to be addressed effectively.

References

Balomenou, N. & Garrod, B. (2014) 'Using volunteer-Employed Photography to inform tourism planning decisions: a study of St David's Peninsula, Wales.' *Tourism management*, 44: 126–139.

Balomenou, N. & Garrod, B. (2016) 'A review of participant-generated image methods in the social sciences.' *Journal of Mixed Methods Research*, 10: 1–17.

Banks, M. (2001) *Visual Methods in Social Research*. London: Sage.

Chenoweth, R. (1984) 'Visitor employed photography: a potential tool for landscape architecture.' *Landscape Journal*, 136–143.

Cherem, G. & Driver, B. (1983) 'Visitor employed photography: a technique to measure common perceptions of natural environments.' *Journal of Leisure Research*, 65–83.

Cherem, G. J. & Traweek, D. E. (1977) Visitor employed photography: a tool for interpretive planning on river environments. Proceedings of River Recreation Management and Research Symposium. USDA Forest Services, 236–244.

Clancy, S. M. & Dollinger, S. J. (1993) 'Photographic depictions of the self: gender and age differences in social connectedness.' *Sex Roles*, 29: 477–495.

Crang, M. (1997) 'Picturing practices: research through the tourist gaze.' *Progress in Human Geography*, 21: 359–373.

Danford, S. & Willems, E. P. (1975) 'Subjective responses to architectural displays: a question of validity.' *Environment and Behavior*, 7: 486–516.

Deale, C. S. (2014) 'Students' photo perceptions of hospitality and tourism in a community: a scholarship of teaching and learning case study.' *Journal of Teaching in Travel & Tourism*, 14: 1–21.

Durrant, A., Rowland, D., Kirk, D. S., Benford, S., Fischer, J. E. & Mcauley, D. (2011) Automics: souvenir generating photoware for theme parks. Proceedings of the SIGCHI Conference on Human Factors in Computing Systems. ACM, 1767–1776.

Emmison, M. & Smith, P. (2000) *Current Trends in Visual Research*. London: Sage Publications.

Garrod, B. (2008) 'Understanding the relationship between tourism destination imagery and tourist photography.' *Annals of Tourism Research*, 35(2): 381–401.

Germain, R. (2004) 'An exploratory study using cameras and Talking Mats to access the views of young people with learning disabilities on their out-of-school activities.' *British Journal of Learning Disabilities*, 32: 170–174.

Haywood, K. M. (1990) 'Visitor-employed photography: an urban visit assessment.' *Journal of Travel Research*, 29: 25–29.

Jenkins, O. H. (1999) 'Understanding and measuring tourist destination images.' *International Journal of Tourism Research*, 1: 1–15.

Jurkowski, J. M. (2008) 'Photovoice as participatory action research tool for engaging people with intellectual disabilities in research and program development.' *Intellectual and Developmental Disabilities*, 46: 1–11.

Keighron, P. (1993) 'Video diaries: what's up doc?' *Sight and Sound*, 3: 24–25.

Linfield, S. (2011) *The Cruel Radiance: Photography and Political Violence*. Chicago, IL: University of Chicago Press.

Lo, I. S. & Mckercher, B. (2015) 'Ideal image in process: online tourist photography and impression management.' *Annals of Tourism Research*, 52: 104–116.

Loeffler, T. A. (2004) 'A photo elicitation study of the meanings of outdoor adventure experiences.' *Journal of Leisure Research*, 36: 536.

Mackay, K. J. & Couldwell, C. M. (2004) 'Using visitor-employed photography to investigate destination image.' *Journal of Travel Research*, 42: 390–396.

Markwell, K. W. (2000) 'Photo-documentation and analyses as research strategies in human geography.' *Australian Geographical Studies*, 38: 91–98.

Pembrokeshire Coast National Park Authority (2003) National Park Management Plan 2003–2007.

Prosser, J. (1998) *Image-based Research: A Sourcebook for Qualitative Researchers.* London: Falmer Press.

Ross, S. T. (2011) 'Show and tell: Photovoice as international travel pedagogy.' *Analytic Teaching and Philosophical Praxis*, 32.

Schänzel, H. A. & Smith, K. A. (2011) 'Photography and children: auto-driven photo-elicitation.' *Tourism Recreation Research*, 36: 81–85.

Sugimoto, K. (2013) 'Quantitative measurement of visitors' reactions to the settings in urban parks: spatial and temporal analysis of photographs.' *Landscape and Urban Planning*, 110: 59–63.

Swanson, K. (2015) 'Place brand love and marketing to place consumers as tourists.' *Journal of Place Management and Development*, 8: 142–146.

Taylor, J. G., Czarnowski, K. J., Sexton, N. R. & Flick, S. (1995) 'The importance of water to Rocky Mountain National Park visitors: an adaptation of visitor-employed photography to natural resources management.' *Journal of Applied Recreation Research*, 20(1): 61–85.

Traweek, D. E. (1977) *Visitor Employed Photography on the Huron River: A Tool for Interpretive Planning.* PhD, Ohio State University.

Tribe, J. & Mkono, M. (2017) 'Not such smart tourism? The concept of e-lienation.' *Annals of Tourism Research*, 66: 105–115.

Urry, J. (2002) *The Tourist Gaze.* London: Sage Publications Ltd.

Ziller, R. C. & Rorer, B. A. (1985) 'Shyness-environment interaction: a view from the shy side through auto-photography.' *Journal of Personality*, 53: 626–639.

Conclusion

Towards truly ethical co-productive research

This book makes a bold claim. It argues that to co-produce research is one of the best ways to involve community partners in health and social care settings. As well as having intrinsic value in and of itself, it embeds a culture of learning, co-production and of valuing research within organisations, and creates a mechanism for developing evidence for monitoring and evaluating other ideas and initiatives that arise from the structures for co-production. The book has argued that the most effective way to conduct research is through a synthesis of participatory research, critical pedagogy, peer research and community organising, a model called Participatory Pedagogic Impact Research (PPIR). This synthesis was designed to address the different flaws and limitations of each approach and bring them together into a complementary framework. Participatory research is often criticized for not having the impact it promises. I think community organising addresses this, making sure that the issues we choose and the recommendations we develop are realistic and realisable, and serve mutual interests. At the same time the approach and its dissemination push the balance of power towards the oppressed, genuinely holds decision makers to account, and makes for real sustainable change.

The strengthening of the critical pedagogic aspects within participatory research builds towards a detailed articulation of what makes for genuinely critical reflective spaces, something unarticulated in sufficient depth in the literature. Combined with some of the insights and approaches of Rancière (1992) into the paternalistic tendencies of critical pedagogy, we address other concerns (Cooke & Kothari, 2001) about the tyranny of the group and of method within participatory research. At the same time PPIR makes identifying issues and applying analysis, something which needs development within both co-production and community organising, far more robust. The book establishes PPIR as an ethnopraxis, in that it seeks to root the framework for research from issue identification, to methodology, to analysis and dissemination, within the local ways of knowing of research participants.

We have also examined what is meant by a peer. We recognise that there is strength in being a 'near peer' and that sometimes the power of a peer is symbolic. This symbolism manifests in different ways. Sometimes the peer can reassure participants that they are going to be listened to and that, as a consequence, the participant may extend proxy trust to the research team, although this will rightly remain contingent. Sometimes the peer is a symbol of the fact that one can be lost and come back from this, that there is hope, and that the skills the peer is displaying are a mirror of the skills that the participants has, but may not acknowledge to themselves or have acknowledged by others.

However as Simone Helleren, Richard Campbell and Beth Coyne say, a peer researcher needs proper training and support and for their roles to be clearly defined. Simone Helleren show how, in the absence of sufficient training and support, sometimes the sharing of experiences led the peer researcher to dominate by taking over the interview in a way that silenced people rather than allowing them to open up. Other peers felt that they had to exaggerate or conflate their experience to establish themselves as a peer researcher, based on an assumed presumption that being peer would give them common cause with clients. Simone Helleren highlights the naivety of assuming that the researcher's 'peerness' will necessarily enable people to open up. This is reiterated by Richard Campbell. Professional researchers can underestimate how the participants' and peers' often traumatic experiences can lead to a culture of silence, not openness. Support seems an inadequate word in these contexts. I have witnessed the anger of both peer and participants as they realize the extent of their, and their community's, systematic oppression, silencing and unresolved trauma gained through the fallout of symbolic and literal violence, combined with frustration at themselves at having internalised the negative dynamics that accompany such hegemonic discourses. Acknowledgment of these things is important in these contexts.

At the same time participants and peers have a consequent resilience and commitment to each other that needs to be acknowledged, cultivated and replicated. Professional researchers also need to reflect on the impact of their privilege from often less visceral experiences. I was struck by Simone Helleren's analogy of a sneeze: it neatly sums up the professional researcher's need to hold their own desire to intervene, and the lack of resilience that makes them want to close down volatile situations, when this is actually the point of breakthrough. As I say in Chapter 4, stigma resistance needs to be held in common and, as professional researchers, we are often far less used to holding such moments of tension. Participatory research requires deep thinking about our subjectivities.

Richard Campbell's account reminded me how, as a professional, I still have a lot of power to relinquish. I have privilege to undo, and the price of privilege is that you have never done enough in this regard. We were reluctant in the Touch project to get peers and participants involved in analysis because we wanted to do it ourselves. On a deeper level we did not really trust ourselves and the participatory process, and did not want to expose ourselves to others in this regard. We therefore did not train peers and participants properly and projected our deficit back onto them, not allowing them to discover their own native analytical skills. Similarly when we asked people to call on *their* subjectivity we needed to have taken account of our *own* complexities and consider how we impose this. Who are we to judge who is fractured and who is a meta-reflector? This can only truly be assessed together. Especially when the experience we, or participants, are drawing on is traumatic, we need to apply sensitivity and humility, make use of our mutual experiences and perspectives, and work with each other to humane ends. We need continually to root our research in peers' and participants' ways of knowing, not our own. Our major role is to act on their will to overcome the hegemonic forces that we have been a part of maintaining, and recognise their knowledge's value and their personal capacity and capability, and seek clarity and consistency in ourselves as much as them, and not to inadvertently undermine them.

Positively what all the practice examples show is that this kind of research can be transformative. As Richard Campbell documents, research can enable peers to recognise and realise their academic potential and cultivate a wish to both enable others to do this, as well as challenging the academy in its elitist tendencies. Beth Coyne and Simone Helleren reiterate this, detailing how individuals have gone on to gain employment they would not have done otherwise, through fundamentally changing their view of themselves. Randy Stoecker, Karen Reece, and Taylor Konkle show how organisations and communities can recognise that they have common ground and common cause, and that the universities need to be *for* the community as well as situated in them, and communities need to hold universities to account for this. Perhaps most fundamentally, as Beth Coyne, Richard Campbell and Simone Helleren show, through undertaking research, organisations and communities start seeing each other in transformed ways, coming to value the knowledge that they co-create and the process by which they do this.

Creating an agenda for change: the engaged researcher

Researchers need to be actively engaged with community members. PPIR needs to set its standard as reaching the most marginalized groups, not just those that are the most articulate. In the process it must also deconstruct notions of power and peer, and, on an operational level, the nature of research itself. As activist researchers we need to be a part of a re-articulation of how research views validity and reliability, what is meant by 'grounded' data and reflexivity, and where ethics come to play in research projects. We need nothing less than a paradigm shift. Our epistemological stance on what constitutes knowledge and how it is to be created needs to shift, particularly within the academy. The co-production of research needs to move from being seen as exotic, radical or added value, to being the only meaningful way to conduct an investigation. We need to move from asking when and if we should involve community partners in a piece of research to asking how. We need to stop seeing the difficulties and barriers to involving community members in a particular research context as reasons for non-involvement, but as obstacles to be overcome.

Positivism still dominates, from the idea that only quantitative research is meaningful research, to funding regimes where at the outset time frames must be set, and methodologies and research questions defined from the beginning. Ethical guidelines remain deontological sets of rules which privilege neoliberal constructions of the individual, rather than looking at wider political notions of what makes for 'being ethical'. This entails working both within and outside of the traditional research mechanisms. We should critically engage in how research is viewed in our institutions and professional bodies and be the voice of change and dissent. We should critically engage in assessment exercises such as the Research Excellence Framework and sit on its panels to ensure that 'Impact' is taken seriously, as is participatory research, and that other voices are not dominated and marginalized by the ever pervasive presence of academics and their discourses.

We should also engage with communities on a day-to-day basis. We should start with those communities where universities are situated. We must challenge the common position where those engaged as university stakeholders are celebrated as being demographically representative of the world, but the institution cannot make such a claim for the square mile where they are located. Local relationships built over time and through mutual self-interest lead to more meaningful integrated research, where long terms impacts can be accounted for and articulated. Such relationships also develop impact and have resonance beyond the local, with national and international reach, as our often diasporic community partners have such reach themselves. My own subject, youth and community work, has always placed an emphasis on working and rooting its approach in the local, and as a consequence has developed organic networks across the world with projects and communities that do the same.

The final word

In the introduction, as evidence of the benefits of the approach I gave space to a commissioner who came to value co-produced participatory research. I would like to conclude by giving space to two people, one a peer researcher and another a front line worker who, as I have said here and before, are often the most marginalized stakeholders within projects. Through research, however, they can come to realize the power and potential they have together.

> The staff in the project really listened to us, our ideas, which was great. It meant they actually cared about what we thought. It's funny because we're all trying to achieve the same outcomes. I think the project has helped staff and probation realise that they need to consult with service users more as they can learn a lot from us.
>
> (Client commenting on the probation based peer research project)

> The greatest success has been the peer research done at the Watford office . . . The work that has come out of this has been fed back to our senior management team and changes are starting to happen.
>
> (Worker commenting on the probation peer research project)

References

Cooke, B. & Kothari, U. (2001) (eds) *Participation: The New Tyranny?* London: Zed.
Rancière, J. (1992) *The Ignorant Schoolmaster: Five Lessons in Intellectual Emancipation.* Stanford, CA: Stanford University Press.

Index